The Bourgeois

THE
BOURGEOIS

CATHOLICISM VS. CAPITALISM

IN EIGHTEENTH-CENTURY

FRANCE

By Bernard Groethuysen

INTRODUCTION
BY BENJAMIN NELSON
TRANSLATED FROM THE FRENCH
BY MARY ILFORD

Holt, Rinehart and Winston
NEW YORK CHICAGO SAN FRANCISCO

FIRST EDITION

Grateful acknowledgment is made to the following publisher who has so generously granted permission to reprint from their publication:
Harper & Row, Publishers, Inc., New York and William Collins Sons & Co. Ltd., for passages from *Pensées*, by Blaise Pascal. Copyright © 1962 in Martin Turnell's translation with the Harvill Press.

Designer: Herb Johnson
8654659
Printed in the United States of America

CONTENTS

INTRODUCTION

A sense of the uncanny seems to me to attach to every aspect of this book.

First—Groethuysen records the birth and the social success of a new sort of man, whose very existence had not previously been remarked by such master sociologists, historians, and philosophers of modern civilization as Max Weber, Ernst Troeltsch, R. H. Tawney, Jan Huizinga, and Wilhelm Dilthey, Groethuysen's famed teacher. Thanks to these pioneers, and other scholars who forged forward in their spirit, we now have a fair view of large tracts of the cultural and religious foundations of our contemporary world order. Yet it is to Groethuysen, above all, that we must turn if we seek to reclaim the interior landscapes of this new middle sort of man, the *self-made, self-reliant Catholic bourgeois*—this worldly yet churchly; worldly-wise *but not free-thinking*—man of Catholic France's Age of Reason, Enlightenment, and Revolution.

Earlier historians and thinkers—Michelet in France, Burckhardt in Switzerland, John Addington Symonds in England—had told about another and a very different sort of "new" man, the *virtuoso* of the Italian Renaissance. Aspiring to become a *"universal man,"* the virtuoso conceived all existence—including his own person, society, nature—as prime matter asking to be fully realized as works of art. In emulation of Prometheus, the artist-scientist of the Renaissance world did not rest until he had appropriated the secrets of the cosmos to the advantage of the fellowship of man.

Max Weber had taken the lead in untangling the spiritual bases of the vocational ethic and institutions of contemporary industrial civilization. The Protestant ethic of innerworldly asceticism, more than the spirit of Mammon, came to be seen as spur and sanction to the rationalized enterprise and scientific "technoculture" of the most advanced Protestant nations of the earth.

More will be said soon of other renderings of the pilgrimage of Western man, including that of the masterly Dutch historian, Jan Huizinga, of whom I hear as many echoes in this book as I do of Dilthey. But let me insist again on our first uncanny fact: no historian or sociologist of culture before Groethuysen— and hardly any since—have managed so well to evoke the puzzling landscapes of the everyday sort of man who claimed center stage when the secularizing *virtuosi* of the Renaissance and the religiously oriented *virtuosi* of the Reformation had spent themselves. Huizinga alone might be said to match Groethuysen in conveying a sense of the spiritual distance needing to be covered before *everyday men* could innocently proceed to go about their tasks in the *everyday world* with the simple conviction that their *everyday minds* were the true and honest measure of *everything* that came their way.

Second—Groethuysen's subtle sense of the cultural and social environments—his awareness of the scenes, settings, and stylized performances, including the clashes and compromises in the ongoing ritual and game of life—all these reveal the eye of the dramatist, portrait painter, and naturalist. He thus quietly wanders outside the somewhat academic frames of Weber and Dilthey, calling to mind the sensibility of Molière, de la Rochefoucauld, and, indeed, of a reflective young Englishman who, serving as a ship's doctor far from his native countryside, was drawn to wonder about the odd transactions of species and their environments and so stumbled on "webs of life," struggles for existence, ecological successions, and the evolution of species through natural selection.

In its sense of locale and atmosphere, *The Bourgeois* outshines many more celebrated works as a guide to the understanding of the changes which traditional and transitional societies and cultures undergo as they become increasingly "technological, industrial, secular"—in short—"modern."

Third—Oddly enough, the story which Groethuysen records with such subtlety is largely unknown.

In the Middle Ages, as Huizinga has shown, hunger, famine, plague, injustice, lust, guilt, sin, despair—all were likely to be the lot of Everyman, whatever his station. Every sort of contrast and conflict abounded. Unlimited vindictiveness and acosmic pity could readily mingle in the same heart, as could the extremes of sensuality and spirituality, lawlessness and devotion to the exacting rituals and rigid forms of law.

Pre-modern Catholic spirituality was rooted in precariousness. Before the advent of a modern corporate welfare society, men—whether warriors, bishops, bankers, lawyers, or peasants—could not securely hope to fulfill life's demands or find justification in their own eyes. Inevitably, they looked to others for aid and guidance in uncovering ultimate grounds, reasons, meanings, purposes, principles, relations, imperatives—what we might call dramatic designs and directive programs—in the conduct of their existence.

Then one day the world seemed new-made—everywhere one turned there were honest—if not noble—fellows, who needed no transcendent power, principle, or person outside themselves as guide, teacher, or comforter—they felt adequate in themselves. From morn to night, they went about their functions, making themselves and the world they called their own, comfortable in the assurance that they possessed *common* sense, were *adequate,* self-reliant, and *reasonable.* They were, in truth, *self*-made men.

But they really didn't need or want to be freethinkers or skeptics—they wanted to be churchly, whether or not they were pious; they believed in good report, good behavior, a good conscience, the Ten Commandments, but not in standing still. Times changed and the sensible man changed with them. They were sure they were at least as sensible and informed as the priests who ministered to them.

The "new men" had a feeling of being at home in the world,

free from the terrors of sin and the burden of guilt. They considered themselves as justified as one needed to be in the sight of God and their fellow-men. They began and stayed at even keel. They were honest, if not noble; prudent if not otherworldly.

Forsaking "perfection" or virtuosity, whether in politics, law, religion, or anything else, the new men celebrated the superior merit of the middling virtues—*mediocrity* in the good sense as well as the unhappy one—*honesty* rather than honor, *common* sense, reason, responsibility, orderliness.

In many ways, the Catholic man of the middle classes was like his Protestant opposite number. He too believed in being frugal, respectful, clean, time-saving, prudent. Yet, the self-made man of Catholic France was in fact relatively free of the fearful anxieties which Weber has ascribed to the Protestant Saint of the sixteenth and seventeenth centuries. He had little taste for agonizing self-reexamination, living on the boundaries in unending quest of the assurance of election.

What wonderful materials Groethuysen provides us for a historical tapestry. The center scene would describe the ambitious burgers and defensive clergy making their faces—public and private—as they carry on their household quarrels over their claims to precedence, authority, power, and wealth. The title of the tapestry might well be—the title of this book might well have been! —"The *Catholic* Ethic and the Spirit of Capitalism."

Fourth—The book circles uncannily around a covert center. The reader is led a chase across country roads, city streets, market places, churchyards only to find in the end that the game he he has been pursuing is himself. The story we are reading is about ourselves! If Groethuysen never sounds like the mad wayfarer who cried out that God was dead, it may be because he wanted to correct a popular illusion. God's withdrawal occurs in unspectacular ways as regularly as clockwork both when men build the *secular city*—and when they don't.

Fifth—We are led to ask about the relevance of Groethuysen's book to the current tendencies in the Catholic world. Can the distinctively bourgeois frames which flowered in the period under analysis be expected to continue in the new environments of contemporary Catholicism? My answer to this vexing question would have to be in two parts:

The paradoxes and dilemmas in these fateful processes of the last two centuries—secularization, secularism, sacralization—have yet to find historians worthy of their challenge. Not being a professional sociologist, Groethuysen feels no pressure on him to spell out the steps in the modernizing development, but he nonetheless goes beyond any contemporary sociologist of culture in offering insights into the shifts of sensibility which needed to occur if the Church of the Middle Ages was to make peace with the new world of the new men.

One fact is important to stress: In each successive act of adjustment the Church seeks to preserve its essential spiritual structures and orientations from impairment. No one will claim that it never stumbled. More than once the interdependence between "religion" and the "world" has been almost total, making it impossibly hard to say where "world" ended and "religion" began. Has Protestantism fared better in this regard, in the countries of its greatest development?

Now in mid-twentieth century the Roman Catholic Church is being challenged to respond to pulsing currents of social and cultural change. Beset from within and without by quarrel, tumult, and crisis, it seeks once again to make itself new—and yet remain ever the same. Who can now say what the outcomes will be? At the present moment the Catholic spirit and the Church seem to be veering away from excessively *bourgeois* orientations in the economically most advanced sectors of the world. On the other hand, tendencies in favor of *bourgeoisification* may be expected eventually in the so-called developing areas of the world, but only after agonizing political and cultural upheavals in which every aspect of Catholic life and tradition will be challenged.

Sixth—and *last*—the darkest mystery of all: how to explain the fact that this remarkable book has been so utterly overlooked even by specialists and that its author's name has slipped the memory of scholars in Germany and France, the two lands in which his work was published in variant editions.

Bernard Groethuysen is little known today because the land in which he was born and came of age underwent a holocaust in the 1930's and 40's. Making his way to France before the full flush of the Nazi onslaught, he fortunately found friends in French literary and artistic society and attained a certain eminence as a leading member of the renowned *Nouvelle Revue Française* circle. Several of his works were written in French, most notably his studies of Rousseau and Montesquieu, and he translated others from the German. He passed away quietly in 1946 at the age of sixty-seven in Luxembourg.

The volume now in our hands appeared in 1927 under the title *L'Eglise et la bourgeoisie* and was described as the first volume of his *Origines de l'esprit bourgeois en France*. A second volume of this study never appeared. One reason might have been that the present work is in fact a fresh condensation of the two-volume German edition. Specialists wishing to check details in the footnotes of his chapters on the social teachings of the Church may, however, wish to look into the second volume of the German publication.*

A final word may be allowed:

Groethuysen carries us beyond Dilthey into a focus of sensibility especially relevant to our day. This fact will grow in importance as increasing numbers of researchers feel inspired to seek to settle accounts with the relations of Catholicism and the ethics of capitalism in the history of civilization, whether of modern

---

* The above statement mainly seeks to evoke the atmosphere—the tone and setting—of Groethuysen's portrait. I have therefore restrained myself from comparing Groethuysen's views with those of many others, notably Marx and W. Sombart, who are strongly identified with the meanings of "bourgeois," "bourgeois spirit," and "bourgeoisie." It may help here to say that in my view the term "bourgeois" is often obliged to bear a heavy freight of unassorted senses in ideological polemics. Finally, readers wishing to look further into the material discussed by Groethuysen from a perspective somewhat different from his are advised to consult the thoughtful study of Robert R. Palmer, *Catholics and Unbelievers in 18th Century France* (Princeton: Princeton University Press, 1939), which includes a considered but all too brief estimate of Groethuysen (p. 227) based on a reading of the first volume of the German edition.

Europe or of Africa, the Near East, the Far East, not to mention
Latin America. Future scholars—with wide interests and sympa-
thies—will look not only to Weber, Tawney, W. W. Rostow, and
others—but also to Bernard Groethuysen.

BENJAMIN NELSON

Graduate Faculty
New School for Social Research

The Bourgeois

PART ONE

*The Church
and the Development of the
Bourgeois Conscience*

1 · THE HUMBLE BELIEVER

"The Church," writes Bossuet in his funeral oration for Maria Theresa of Austria, "inspired by God and instructed by the Holy Apostles, has arranged the year in such a manner that we find in it, together with the life, the mysteries, the preaching and the doctrine of Jesus Christ, the true fruit of all these things in the admirable virtues of his servants, and in the examples of his saints; and finally a mysterious epitome of the Old and New Testaments and the whole of Church history." The people derive their religious instruction not only from the feasts, which are "as so many sacred events, annually recalling to us the mysteries and principal articles of our belief," [1] and "which may therefore be regarded as a kind of catechism whereby the principal virtues of the Christian faith are engraved in the memories even of the rudest men," [2] but from everything related to religious observances.

"The first object we see from the outskirts of a Catholic parish is the tower and the cross. This cross, raised in the most prominent place, sums up our faith." Go next "into the parish churches, go into the old abbeys, into the principal church of the diocese or other cathedrals, and you will find there the same objects and the same instruments, small here, of splendid and magnificent appearance there." And in these objects "the whole of the Catholic religion is clearly expressed." If, next, you leave the churches, "where the whole of religion is retraced before your eyes, even without books or pictures, you find a last lesson in the place consecrated for the burial of your families. . . . It is thus that the usages of the Catholic Church, together with the painted figures, are a book that is always open to you," writes Abbé Pluche,* who often gives us very interesting insights into the mind of the humble believer.[3]

In the ceremonial, then, and in the "painted figures," the un-lettered Christian learned his religion even before he learned the text. "Thus before your pastors have given you any instruction, the exterior of the Catholic church has already taught you the selfsame principal truths. What the books say, the ceremonies echo in a hundred ways, and the more the whole is repeated, the more firmly the meaning is rooted." [4] After symbols come words. "While the ceremonies of religion speak to your eyes, we cause the holy truths to resound in your ears, truths which you have learned from infancy and which the Church recalls to you in the celebration of its feasts." [5]

Thus the Church created a whole universe for the believer, a universe which, like the other one, called upon all his faculties and surrounded him completely. But whereas in the world of appearances he knew only what he saw and was ignorant of the whole, the insights of faith, for him, formed a variable universe, the only one which he knew and was able to define. "The most famous men in history and in the conduct of temporal affairs are for you as though they had never been. Whether I speak to you of the ideas of Plato or Confucius, or of the victories of Hannibal or Tamerlane, you know nothing of these men, and you lose very little by not knowing. But you rejoice in the birth of the Precursor; you leave your work to come to sing the victories of Stephen the Deacon, of the holy Apostles, and of those who confessed the marvels of the apostolic preaching in the midst of torment." [6]

Thus the world in which the unlettered believer was really at home was the next world, while he remained ignorant of this one; or, rather, what he knew of it he understood only in terms of visions of the other world, which interpreted to him the why

---

* Many of the major sources of this book will be unknown to the general student of French history but can be adequately identified in the *Diction-naire de Biographie Française* or the *Nouvelle Biographie Générale*. (Tr.)

and wherefore of things, teaching him whence he came and whither he was going and revealing to him the secret of death. Had he broken loose from his Church, he would no longer have known his way about this world; everything would have been different and unfamiliar; he would have found in it only the unintelligible signs of a language which was not the one in which he had learned to think and feel.

Bossuet explains how a child, as yet incapable of reasoning, can nevertheless have faith. "It should not be thought," he writes, "that children in whom reason is budding are incapable of experiencing the impression of truth merely because they are unable to marshal their arguments. We see them learn to speak at a still earlier age; yet neither they nor we, who learned in the same manner, can explain the process by which they learn, by what means they distinguish between noun and verb, substantive and adjective, so deep and hidden is that process. We learn the language of the Church in much the same way. . . . A hidden light leads us to one state as to the other; there reason, here faith. Reason develops gradually, and faith, infused at baptism, does likewise." [7] And, we might add, the humble believer, like many who speak their own language but never learn the rules of grammar, could live his Catholic faith while remaining more or less ignorant of his catechism.

"Everything in the Catholic Church is a form of preaching; the external forms of worship are a perpetual instruction." The Church "speaks little itself, and teaches us many more things than it says every day. It causes us to conceive of and meditate on a great many truths through its various external features, where everything has a clear meaning and a distinct relation to faith." [8] In this way, the Church creates a language intelligible to all. "Our sacred rites flow from our dogmas; they are a tangible and public profession of faith in those dogmas. Within the grasp of the simplest, they unite in a single doctrine the learned man who would lose his way among his own thoughts, and the ignorant man incapable of forming a thought at all." [9]

2 · THE "ENLIGHTENED"

"It is a mistake to imagine that analysis must always precede belief," writes Bossuet. "The good fortune of those who are born, as it were, in the bosom of the true Church, is that God has given the Church such authority that we first believe what it proposes, and that faith precedes, or rather, excludes analysis." "Blessed are those," he writes again, "in whom human notions are linked with the true belief which the Holy Spirit has infused in men's hearts. They are spared a great temptation."[1] Unable to conceive of being anything but Catholics, they will not question a faith common to them all. This is very well explained by Abbé Pluche, an eighteenth-century scholar, less concerned with theology, who often argued as a sociologist. The faithful, he says, "do not ask for proofs of dogmas, or of the Gospel, or of the ministry, any more than they ask for proofs of the acquisition of their patrimony or of the establishment of the magistrature. Proof would be easy to give; but what is the point of proving what is not challenged?"[2]

So let us set aside books, files, and documents and confine ourselves to palpable proofs, to the living argument which the Church daily provides by its mere existence. "Those who want to gain a thorough knowledge of the rights and usages of the London Parliament, or of the Catholic Church, turn to books which have spoken of them through the ages. They may write new ones themselves. But those great institutions needed no books to develop or exercise their rights, or make them known. They anticipate the books; by the brilliance of their luster, they destroy the petty objections to universally recognized maxims which might be advanced by this or that writer." [3]

The Church was a social reality. The same feasts, repeated, "bring with them, from one week to the next, from one century to the other, proofs of the Church's saving mission. . . . Ever the same altars, the same vessels, the same liturgy, the same authority, a mission and a significance which cannot change." [4] The believer knew himself to be in peace and security in a world that did not change and had never changed; he had perfect certainty that, in his Church, he would always find "the true ministry and the proper preservation of the deposit of faith." [5]

So might argue the believer who had preserved the simplicity of faith, which for him took the place of knowledge. "We sometimes find among the common people," writes Abbé Réguig, the Pastor of Gap, "souls whose innocence, rectitude and true piety serve them in place of teachers. . . . We theologians, well-informed, studious men, with our libraries, we leaf through many books, we define everything, we explain everything, we argue about everything. That good soul is unable to define or explain anything; he argues about nothing and practices everything. We hold the key of knowledge and remain outside; he, without study, without books, enters and penetrates into the sanctuary." [6]

Thus, we are told, the Church loved the simple believer who believed without understanding. The simple left doctrine to those in authority; they were content to go on speaking the language of the Church without quibbling about words. On the one hand, we have the theologians, qualified guardians of the faith; on the other, the humble faithful satisfied simply to believe. The duty of the former was to clarify doctrine, enter into discussion with opponents, guard the purity of the faith; the latter should transmit to their descendants a faith born anew in each of them, without anyone being able to say when he had first begun to believe, or why.

But alongside these two types of Catholics, each representing a perfectly legitimate form of belief in their Church, we find a new breed of men emerging in the eighteenth century. They were men who, without being qualified to take part in the government of the Church or to serve as "teachers," had lost the character of ordinary believers. These were people who argued and wanted to analyze before believing. They entered, Massillon writes, into "contestation with God";[7] they questioned, they asked for an accounting. Hecklers, we might call them, people with curious minds who interrupted the authorities at any moment they chose to put this or that question and raise problems. Who were they, and whence did they come? Certainly not, primarily, from the populace. They were the educated, the literate—people of some standing who, knowing what was their due, dealt with their pastors on equal terms.

The Pastor of Gap was highly skeptical about the usefulness of education for the populace. "Your children have been to school; they have learned to read and write. . . . Does that make them more proficient in tilling the soil? . . . . Do those of you who have been to school frequent the bars less than others?" What worried the pastor even more was that those who had been to school were not the most docile members of his flock. "After surveying the situation more carefully," he continues, "I find, as do my colleagues, that the largest part of the least Christian element in our parishes is made up of those who have been to school; whereas the simplest, the most innocent, the most Christian can neither read nor write."

And why should those who could read and write be less good Christians than the rest? Some among them, the Pastor of Gap tells us, had read "those miserable tracts which are capable of corrupting purity of morals and simplicity of faith alike" and which were hawked even in rural areas. But others had read only very orthodox writings, yet had ceased to be docile and submissive Christians. "There's good and bad in my parish," writes the Pastor of Gap, "as in every other." There are souls "who listen to the word of God with simplicity, who believe without reasoning all that faith teaches us; there are others who like to reason as to the why and the wherefore, who play the pundits, who think they know as much as their pastor because they own an old Bible and the big *Lives of the Saints,* out of which they read, or imagine they read." [8]

Those who reasoned thus were all "persons of a certain sort," as the Pastor of Gap called them, "respectable folk," whom he addressed individually, not without irony, as "monsieur." "And where, indeed, do we find the beautiful and precious simplicity of the faith? Is it not commonly among the populace? They believe, without reasoning, what their fathers believed, what their pastors teach them. They don't argue about the why and the wherefore; they stick to their catechism. . . . Whereas you, Monsieur, you argue without rhyme or reason about religion and its mysteries." [9] This "monsieur" was a somebody and wanted to be personally convinced. He believed himself entitled to ask for an accounting of a belief which the common people accepted because everyone else did. He was a bourgeois, aware of himself, knowing what he owed himself; he was no longer the more or less anonymous believer who allowed himself to be led with docility along the beaten track.

The clergy were at a complete loss in the face of the pretensions of this new man. In theory, at least, the Church could not grant the bourgeois an exceptional position in regard to faith. "The simple will always have to blush at their ignorance; but the comforting veil in which faith is clothed ignores this distressing inequality; from the point of view of faith, all are scholars and all are unlettered; the same mysteries are for all, and there is therefore no more pride for these nor shame for the others; the Church is like a good mother who permits no pre-eminence among her children, and whose only predilection is for the more docile." [10] But the bourgeois wanted no part in an equality which would strip him of his prerogatives as a thinking man, and he continued to question God and his servants and to ask for explanations. Belief, for him, was to become increasingly an intellectual problem. Faith was no longer bound up with existence itself; he did not find it "natural" to believe. In time, therefore, he came to consider belief as assent to propositions submitted for his examination, placing himself outside the faith and forgetting that he was a Catholic.

Hence, the silent language of symbol, which still endured, and was handed down from generation to generation, could no longer suffice for those who wanted to get to the bottom of things. In order to believe what the Church taught, they had to be convinced that what the Church said was true.

The Church speaks little itself, Abbé Pluche had said. Yet how should it remain silent before those who questioned it and for whom the testimony of buildings and ceremonies no longer sufficed? If these outsiders, who sought the precise meaning of words and raised the question of truth, were to be brought back to the faith, the Church must at all costs find definitions and clarifications. It must tell these "persons of a certain sort," these bourgeois who did not want to be identified with the mass of the faithful, what they must believe and why they must believe it. Doctrine would no longer be directly identified with objects. The sermon would be carried outside the church precincts, and words would no longer be enveloped in that aura of mystery which shielded them from too glaring a light. Faith would become a doctrine to be known and presented in a language which was not the common idiom and which would have to be learned in terms carefully chosen and defined.

3 · BOURGEOISIE AND POPULACE

COLLECTIVE FAITH AND INDIVIDUAL ASSENT

"That individuals should be ignorant of certain articles of faith," writes Bossuet, "I readily admit; but the Church conceals nothing of what Jesus Christ has revealed; and that is why the faithful who do not know certain individual articles nevertheless confess them all in general when they say, 'I believe in the universal Church.'" [1] The Bishop of Meaux was very cautious in his treatment of a subject which, on closer examination, might give rise to awkward questions. Other, less sagacious theologians sought to give definitions and make the necessary distinctions between what the believer knew and what he believed without knowing. Distinguishing between implicit and explicit faith, they endeavored to determine what was required in each of these two ways of believing.

"We term implicit faith belief in the consequences of an article of faith, even when those consequences are not clearly perceived. Thus a Christian who believes that Jesus Christ is God and Man believes implicitly that he has two natures and two wills, because the second truth is implicit in the first," writes Abbé Bergier. A harmless enough assertion, which might be reduced more or less to a rule of logic, applicable to every kind of deduction. But let us read farther. "The simple believer, who believes in the infallible authority of the Church, and who is predisposed to believe all the truths which the Church will teach him, believes all those truths *implicitly;* he will believe them *explicitly* once he knows them distinctly and professes them formally." [2] An altogether more significant statement, which might even lead to certain embarrassing conclusions. For if it sufficed to believe in the "infallibility of the Church" and to be submissive to its teaching in order to have "implicit faith in all the truths it teaches," might not the believer remain ignorant of all truths save only one, namely, that the Church is infallible, and consider himself a perfect Christian?

Theologians were, therefore, careful to add that "implicit and general faith does not suffice" and that there were "individual truths which the Christian is obliged to know and to believe with an explicit faith." [3] In other words, there were certain "fundamental articles or dogmas" which the believer must know and believe "on pain of damnation." [4]

A distinction had to be made, therefore, between what must be believed explicitly and what might be believed only implicitly. According to the Theological Faculty of Paris, there were articles "necessary to truth and useful to the whole Church, but of no utility to many. Although articles of this kind belong to the public revelation and are known by the learned, it is nevertheless not customary to propose them expressly to the faith of the simple and ignorant, for whom it suffices to have an implicit faith." [5]

Thus the faithful might have "an implicit faith in certain Christian verities which they do not know distinctly." Hence there would be "certain revealed truths whose knowledge is not absolutely necessary to salvation, and which are neither major dogmas, nor contained in those dogmas." For these, "it suffices that the simple man should believe in general all that the Church believes; and then his faith, although implicit, is not without an object, since he knows, by revelation, that the Church is the depository of all Christian truths, and that it cannot be deceived in its belief or in its teaching, or in its decisions on dogma and morals." [6]

The theory of implicit faith, as applied in the eighteenth century, was, in a way, designed to compensate for obvious gaps in the principle of authority as such. The believer could not believe all that the Church taught, but he could believe the Church.

However, in believing the Church, what did he really believe? That was the question which of necessity had to be raised and which took on particular importance in the eighteenth century. So long as faith remained a living unity, it was less important to specify what one believed and how one believed. One truth would be present in the mind, another forgotten, but the believer would nonetheless be persuaded that he believed everything, without taking into account the frontiers of his present belief and its variations according to circumstances. "I believe the Church" and "I believe what the Church says" were, then, basically the same thing, the first constituting the enduring faith, the second individual and variable acts by which the believer concentrated now on one object of the faith, now on another, without its being really possible to distinguish between those two modes of belief.

It became necessary to establish distinctions, to define the area of what each man believed, and might not believe, and to discern the modes of belief. "I believe the Church, but do I really believe all that the Church teaches? I am ignorant of such and such a truth. May I believe what I don't know? I don't understand this or that mystery, and find it very hard to believe. May I be presumed to believe it, although in fact I don't? Is it enough for me simply to trust the Church? What do I have to believe in practice, and what need I not believe?" These were the terms of the question for those who believed on their own account. Faith, for them, was no longer a unity; it was divided, fragmented.

In order to restore the unity of faith in consciences, therefore, the Church had to resort to a series of fictions. "By submitting to the authority of the Church, you will continue to believe what you can no longer believe." That was the first fiction. But how could the believer thus believe what he was reluctant to believe? How was it to be shown that this particular verity, for which he had no use, nevertheless belonged to his belief? The explanation was that he would believe with an implicit faith what he could not believe with an explicit faith and would thus remain, as it were, a Catholic in spite of himself. Here was the second fiction, added to the first and completing it.

The Catholic always knows very little about his faith, and what knowledge he has gained has become very imperfectly his, and may have assumed forms which debase its purity. There has thus necessarily been a problem at all times for all who are not theologians. But why, in the eighteenth century, did this problem take on particular importance? And why did it seem necessary to resort to so many distinctions in order to resolve it and thus enable "respectable persons" to continue to call themselves Catholics? The humble, who continued to believe as their fathers had believed, knew their religion very imperfectly, too. Indeed, they knew it generally even less well than the bourgeois who had received a certain degree of education, and yet the problem for them seems to have presented far fewer difficulties.

"You will find good folk everywhere who have been going to church for forty or fifty years, and assiduously attending services and sermons, yet who are still ignorant of the basic elements of Christianity," says Abbé Fleury. "Most of them think they know the catechism because they learned it as children, and don't realize that they have forgotten or never really understood it." [7] In the same vein, the Pastor of Gap notes that "you find old men among the people who don't know even the first principles of the catechism, and who say they have forgotten it." [8] The position of these old men who had forgotten their catechism was regarded as very grave, for "holy Church cries loudly to all the faithful that whoever would be saved must first have a knowledge of the Catholic faith," [9] that is, know his catechism thoroughly, for it contains "the dogmas which we are absolutely obliged to believe to be saved." [10]

So those humble believers, however faithful throughout their lives to attendance at services and sermons, could not hope to avoid hell, since, whatever their other merits, the fact remained that, "without knowledge of the principles of religion, we are damned." [11] And since there was no doubt that ignorance reigned "among the common people, and particularly in the rural areas, through lack of instruction," [12] only very few of these simple people, whom the Church ceaselessly proposed as models, would be found among the elect.

In my view, however, the Grand Archdeacon of Evreux, Monseigneur Boudon, and so many other rigorous theologians were asking the question in the wrong way. They seemed to take each of these unlettered believers singly and question them separately on what they knew or believed. It was the community which believed, the community which knew, and not this or that particular individual, and it was for the community to answer for each individual. The Church believed for this unlettered man who had never really learned his catechism and had eventually forgotten it altogether, the Church which knew everything, believed everything, and never erred.

But what was true regarding the ordinary believer no longer applied to the enlightened bourgeois. Either he knew or he did not know. Either he believed or he did not believe, without being able to appeal to his implicit faith, to cite for his personal advantage what belonged to the common belief. He believed that of which he was convinced, and nothing more. Hence, when it became necessary to work out "catechisms adapted to the capacity of forty- or fifty-year-old children," [13] as Abbé Champion de Pontallier put it, the fact that the bourgeois had forgotten the principles of faith was to have an altogether different significance. For what would have disappeared from the consciousness of the bourgeois was not this or that truth, hard to understand when formulated in precise terms, but a whole universe . . . the universe of faith; the bourgeois would have forgotten how to believe.

The unlettered Christian was a believer; without always knowing what he believed, he lived in a world which was that of the Church and which he could not abandon to live elsewhere. Sometimes he knew little indeed about it; the Archdeacon of Evreux charged the country folk with committing some deplorable errors on the subject. "More often than I can say," he tells us, "I have found elderly persons who have replied, not by mistake but through lack of knowledge, that they loved the most holy Virgin as much as God . . . others said, more than God." Others had told him "that the glorious Virgin is God . . . that she made God; that she has always existed, and similar, altogether ridiculous things." [14] To Monseigneur Boudon all this appeared very grave; he feared for the salvation of the ignorant.

Yet was not this world of the simple identical for all who believed, unlettered and lettered alike, however varied the interpretations placed upon it, whatever the misjudgments or errors of perspective made concerning it? The Virgin was a part of it just as the good Lord . . . and also the devil; everything about it was supernatural and miraculous. The Archdeacon of Evreux accused the ignorant of failing to attach sufficient importance to what was set down in the catechism, and the clergy of failing to explain it to them well enough. "Truths are learned merely by rote; I say 'merely' because people repeat them like parrots, without understanding, which is altogether illusory; for after all, these truths must be understood. . . . It is not enough to repeat definitions correctly if those definitions are not understood." [15] But were not the unlettered at home in a world where both what could and could not be said were true on the same basis? That was also why they were not so concerned to know the terms in which the mysteries could be expressed.

Some people, the Archdeacon of Evreux tells us again, "say and repeat that there is one God in three Persons without any respect, as though they had learned that there were three trees in their garden. If I taught a parrot that there was one God in three Persons, it would repeat the words one hundred times a day. I teach them to a man; and if I don't explain them, and he simply repeats them, who will distinguish him from the poor animal?" [16] That three were one and one was three did not seem to interest the inhabitants of the countryside, to the indignation of the worthy archdeacon. But were they so much to be blamed? The world contained so many more mysterious things which they accepted without difficulty, things more likely to appeal to their imagination.

The ordinary believer believed too much, and in too direct and spontaneous a fashion, to be very interested in knowing what he believed. The bourgeois, by contrast, no longer had sufficient faith to wish to understand what he was supposed to believe. The former, believing in mystery, was unconcerned to establish a complete and detailed accounting of all the mysteries and to define the meaning of each; the latter, no longer believing in mystery, was at a loss about what to do with the mysteries presented to him.

The Archdeacon of Evreux, speaking of the poor villagers, deplored the fact that "they don't know God," that "they know him less than they know their household animals." [17] But this divinity whom the peasants represented to themselves was nevertheless recognizable under the often outlandish images they used; it lived with them, it was their God. Continuing to enjoy unlimited power over them, God dispensed rain and fair weather; he caused the crops to grow and accomplished other marvels in a world which was still his.

In the bourgeois' world, on the other hand, although his concepts of God were often much loftier, neither God nor his age-old antagonist, the devil, were at home. The devil was ridiculed, and, if some respect was shown to God, it was on condition that he in turn would respect the general laws governing the universe and refrain from acting contrary to the plans of the middle class, who used their reason and demanded their share in the government of the world. While the faithful had preserved the vision of a Christian universe and erred simply as to persons and titles, the bourgeois had taken away heaven and hell from the God of the Christians and conceived of him without his legendary power. A divinity without a name of his own and without personality, his role was increasingly reduced to that of an abstract and colorless principle in a world which he was supposed to have created but which he must no longer inhabit.

Thus, within the framework of the Christian religion, two worlds evolved, whose inhabitants, while often using the same terms, no longer spoke the same language. Some still used a Church jargon, and were often accused of lacking in dignity and accuracy in what they said; others, although expressing themselves in a chastened and correct style, did not know, when they tried to speak as Christians, the true meaning of the words they used. In speaking of God in traditional terms, they were guilty of a kind of neologism. In the language still spoken by the humble, all words, whatever their particular meaning, signified mystery; in the modern language of the enlightened bourgeois, since the words no longer had their common meaning, everything that was said meant something different.

The Church thus had to deal on the one hand with the ignorant, who preserved the spirit of the language spoken by their fathers but were often guilty of deplorable misconstructions which the Church could not let pass, and on the other hand with "persons of a certain sort," who ostensibly spoke the language very correctly but had changed the meaning of the words.

FAITH AND SUPERSTITION

You have to "know the people of our rural areas," writes a contemporary observer, "and especially the peasants of our remoter regions, to get a true picture of the ridiculous superstitions and prejudices of all kinds which their ignorance and simplicity cause them to adopt and to believe." [18] The humble believer, who had retained his sense of wonder and did not always find in the faith preached to him the wherewithal to satisfy it, would put God and the saints to work to produce new miracles. The result, as Bossuet notes, derogated from the "order of true religion, chaste, severe enemy of the senses, and solely attached to invisible possessions." [19] But were these poor people so much to be blamed if they sought to see with their own eyes, if they wanted to apply the faith to themselves and their own particular needs?

While "the scientists are too slow to believe," says a contemporary preacher, "the people believe too much." [20] But from the Christian viewpoint, the people were to be preferred. The man of the people believed in miracles, he still hoped in the intercession of the saints. "Secret miracles," says the Pastor of Gap, "miracles unknown to those who are called persons of a certain sort, who don't believe them, mock at them, and ridicule the pious simplicity of the believer, whereas the latter asks for and receives them." [21] Réguis charges the bourgeois with "treating with contempt, and turning to ridicule certain practices authorized by the Church . . . as fashioned only for the people." He cites as examples "that good woman telling her beads, that husbandman who plants crosses in his fields," the humble believer "who attributes to the sound of bells the virtue of warding off storms" or who "carries on his person, or respectfully keeps in his house, relics, crosses, images, or other objects consecrated by the prayers and blessing of the Church." [22]

The enlightened bourgeois would have nothing to do with

things of this kind. He had managed to put a certain distance between himself and heaven, thereby preventing excesses. The man of the people, on the other hand, "in whom religious impressions are not counterbalanced by the distractions of luxury, or by the society of enlightened or frivolous men," believed in the real presence of the objects of his belief. "He puts nothing between himself and the divinity, so that religion comes to weigh on his imagination, acting upon it with full force." [23] Religion for him had colors which the more drab religion of the bourgeois had not. If he did not feel the need to understand everything, he wanted to be able to represent to himself the things of faith, to have them, so to speak, at home. The bourgeois had arranged a religion for himself which did not require much effort of thought or imagination; the people, on the other hand, maintained a certain vitality in the religious sphere which their pastors, whom it sometimes appalled, were nevertheless compelled to take into account.

Religious activity seems to have been concentrated in very many places, in congregations and confraternities, often founded by humble laymen for whom the traditional forms were insufficient. The enlightened bourgeois often complained of them. "Let's have none of those associations," they said, "which, by persuading the common people that their confraternities are the focal point of salvation, turn them away both from the essential duties of religion and from the work pertaining to their station, making them intolerant or superstitious, and even inculcating a spirit of partisanship." [24] And abuses certainly appear to have existed. "What should I say," exclaims the Pastor of Gap, "of those special feasts which certain societies are accustomed to celebrate in honor of their confraternity's patron saint? Apart from the few moments devoted as a matter of form to the celebration of the holy mysteries, is not the day spent in frivolity, sometimes even in libertinage? And please God that the dues of the confraternity are not spent on banquets and altogether worldly practices!" [25]

The people, in their devotion to God and his saints, seemed always to combine considerations of a more secular order with their religious aspirations. But this combination was perhaps not as bizarre as the bourgeois imagined, taking into account the spirit in which the humble inhabitants of the countryside regarded the solemnities of their religion. They put into it what appeared irreconcilable: adoration of mystery and a zest for life, combining in a single sentiment all the emotions which transcend the monotony of the daily round.

The bourgeois was quite incapable of the same kind of sentiment, but if his religion was purer, or more sober, than that of the unlettered people, it was also far more sterile. He did not feel the urge, which possessed peasants and craftsmen, to seek all kinds of ways of manifesting his faith. Popular Catholicism, in the eighteenth century, still preserved its distinctive life. We find in it a spirit of action which seemed to break down the guidelines set by the Church. But this activity must have shocked the bourgeois, for there was always something haphazard about it, and it was linked with superstition. The bourgeois felt all the more justified in thinking it reasonable to go no farther, in religion, than moderate ideas and sentiments which could not rouse the imagination.

But those who were constantly attacking superstition were really attacking faith or, rather, the application of faith to daily life. The people wanted faith to pay dividends, they wanted God and his saints to have some part in the things that concerned them; they wanted to associate them with their lives. The bourgeois, at first glance, was more discreet, but actually he did not believe enough for his faith to have any practical application. His faith could no longer be a thing for daily usage, pertaining to individual events; he could believe only "in general," and it might even be dangerous for him to apply faith to this or that occasion of his life, for he realized, then, that he did not really believe at all or that he did not believe what he thought he had believed hitherto.

This explains, at least in part, why the bourgeois, while remaining a Catholic, did not want his religion to go too far. He did not want to be confronted in too explicit or detailed a fashion with what he was supposed to believe. Consequently, when presenting the faith to him, the clergy proceeded with great caution. Many preachers, addressing the enlightened on the eve of the Revolution, tended to drain religion of all its tangible properties "on the pretext of making it more spiritual," going so far as to abolish devotions "authorized by the Church and consecrated by the piety of the people." [26] The worldly Christian must not know too much of what he was supposed to believe, and a certain ignorance might even be useful. Above all, the objects of faith must not be brought too close to him, associated with the things of life, for his faith was no longer sturdy enough to be confronted with realities; if he tried to use it, it might be destroyed altogether.

"Without losing our faith completely," Massillon had written earlier, "we allow it to weaken within us, and make no use of it." [27] The enlightened bourgeois who appeared to be accusing the humble of misusing their faith was really attacking them for using it at all. His objection, the bourgeois said, was to those "little devotional practices," which did not evoke the "great ideas of religion." [28] But what he was really attacking was the devout themselves. The reason he did not want God to be too much involved in the affairs of this world was that he no longer believed that the deity had much connection with them.

So we have to be wary of the bourgeoisie when it assumes the defense of religion against the "people." The bourgeois, for instance, found it comical that country priests, after daily saying Masses that the grapes might be preserved from hail, should then demand their share of the crop. At first, the "enlightened class" seemed merely to have been objecting to a practice unworthy of the sacred character of the ministers of the Church. Then they began to feel that the practice itself was perhaps a trifle superstitious. But basically, the bourgeois no longer believed that God had anything to do with good and bad crops, whereas the faith of the humble found it inconceivable that God should not be concerned with them.

Thus there developed two social classes, both presumably believing the teachings of the Church, but no longer understanding one another. One continued to apply and even extend the application of the faith; the other feared to touch it at all. The misuse which the humble inhabitant of the countryside sometimes made of faith incited the bourgeois to the utmost discretion on the subject; it was preferable, he felt, to be unbelieving rather than superstitious. We might even go so far as to say that the bourgeois never felt his own identity more keenly than in comparison with the humble inhabitants of the countryside, who continued to believe with simple and sturdy faith. He knew himself to be a bourgeois, an enlightened man, and the proof was that he knew the score and no longer expected God and his saints to interfere miraculously in the events of daily life.

TWO WORLDS

"You find Christian philosophers everywhere these days," says Massillon, "and believers who pontificate about the faith. Everything is toned down; everything is given an air of reasonableness; by retaining the fundamentals of the Christian doctrine and of hope in Jesus Christ, people think they are producing a more wholesome religion because it is clearer and more intelligible; they are wary of anything that savors even remotely of the miraculous or the unexpected." [29]

In the world which the bourgeois had built for himself, there was no longer any room for the marvelous; it was a world closed to miracle. The enlightened refused to believe in mystery as such; the universe of the Christian God and his saints now appeared to them as altogether remote. "Deliberately, on principle, systematically, nothing supernatural must be believed; the mere mention of miracle must provoke mockery among worldly people, and they must feel sorry for people like ourselves, who believe in miracles when they are obvious," writes Abbé Molinier.[30]

The apologists of religion argued with the worldly-minded; they cited witnesses to prove the truth of miracles, as though they were dealing with some perfectly ordinary fact which could be established by appeal to authority. Religion, they said, "concedes that it proposes incomprehensible things for our belief," but it "offers to prove their truth by factual evidence, which it is willing to submit to examination." [31] But the facts on which the mysteries are founded are themselves "miraculous facts," [32] and consequently the worldly, however submissive they might be to the authority of the Church, were unable to believe in them. They continued to reject miracles "in a religion founded only on miracles, and which is itself the greatest of all miracles." [33] And if the defenders of the Church persisted, its opponents asked why God did not "perform miracles nowadays" and added that if he did, they would believe.[34]

The question they put to their pastor was one of deep significance. The modern world brooked no more miracles; faith had become "the heritage of the credulous common folk.[35] "All faith is regarded as simple-mindedness," says the Bishop of Langres.[36] "How naïve of you to believe everything the priests say," the secularist told those who continued to believe as before. "Do as I do; I am not so credulous. I believe what I see, what I understand; that is the proper way and the right philosophy." [37] In speaking thus, the secularist may not have intended to oppose all religion; he left "to the people," as Massillon puts it, "belief in so many marvelous happenings which the history of religion has preserved for us," [38] and retained for himself what was "reasonable" in the faith. Hence he continued to be able to speak highly of Christian morality and to assert his belief in God, while rejecting all mystery and marvel as so many fairy tales.

"In order to destroy ancient superstitions," asks a contemporary preacher, "is it necessary to destroy religion itself?" [39] The worldly were no longer capable of making the distinction, and many of them dared "treat as superstitions and daydreams the very dogmas of the Church," [40] or, if they accepted them, would strip them of that mysterious depth no longer tolerable save to "Gothic personages, attached to ancient prejudices." [41] They were on their guard against the marvelous and were reluctant to believe at all, for fear of being credulous. "For them, wisdom and the proper use of reason consist only in not believing," comments Abbé Molinier.[42]

Again we see two attitudes subsisting side by side; two worlds, we might say, the old and the new. The bourgeois, to assert himself, needed to become an unbeliever; the lack of faith of which the preachers accused him was a part of his class consciousness. There were two sorts of people: the "good folk" and the "man of the world" capable of using his reason, the populace and the bourgeois.

The people, then, would go on believing, believing in what was mysterious both in religion and outside religion. There were still in France "whole classes which do not even realize what efforts have been made to destroy it," as the Archbishop of Toulouse, a deputy to the National Assembly, remarked.[43] "Shall it be said," asks Jauffret in 1790, "that the people have ceased to believe?" But it is not true, he replies, "that the greater part have ceased to believe. I can cite the testimony of the pastors of our rural areas to this effect, and even that of the pastors of the cities. They will all assure you that the mass of the people still believe, often to the point of superstition. It is true," he adds, "that the most enlightened elements among them are also the most unbelieving."[44]

Sometimes, too, elements from among "the people," though having a less developed sense of class than their masters, became aware of the difference separating them in the area of faith. We read in a document of the time of the Revolution, "This is how the worthy pastors speak to their flocks on the subject: 'Alas, my dear brothers, there is no more faith or religion in the cities, we are told, so let us make every effort to preserve this sacred deposit which God has entrusted to us in our villages.'"[45] Then the people might turn against the bourgeois and hurl "many insults at them, among others that they want to change religion and even God himself," and accuse them of having "no religion."[46]

It would nevertheless be false to regard the two social classes as wholly separate, the one made up of believers whose faith was intact, the other of "philosophers" who believed nothing. "The people—the craftsman, the inhabitant of the countryside—are throwing off the yoke of religion," asserts a contemporary writer.[47] "Religion is judged in the workshops! Philosophy, which has descended to the lowest ranks, has made thinkers of everyone," says another.[48] This observation, of course, must not be taken literally. It is nevertheless true that the time was past when it could be said that "it is hardly necessary to write books to prove to the people . . . the truth of Christianity. They do not doubt it and, if they do, then stupidly, and without being able to argue the point for lack of basic principles. Consequently it is either a waste of time to try to argue with them, or an undertaking which is not necessary at all, because they are so little inclined to have doubts, and for them proofs of conscience and sentiment are more effective than the soundest theology and philosophy." [49] Things had changed indeed. The Pastor of Gap complains that "hawkers distribute in the country areas as in the towns all kinds of miserable tracts which are capable of corrupting purity of morals and simplicity of faith alike." [50]

It might be wondered how pamphlets could influence almost illiterate peasants. "But these people have eyes, and they see, and they have ears, and they hear. This servant attends Mass in his parish church and listens to his pastor's sermon, explaining the Gospel to him and telling him very good things. When he returns home, he finds a master or a mistress who tells him very bad ones." Or again, "This peasant cannot read," but "this 'monsieur,' who left his village long ago to seek his fortune and who, after making it—no one knows how!—has come back to show himself in his new plumage, this 'monsieur' has read, and if he has not read, he has seen, he says, and heard what the right people think, the enlightened people, the intelligent people. So now he comes to enlighten his fellow villagers: 'What, you do this! you believe that! what simpletons you are!' That suffices, sometimes, to corrupt a peasant's mind, and to make him doubt the most holy truths of religion." [51]

The Church could not prevent the influence of the middle class from affecting the attitude of the common people. The prestige which the bourgeois enjoyed rested on a series of moral and economic conditions which the Church was powerless to alter. Hence if those who had formerly been simple believers adopted the language of the enlightened, it was in order to prove to themselves and to others that they belonged to a higher class, that they had become in their turn "persons of a certain sort." This was additional proof that religion had become a thing for the common folk. The man who "looks with contempt and as though from the height of his own eminence at the wretched people who assist respectfully at the sacred mysteries," this man who "believes himself to be a distinguished personage because he does not bow, or genuflect, or say prayers like the rest," and who says to his pastor, "in a tone of pride which is pitiful, 'you can't frighten me with the devil—I'm not one of the *people;* devotional books are for the ignorant, and the rosary for good women,' " [52] while he was denying his religion, was at the same time establishing a distinction between two social classes and making what might be termed a declaration for the recognition of his rights as a member of the middle class.

And that, too, was why the clergy's campaign against the incredulity of the bourgeois was vain; the bourgeois would not give up his rights. To believe, for him, would have been to detract from his newly won dignity, to descend instead of to climb, to see himself assimilated into that anonymous mass, the "common people," from whom he wished to be quite distinct.

Thus disbelief became identified with the idea of the bourgeois; it became, in a way, the hallmark of a class. The unbeliever, originally, had become one on his own account, and the Church had accused him of a desire to be different. He was not like the others, who continued to believe; he had rid himself of his prejudices, which he knew were those of the common herd. The parish priest could point to him; he was the lamb which had strayed and which should be brought back to the sheepfold. True, he was not altogether alone; he had found others of like opinions; he had his group. But those belonging to it had more or less deliberately placed themselves outside society, and most of the time they defied not only its religious prejudices but also its moral sentiments. The parish priest denounced them to the others, who wished to remain respectable and continue to live the common life.

But gradually disbelief became respectable. It acquired a moral character. By the mere fact that it was an integral part of the consciousness of a class—of the bourgeoisie—it became bourgeois. From an individual phenomenon, or a phenomenon confined to certain isolated groups, it became an expression of collective life.

Faced with this new form of disbelief, the Church was at first at a complete loss. It saw only an appalling number of unbelievers, which was growing larger every day. "An unassuming pamphlet, attractively written, makes a thousand unbelievers in a day," writes a contemporary apologist.[53] The Church would have liked to turn to each of those thousand unbelievers separately, to show him that he was wrong, that he had allowed himself to be led astray by his passions, that he had everything to fear in the next life, and so forth. But it was not he, really, who had become disbelieving, it was his whole class, and it was his class consciousness which replied for him when he was addressed individually.

Was he a sinner? Possibly. But could his class, the bourgeoisie, be condemned as a whole? The Church did not realize how secure he felt when it spoke to him of damnation. Would God send a whole class to hell, the class of the respectable? Who, then, would be in heaven? The common people? That would be hard to imagine!

And in any case, just because the common people were believers, were they any the better for it? "They go to the sacraments, we are told, but honesty and integrity are very rare among them. They wouldn't miss a service, they go to all the processions, they belong to all the confraternities; but they get up at night to pillage our gardens, to steal our fruit, to harvest our vines. . . . They are devout in church, they pray at length, they clasp their hands, they kiss the ground; but on leaving they go to the bars, get drunk and have nothing but oaths and vile language in their mouths." [54]

Faith was a phenomenon of a collective nature. The same was to be true of disbelief. The battle was now joined between two powers, each of which had a collective character: the Church and the bourgeoisie. The bourgeois might very well say that religion was necessary "for the people" and even admit that Christianity was "undoubtedly the best that can be given them." [55] But in saying this, he was proving that he knew how to distinguish between those who were of his class and the others who were not. For if religion was good for the people, and even necessary, he could do without it, while remaining what he was, a perfectly honest man. The difference between the two classes, bourgeoisie and people, was an established fact, and the distinguishing characteristic was specifically the attitude of each toward religion.

This does not mean that every bourgeois was necessarily an unbeliever, while the people remained faithful. What it does mean is that if the bourgeois retained anything of the traditional faith, he did so on his own account and not in his capacity as a bourgeois. The common folk continued to say, *"we* believe"; the bourgeois always said only, *"I* believe." And what he believed was always something added to his life, which did not modify his secular status. But for the people, faith remained integrated in life and identified with it.

Describing the peasant spirit of the Vendée, two deputies of the National Assembly reported on October 9, 1791, that "his religion, or religion as he sees it, has become for him the strongest and, one might say, the sole moral force of his life." Religion, for the mass of the people, was intimately linked with the collective life, of which it was one of the foundations. A man no longer felt at home, no longer was in community with his neighbors, if he ceased to belong to the Church. He was a Catholic as he was a subject of the king, or as he bore a name, or as he belonged to a town, a village, or a family. The fact of being Catholic, for most, was a very natural thing, like everything which linked the individual to his environment, his community, his country.

Hence the unlettered faithful could not do without their religion, which created their communal life and made them feel that they belonged to a community. It was in church that they gathered; on special feast days, those who lived far from one another would meet in church and unite in the same sentiments. "In the sparsely populated areas, where the inhabitants are widely scattered, they can gather, receive instruction, and make public profession of their Christian faith only on feast days; were they to be deprived of this, they would soon become completely brutish." [56]

The country dwellers thus remained attached to their religion. "It is untrue that external worship has become a matter of indifference to the people; the contrary is proved by the crowds gathered in our churches on feast days, to the great disappointment of unbelievers. In the rural areas, where the inhabitants are more devout than in the cities, no individual fails to attend divine service when he can, and he often attends Mass even on weekdays." [57] The populace, attached to their ancient customs, did not want the least change in them. They cried out "against our lords, the prelates, because they had wisely curtailed certain feasts." [58] Everything pertaining to worship in their parish churches was their business. "The parish church is thus the true house of the faithful, and as parishioners they have an acquired right to all the treasures with which it is filled; an acquired right to the sacraments administered there, to the prayers recited, to the instructions given, and to all the graces distributed there." [59]

The bourgeois, too, to a great extent, retained certain religious traditions. But if the bourgeois continued to go to church, did he still belong to the Church? It was his Church, of course, for he remained a Catholic, but he was a bourgeois and a Catholic rather than a Catholic bourgeois. The Church, for him, had ceased to be a great community in which a man lives and dies. One might say that he retained his secular character even in church; he was there only in transit; he was a stranger, as the preachers were ceaselessly to repeat. He was not of the community; he was not at home when he was in church.

Thus a separation had been established between bourgeoisie and Church. The bourgeois who spoke of the Church praised or blamed it as one who did not belong to it. He no longer judged it from within. When, later, during the Revolution, he had to consider what to do with the Church in the new social and political order, he put the question less for himself than for those who were not of his class, for the populace on the one hand and for the clergy on the other, the two being intimately linked in his eyes, whereas he himself, standing outside the Church, judged of the usefulness of religion as an impartial observer.

4 · PRIESTS AND LAITY

"If we consider the Church as the Mystical Body of Jesus Christ," says Fénelon, "we must always find in it the image of the natural body of the Saviour, which it represents. . . . The Holy Spirit animates and organizes the whole of this great body; he impresses on the whole body a movement of submission and docility toward the principal parts, which take the place of the head; he impresses on those whom he thus makes leaders of the whole body a movement of wisdom, of intelligence, of authority and of direction; he gives the eyes the power to see and to enlighten the rest of the body; he gives the ears the power . . . to be the common hearing of all the members; he gives the mouth the power to speak for all and to all." But it would appear that now, in this Church which, "animated by the Holy Spirit," was "a real unity, a living body with its organs," [1] there were circulatory disorders, that the organs no longer functioned in harmony, that the same life no longer animated both head and members. The bourgeoisie, to a large extent, led a life apart; it had eyes to see, a wisdom, an intelligence of its own; it confronted the Church and judged it from without.

At all times the Church had had to make a distinction between head and members, between the "teaching" and the "listening" Church, the former consisting of the bishops and priests, the latter consisting of the faithful, who had to receive with docility what their pastors told them. Thus "the faithful should not concern themselves with reasoning or criticizing; they should listen to what they are taught with complete submission." [2] Such a distinction seemed to have become more necessary than ever at a time when so many indiscreet laymen were meddling with the things of faith. "If the insistence on the distinction between the teaching Church and the Church which believes the things that are taught has become more general in our day, it is because this distinction has to be made to counter errors either newly born, or repeated with new-found passion." [3]

But however necessary this distinction might have appeared, it was bound, if pushed farther, to break the unity of the Church. After all, those who listened were not the Church in the same sense as those who taught. They might listen, or they might not; they might take it or leave it; but they all spoke of the Church as of something external to themselves, as of an organization existing outside themselves, represented by a group of persons whose job it was to preach religion, to defend the faith.

"I know," says Père Berruyer, "that the unbelievers flatter themselves that they can escape our just reproaches by replying to them, in that bantering tone which they excel at using to cover their weakness, that persons of our profession . . . are not credible on the subject of religion, that in defending it we are simply doing our job—for that is how they are pleased to put it—and that we are paid to talk the language of devotion, to sound the pious note." [4] The Pastor of Gap comments, "Nowadays among most Christians, we find nothing but indifference, a fatal insensitiveness to the weal and woe of the Church. We are dead members, since we no longer feel either the health or the sickness of the body to which we belong." [5] People continued to call themselves Catholics, but this appellation had little relevance to their convictions.

"Whence comes it," asks Champion de Pontallier toward the end of the century, "that the faithful, who formerly were soldiers, have now become idle spectators in the relentless war waged against our Mother?" The Church can no longer count on its children, he says; it lacks officers; it no longer has brave soldiers prepared to defend it. "Those who strike the most dangerous blows at the Church are not the impious and the avowed libertines, nor the souls unfortunately and notoriously given over to deception and baseness, but men undecided in their conduct as in their sentiments. The Church is a great army corps always on the march and in battle formation. The turncoats who go over to the enemy, or the deserters who leave because they are discontented, hardly weaken it at all. It suffers infinitely more from those cowardly soldiers who retain the uniform of good people but yield at the slightest shock, break their lines, and thus lead to the rout of most of the troops." [6]

But why should the laity act as defenders of the Church, which for them had become little more than an institution run by priests, whose business it was to defend their own interests? The clergy were necessarily regarded as rivals by the bourgeois. "It is not unusual," writes Beurier, "to find even among those who still have a grain of religion in their hearts, men who . . . repeat after [the unbelievers] invectives against the ministers of a religion which they do not hate." [7]

These were the antipriests, as Beurier called them, and they were numerous among "persons of a certain sort." "There is a certain type of social gathering where one finds so many of those men for whom nothing is sacred, who respect neither popes nor cardinals nor bishops nor, of course, priests or men or women in religious orders. . . . A particular man whom they might like, were he not a priest or a monk, will become the object of their aversion because he is one or the other. The very virtues of these men, devoted to the service of religion, are turned to ridicule, or attributed to a false or hypocritical piety. Their good works are labeled cant or bigotry." [8]

The antipriests, we are told, were always on the lookout, taking a malicious delight in tracking down the errors of the servants of the Church. "They seek to ridicule and disfigure them with a thousand biting barbs of satire and mockery; every weakness is exposed; everything they do is regarded as a crime, so that all the attacks on them may be turned against religion itself." [9] "If the clergy happen to commit some faults—because for all that they are consecrated to God they still remain human —instead of keeping silent about it, as charity would require in the case of any citizen at all, they take a criminal pleasure in broadcasting them, sometimes even improving on them." [10]

The bourgeois was ruthless. This struggle against the clergy was the first one he undertook to establish his superiority. In these skirmishes, a thousand times repeated, where he pitted himself against the servants of the Church, he was preparing himself for his great conquests. Through scoffing at priests who were hard put to answer his mockery, he became conscious of his own value. He had been told not to concern himself with the things of religion and to submit to what his pastors told him. But were the servants of God better or more intelligent than he? He insisted that it was much better to be an honest man than to try to be a saint.

Often, too, the bourgeois found that the pastor, although vested with divine authority, which should make him superior, was in many respects inferior to him. "They are boorish men, of little intelligence, no education, and no manners," the bourgeois said, referring to the country clergy. "And suppose all this to be true," rejoins the Pastor of Gap, "what has that to do with the august character with which the priest is invested?" [11] Nevertheless, the priest should have been able to answer when the "enlightened" asked him questions and, to the extent of his moral and mental capacity, to have been at least on a level with the bourgeoisie.

The apologists, in this case as in others, misunderstood the social aspect of the problem. They explained that this or that human deficiency could not detract from the sacred character of the priesthood. But that was not the point. The point was that the development of the bourgeoisie was bringing about profound changes in the relations between pastors and their flocks. "A pastor," writes the Pastor of Gap, "is like the father of a large family in which there are all kinds of mentalities, moods and characters." He then describes the methods which the pastor must use to maintain harmony in the big family and provide for the salvation of all. "He is responsible before God for all these souls, and must never lose sight of them." Thus "his thoughts move, so to speak, from family to family," and when, finally, "alone in his room, he opens the parish register and goes through it, good Jesus! what sorrow, what sighs, what tears." [12] Or, to quote another authority, the unlettered Christian "sees before his eyes his pastor and his brothers; he unites himself with them with all his heart, and through them with the great society of the Catholic Church, whose dimensions he is incapable of knowing. He is united with his pastor, his pastor with his bishop, and through his pastor and his bishop he is united with all Catholics scattered throughout so many provinces and kingdoms to the ends of the earth." [13]

But this "big family" no longer existed. The enlightened bourgeois was no longer at one with his pastor, and therefore the union which should have embraced all members, both those who taught and those who listened, was for many Catholics so much empty talk. Bourgeois and priest belonged to two different and necessarily competing worlds. "Those who have made money," notes the Pastor of Gap, "have a marked aversion for the ministers of the Church." [14] The "people of a certain sort" were not prepared to concede to the clergy a superiority which the humble readily acknowledged.

This was the starting point of the long struggle which each bourgeois seemed to wage individually, and was also the struggle of a whole class. It was to end only when the bourgeois felt sure of his victory; that is, when he no longer felt any need to attack the clergy to prove that he was an enlightened man, a gentleman. Once his social status was assured, he no longer felt under the same obligation to demonstrate to himself and to others that he was different from the common people. He then stopped arguing, or argued less, with the clergy, and might even speak very highly of them.

By the eve of the Revolution, the bourgeoisie was sure enough of itself not to feel a need to get the better of the clergy, and it generously proposed an alliance with them. It would support them in their struggle against the higher clergy and, on the other hand, would appoint them its delegates to the populace. Since the clergy were "of the people," they were able to play the part of mediators between the bourgeoisie, which had no use for religion, and those simple folk who needed it.

Thus the bourgeoisie achieved its autonomy vis-à-vis the Church. In the long debates between the servants of the Church and the "persons of a certain sort," the bourgeois pleaded his own cause and developed the moral code which ensured his independence, however general and abstract the terms in which he posed the problem. This might be called the social aspect of the religious emancipation of the eighteenth century. When the enlightened attacked the Church, denied the faith of the simple, or jeered at the clergy, they were doing so not like the *philosophes,* speculating on problems of metaphysics and arriving at conclusions different from those contained in the theology manuals; they were defending their own cause, demanding their rights, creating the new man.

In this way, there gradually developed, alongside the Church, another autonomous moral power, which defended its rights step by step by opposing its modes of life, its ways of thinking and feeling, to those drawn from religious tradition. But before reaching that point and being able to settle down in a world which belonged to him, the bourgeois had had to make a long and continuous effort to modify ideas and sentiments inherited from the past. He was accustomed to religion; he feared hell; before becoming what he was later to become, he had been, in the religious sphere, one of "the people"; and profound changes must have taken place in him to modify attitudes which he had held in common with all the faithful. An interior emancipation had had to take place before he could challenge the ministers of the Church and follow his own paths. He had experimented with unbelief before becoming an unbeliever; he had questioned the ministers of the Church to learn how he might still believe, finally achieving the "security" which disconcerted those who were terrified by the infinite and which was to give him the freedom he needed to carry out his task in the moral and economic sphere.

PART TWO

God, Sin, and Death

5 · THE TRANSFORMATION
OF RELIGIOUS IDEAS

THE CRISIS OF BELIEF

Bourgeois emancipation in regard to religion might seem to be easily circumscribed in the terms "I believe" and "I don't believe," constituting respectively the starting point of a process and its consummation. Thus a man could have said, in the latter half of the eighteenth century, that whereas formerly he had been a believer, now he was not. The important thing, here, is the meaning of the historical phenomenon which we call bourgeois emancipation, and not the question of whether it involved all bourgeois, or only some of those who lived in the age of the *philosophes*. And to determine this, it would seem that we must first of all define what is meant by believing or not believing.

Formerly, we are told, the layman had believed; now he had lost his faith. But what, actually, did he believe when he had the faith, and what did he give up when he lost it? If we take the term "belief" in its strict sense, he might be said to have no longer believed anything. Nevertheless, it would clearly be untrue to say that in the past he had accepted the faith in its entirety and now completely rejected it. Faith cannot really be regarded as simply a content of conscience to be found equally among all laymen, a system which people either accept or reject, as they would a particular opinion or doctrine clearly understood and subsequently assessed.

So long as people could call themselves believers, they believed before they knew, and what they subsequently found out about their faith never represented it completely. As time went on, the beliefs of the laity continued to change. Some were forgotten, some were singled out, some were toned down, and all manner of transformations took place in regard to the extent and even the quality of the professed belief. But just as it cannot be said that people had ever believed everything, so it cannot be asserted that in the end they no longer believed anything. Indeed, in that respect there was a difference of degree rather than of kind between the position of the layman at the end of the eighteenth century and that of his forebears. Although the bourgeois had eliminated certain truths or, rather, allowed them to wither in his soul, he had retained others, transforming them by taking away their specifically religious character and secularizing them by integrating them in his nonreligious world.

Thus a bourgeois did not say, simply, "I don't believe in God." Indeed, he might readily admit the existence of God. But his concept of God was different. Not that the layman had forsaken the Christian God for the newly invented deity of the *philosophes*. It might be truer to say, taking the view that the Christian God lends himself to many interpretations in the minds of his adorers, that the layman had secularized the traditional deity rather than created or adopted a new one.

It would be altogether misleading, therefore, to reduce the religious problem of bourgeois emancipation to the terms "I believe" or "I don't believe." It would be more accurate to speak of a continuous movement, punctuated by sudden jolts both on the individual and on the collective level, but one which on the whole developed less in the form of great battles in which the adversaries pitted principle against principle, than through successive and constantly renewed struggles in the course of which the bourgeoisie often took over certain positions of the other side and incorporated them in its own. These struggles, moreover, did not always take place between two clearly defined opponents. Often, indeed, it was rather a matter of tension and conflict of conscience in the individual who was gradually becoming emancipated and of changed prevailing attitudes, of which the individual was not always aware and which he could not have defined exactly.

If we are to understand the essence of these great transformations which gave birth to modern man, we have to begin by distinguishing two factors which gradually modified the religious perspective. On the one hand, there was a weakening of faith, a change in the manner of believing itself; and on the other, a shrinkage or contraction of faith, a progressive elimination of certain articles of faith to which credence could no longer be given. Thus the bourgeois believed less strongly and believed fewer things. Or, to put it another way, there was both elimination and watering down of faith, or what remained of it. Or again, if, by virtue of his submission to the authority of the Church, the believer might still be regarded as believing everything, both that which he had set aside and that which he had retained, the area of his implicit faith would have expanded, while that of his explicit faith would have contracted, and what he still explicitly believed he believed less firmly.

While both a weakening and a contraction of faith could lead to more or less complete emancipation, a distinction should be made between them. There might be a weakening of faith without contraction of the content of faith, or the area of faith might be contracted without any diminution in the zeal of the believer.

Thus an individual Catholic, a product of Jesuit training, might no longer experience anything but the fear of hell, but believing in that with all his might and incapable of thinking of it without trembling, he believed in it just as fervently, if not in the same manner, as his ancestors, who had still believed in a number of other teachings. Another Catholic, having retained a certain inclination for the mysteries as a whole and having consequently a much broader faith, believed much less firmly in what he in fact knew of the truths of the faith; and having allowed his faith to decline progressively, he eventually replaced definite convictions by this or that emotion, this or that means of achieving religious experience, without directly participating in it. This, incidentally, enabled him to show a broad-mindedness which the believer whose only tenet of faith was hell, but who believed in that wholeheartedly, was unable to display.

We find the first type quite frequently at the beginning of the modern movement of emancipation. His diminished, rather drab, abstract, and desiccated Catholicism enabled him, by concentrating his faith on a single point or on a limited number of truths, to confine himself in his everyday life to altogether secular attitudes. Thus, for example, while believing in God and fearing hell, he did not put his trust in Divine Providence in connection with his business; he did not believe in miracles, and so forth. This was an emancipation by contraction of faith, permitting the layman to remain a "believer" while looking exclusively to the rules of prudence and good sense to regulate the details of his life. Save in one point, he could belong wholly to this world. He might be as little inclined as the most emancipated of his contemporaries to believe what no longer corresponded to the spirit of the times, such as legends and miracles; yet the vision of the fires of hell remained so vivid for him that he preserved his former capacity for belief, though in a strangely indigent and lifeless form.

This bourgeois was a curious product of eighteenth-century religious evolution, reflecting as he did the spirit of his class and, at the same time—though all he retained of the wealth of legend and mystery which made up the former Catholic universe was a single somber and brutal vision—sometimes experiencing a resurgence of the faith which might have been thought extinct. But such faith, made up of fear and cut off from all the rest of the insights formerly derived from those mysterious depths so disconcerting to the modern believer, could not subsist for long, isolated in the midst of the ideas and sentiments of the modern world.

As for the second type of Catholic, he was rather to be found among the faithful of the close of the century, and especially later. Preferring to cultivate "religious sentiment," this Catholic had no sympathy for the shrunken and dried out Catholicism of those who limited themselves to a few simple concepts and whose only real concern was to escape damnation. He did not like anyone to talk to him of hell, and the idea of being in hell himself was repugnant to him, seeming contrary to good taste and the loftiness and nobility of his sentiments. In his everyday life, he was more or less like everyone else; his religious sentiments were in a world apart, and were sufficiently distinct from that encompassing the motives which normally inspired him to prevent any possibility of confusion; his religious emotions readily found expression in literary and other forms appropriate to them.

Thus we may distinguish two aspects of the dissolution of faith. At one time the believer might say that he did not believe everything, at another that he was not a fanatic—which usually meant that he did not want to believe "too much," that he wanted to temper the ardor of his faith in order to leave room for other preoccupations. The two manners of watering down faith might readily be combined, and were sufficient to explain the changes produced in the religious attitude of the bourgeois, who boasted of having become less "fanatical" and "superstitious," meaning that he attached much less importance to what he believed or was supposed to believe and at the same time had eliminated from his consciousness a number of concepts, held by the unlettered, which he considered beneath the dignity of a man of his time and class.

The bourgeois might thus succeed in limiting himself to a faith which gave him less to believe and to which he need cleave less firmly. This, however, might have meant that he had really preserved the traditional faith unchanged, after eradicating from it what must necessarily shock him and contriving to believe more moderately in what remained. But the changes which took place in him were not, in fact, confined to a reduction in the number of truths to which he adhered and a diminution in his capacity for belief; his very religion, the religion which he could still profess, changed in character. Not only did he believe less, but he believed something different; what took place was a change not only in the quantity and intensity of faith, but also in quality. The Catholicism of the worldly-minded was in many respects, and perhaps even in its essential characteristics, a new Catholicism.

This is readily understandable if we consider that all the mysteries are linked and that it is hard to eliminate one of them without affecting them all. Let us suppose, for instance, that the believer has gradually ceased to believe in predestination, or that the number of the elect will be small, and that at the same time he is not very clear about how to reconcile the action of Divine Providence with the ways of thinking and acting which motivate him in his daily life, and he finds miracles barely credible. Yet he still believes in God. But will this be the God whom Catholics adored when they still believed in a whole series of mysteries which they have now abandoned?

At first glance, it is not self-evident that the circumstance of believing more or less can change the nature of a truth. Yet nothing is more certain. The man who believes with his whole soul and who, far from tolerating any diminution in his faith, is always accusing himself of not believing enough, not only will not let himself be put off by what appears most contrary to reason and human sentiment in faith, but will even seek it out in order to believe more firmly. If the believer's faith is already shaky, what he still believes must be more suited to the modes of believing and feeling which motivate him as a denizen of this world. Hence, when the worldly come to believe less in God, the deity, in order to be believed in at all, must present itself under infinitely more amiable and human features than it does to those who are prepared to sacrifice their reason and their worldly sentiments for the sake of believing in it with all their souls.

Not only did the eighteenth-century layman believe something different, but he also believed differently; that is, his religious experience as such, the emotions which formed a necessary part of it and were bound up with it, changed with time. Since all the truths of the faith do not produce the same reactions, religious emotion varied as the believer ceased to believe this or that particular mystery or emphasized one doctrine at the expense of another. Thus the believer who limited himself principally to a vision of hell progressively narrowed down the emotional sources which fed his faith, until that faith came to consist only of sentiments of fear. It was an emotional impoverishment of religious experience, which necessarily accompanied a contraction of faith. A similar deterioration of the religious experience, although of a different kind, took place when the deity, increasingly excluded from the affairs of everyday life, was finally reduced to the figure of the architect of a presumably perfect universe. The believer could then confine himself to a sentiment of awed admiration before the Supreme Being, and while he displayed great gratitude to the divinity, he at the same time eradicated from his faith all anguish and everything that attached him most intimately to a God from whom he hoped to receive salvation. The Catholic of the end of the century not only believed something different from his ancestors, and believed it in a different manner, but he also became different himself; he was a new man, who sometimes liked to boast of an ancient title.

THE CRISIS OF DOCTRINE

Should it not be said, perhaps, that the various changes affecting the whole complex of sentiments and insights that make of faith a living thing and characterize individual religious experiences through the centuries really apply only to the faithful, and not to the Church as such? According to this view, repeatedly propounded in the pulpit, the laity may change vastly in respect of the manner and content of their belief, but the faith of the Church cannot change. In this case there are two quantities in religious evolution, one that is fixed and another which is infinitely variable, and the whole problem becomes one of describing the different ways in which the faithful of different eras have conceived of truths presumed to be immutable.

Be this as it may, there can be no doubt that even if the truths themselves do not vary, they may be presented in very different ways even by those whose duty it is to teach them to the faithful. Preachers may decide not to speak of certain truths, or to speak of them less, or to soft-pedal them while putting the spotlight on others, which then become central to their preaching.

There is selection in sermons, as in consciences. If the believer says, "I don't believe everything," the preacher must admit that he does not preach everything. The relations between the two sets of variations are often quite complex. The enlightened bourgeois of the eighteenth century questioned; the clergy replied. In replying, the clergy accused the bourgeois of wrongheadedness, but at the same time could not avoid adapting themselves to their attitude. These controversies persisted throughout the eighteenth century, and most of the sermons testify to the fact. Between immutable faith and varying beliefs, preaching was to be a form of intermediary, providing a series of necessarily variable images of a faith which by definition was constant.

But is it true that faith has always remained unchanged? It is certainly not true of the seventeenth and eighteenth centuries. The crisis was one not only of individual beliefs but also of faith. There was disagreement about doctrine. The variations were not confined to the ways of presenting the faith or to the transformations to which individual consciences subjected it according to their capacities and needs; the dogmas themselves were at issue, that whole complex of concepts transmitted from generation to generation which should never change . . . the deposit of faith.

What was changed was not only the Catholic but also Catholicism. To the crisis of belief was added a crisis of doctrine, and it was impossible to tell, at first, whether one had necessarily to lead to the other. Surely the believer who admitted to not believing everything and whose belief had undergone various modifications was really admitting that there was a faith which contained both what he believed and what he did not believe and which remained unchanged, whereas he himself had changed. And even after he became altogether unbelieving, he could perfectly well admit that what was proposed for his belief was what had always been believed, and he could even argue from that to not having to believe any more, since he regarded himself as belonging to modern times. Similarly, if he simply said that he was not a believer, he did not have to give any further explanations, since he was referring to a set of doctrines which had remained what they had always been.

But if we look more closely at the circumstances in which the religious crisis developed in the eighteenth century, we see that the question of faith cannot be put in such simple terms. The question facing the worldly-minded man was not merely what position to take in regard to a faith whose content had been determined once and for all; the question, really, was what to believe. For to believe in the manner of the Jesuits was not the same as to believe in the manner of the Jansenists, and he might even argue from this difference that there was no point in believing at all, since those who should tell him what he ought to believe were not in agreement among themselves.

The changes to which we have referred so far seem to have related primarily to the layman, and particularly the layman of a certain class, the bourgeoisie. The bourgeois, whether he was still religious or more or less religious, was certainly no longer what the believer had been in times gone by. So it would seem that the bourgeois had changed, not the Church; that beliefs had been modified, not the faith; that there was a modern Catholic, but not a modern Catholicism; to use an analogy, that the ancient Gothic cathedrals had remained exactly as they had always been, while those who passed through them had changed.

But in fact there were two kinds of variations, one which took place in the consciences of the faithful and the other in the area of faith itself, one which was primarily produced by laymen, whereas the other more particularly concerned the theologians. Neither, of course, could take place independently of the other. The new theology took account of the changed attitudes, and the believer could modify his beliefs according to what was proposed for his consideration. But the two movements did not always coincide. The faithful did not always believe what the new theologians told them, and the latter were not able simply to formulate a new religion which in all points corresponded to the attitude of the faithful. Nevertheless, what happened in the course of time was that the faithful, when they wanted to know what they should believe, consulted the new texts instead of the old ones, which they had more or less forgotten.

All this goes to show how complex was the religious crisis of the eighteenth century; indeed, to see every aspect of it, we have to take account of many different factors. No longer able to believe all that the Church taught and allowing largely for his secular preoccupations, the bourgeois nevertheless often began by supporting the most intransigent theologians, preferring them to those who were prepared to make all manner of concessions. But a little later, all the concessions which the Jesuit Fathers were prepared to make were still insufficient for him, and he wanted to believe even less.

Yet in the midst of all these conflicting tendencies, the bourgeois continued on his way. Jansenists, Jesuits, and *philosophes* battled for his mind. He was partial to the Jansenists, but did not follow them for long. He never had much affection for the Jesuits, although they taught him a great deal. He considered the *philosophes* to be his true guides, which did not prevent him from taking good care not to adopt their teachings once he realized that they might be damaging to the interests of his class. In fact, in the years immediately preceding the Revolution, he was no longer inclined to hear ill of the Church and was bored with discussions on God, matter, or the origins of the world. He seemed quite disposed to make his peace with the Church, now that he was sure of being sufficiently emancipated to be able to live his life as he chose. To go farther, he feared, would be to act contrary to the interests of his class, for disbelief, by spreading among the people, might eventually endanger the principles of the social order which the bourgeoisie needed to establish its domination.

But to what extent did the bourgeoisie, which had achieved its autonomy through the vicissitudes of the great religious crisis of the eighteenth century, retain any elements of Christianity? While the "enlightened" maintained that they had no use for the mysteries of the Christian religion, they often asserted that they loved and desired to adopt the moral teachings of the Gospel. Can it be said that the late eighteenth-century bourgeois, though having lost his faith, remained a disciple of Jesus in the matter of morals?

Put this way, the question rests on a misunderstanding, for there is no Gospel morality in the sense understood by the eighteenth-century bourgeois, and his concern to turn the Gospels into a manual of ethics is more revealing than anything else of his ignorance of religion, just as his attempts to transform into moral maxims teachings which he could no longer experience as expressions of faith may be accounted among the most significant symptoms of the progress of unbelief.

What the bourgeois might have had in mind when he distinguished between morality and doctrine was that the Christian might very well know what he should do and how he should act in a particular circumstance, without possessing any profound knowledge of dogma. And he might cite in support of this view the example of the humble faithful whom the Church was always lauding and who, for all their ignorance, were deemed perfect Christians. In fact, however, what motivated the ignorant was not moral maxims as such, but rather a whole complex of modes of thinking and feeling peculiar to a "naturally" Christian soul, which the believer himself was unable to formulate in any very definite manner. Such modes of thinking and feeling developed in him independently of any reflection and made of him the man he was, a man identifiable with a particular group and of known origins. Thus, without going into principles or engaging in elaborate discussion, he was humble and submissive, naturally averse to any tendency to revolt; he placed very little trust in his own powers and did not wish to rise above his station. All this, determining the character of his life, made of him a Catholic. It might then happen that certain habits of thought and action which originally had flowed to a greater or lesser extent from a whole series of religious convictions deeply rooted in men's minds, forming a quite specific social heritage, would survive the vicissitudes to which faith had been subjected.

In this sense, then, it is possible to understand and, up to a point, justify the distinction which the enlightened bourgeois liked to make between theory and practice, between doctrine and what he called "morals." It may be possible to recognize a Christian in the quality of his life, down to its least details, without these characteristics necessarily flowing from this or that particular religious conviction. The question that then arises is whether, and to what extent, the enlightened bourgeois of the eighteenth century retained certain religious attitudes after losing his faith; in other words, whether it was still possible to recognize in the unbeliever the Christian who continued to live as a believer, however ignorant he might have become of doctrine.

Here we touch upon one of the most essential aspects of the religious crisis of the eighteenth century. The reason the bourgeois lost his faith was precisely that the approach to life and action which Christianity offered him no longer satisfied him. The Church, sensing that the middle class was slipping out of its grasp, certainly tried to create patterns of living which would enable the bourgeois to remain a bourgeois as well as a Christian; that is, to carry out his economic and social functions while preserving the features of a son of the Church. But it never succeeded in hallowing the aspirations of the new middle class by giving them a religious basis.

It is precisely in this discordance between the Christian life and the bourgeois life, between the man of tradition and the new man, that we have to seek the causes of bourgeois unbelief. How should the bourgeois have continued to believe in mystery, legend, and miracle if all his effort was to excise from his life any vestige of the nonrational? How should he still have acknowledged a Divine Providence and persuaded himself that God ordered all things, when confidence in his own powers and prudent foresight were the guiding principles of all his action? Above all, how should his imagination still have rendered the invisible visible to him and aroused in him a nostalgia for another world, which was in perpetual negation to this world, when everything inclined him to establish his dominion here below and not to give overmuch thought to death?

The differences between the Church of tradition and this new middle class were too great to allow of any reconciliation. One of the two must change, either religion or the bourgeois mentality. Attempts were made to change both, and the attempts failed. But in the very conflicts which ensued, in the interminable discussions in which the old and the new dispensations confronted one another in all their manifold aspects, the modern bourgeois consolidated his position. He had not found ready-made his modes of seeing and feeling, his ideas and his values, the standards by which he judged and shaped his life. It was by gradually separating his convictions from whatever conflicted with them, by rejecting one idea and transforming another, by frequently changing the meaning of a particular term to fit in with his own views, by modifying and reorganizing his emotive criteria, that he developed his mentality, the new mentality characteristic of his era, which was the era of the French Revolution.

6 · DEATH

THE TRIUMPH OF DEATH

Eternity

"Nothing," writes Bossuet, "establishes more firmly, or provides better proof of the sovereign being of God and his dominion over us, than death." This was to be the theme song of the clergy of the period. Life, they said, asserts itself and seeks to expand, the creature lifts itself up and grows powerful, but nothing can withstand death: "it breaks, it crushes, it destroys, it wipes out everything—greatness, power, glory, kings, emperors, sovereigns, the great and the small of the earth—none can escape it." [1] "Oh God, I adore the sovereign hand which destroys all at a single blow!" [2]

Death, in this view, is the supreme challenge which the Church can hurl at the world, its war cry, its song of triumph. The Church must necessarily feel strong; it is sure of victory because it has death on its side, and death is stronger than life. "Death puts an end to all, destroys everything, reduces us to nothingness, and at the same time shows us that we cannot escape this nothingness . . . save by reaching toward God, by cleaving to God through a deathless love." [3] To "those wretched lovers of human glories" [4] the Church showed their nothingness, and the human soul, seeing its illusions fade and returning to itself from a long way off, found, at death's door, the emotions binding it to its religion.

To quote Bossuet again, there is no "truer interpreter or more faithful mirror of human things" than death.[5] The soul facing death makes "a true comparison of time and eternity" and sees clearly "that all its previous ideas were infinitely removed from the truth; that its imagination had given time and temporal things a fantastic duration and importance, while destroying eternity and eternal possessions through the inadequacy and obscurity of the picture it had formed of them. The soul therefore condemns all these thoughts; it is astonished at its blindness, and changes its views and judgments completely." [6]

Before this "immutable presence of eternity, always firm, always permanent, erasing in the infinity of its extent all differences of time," [7] the creature recognizes the vanity of life. In "that last moment in which, when it comes, all the rest of our life is convicted of illusion and error," [8] man realizes his littleness in the immensity of time. He is crushed in the presence of the infinities which surround him on every side "like an atom and like a shadow which only lasts for a second that will not return." [9] But in the face of this "eternity which endures," [10] does he still think of dying, does he still think of his own personal end as occurring within time? "If I look before me, what an infinite space where I am not! If I look back, what a terrible sequence in which I no longer exist! And how little space I take up in this immense abyss of time! I am nothing; so small an interval cannot distinguish me from nothingness; I was sent only to help make a crowd. . . . How small is the place which we occupy in this world! So small, certainly, and so unimportant, that I am sometimes in doubt whether I am asleep or awake." [11] But if life is an illusion, is not dying another, the last of a soul not yet fully awakened, which clings to life?

That is not the Christian position. The visions of eternity and the infinite cannot cause the Christian to forget that a day will come when it will be his turn to die and when he will find himself in the state where "we have only an hour or two left to live, and it comes to our minds, 'in two hours' time, there will be no more time for me.'" [12] He will recover himself when faced with the destruction of his being, and he will never feel more fully himself than when everything speaks to him of his littleness and of the small space which he holds in this world. He will thus show, for the last time before he disappears for good, how interested he is in himself. He will fear death, and, thinking of what awaits him, he will substitute for the infinite spaces and the sublime vision of eternity the picture of a dying man who does not want to die and trembles before the unknown.

So it must be, and the Christian, in a universe where all things pass, must always be brought back to himself and, seeing the destruction of all things, must not lose sight of that which concerns his salvation. *His* death, *his* eternity is always before him; the vision of death and eternity should never let him forget the *I am dying;* he must never lose sight of the dread hour when he realizes that he is dying. Only thus will he be a Christian.

Death and Remorse

"It is useful," writes Nicole, "to be present at the death of men, and even to represent it to ourselves and impress our imagination with the attendant circumstances." [13] Preachers did not fail to evoke the image of the dying in the souls of believers, an image well calculated to move the most hardened hearts. "It suffices to observe a dying man on his deathbed to realize how terrifying is this spectacle: his hands and arms limp with weakness, his chest weighed down by a choking inflammation, so that he can scarcely breathe, his head no longer capable of remaining erect, his lips covered with foam, his eyes dim, his face covered with a cold sweat and mortal pallor." [14] How should the creature remain insensible before the spectacle of a man at grips with death, before this "destruction" which "begins in his bed and is completed in the grave; for who does not know the change that takes place at the moment of death in the most beautiful person in the world? The head falling limp and glued to the chest; the hair, still moist from the sweat of death, in disarray; the temples drawn together, the ears sagging, the eyes sunken and horribly open, the cheeks fallen in and as though stuck to the bones, the nose sharpened, the lips drawn back, the tongue dry, the color livid, the whole body cold and motionless, like a marble statue. The spectacle is so sad," our preacher adds, "that I defy the most frivolous person in the world to view it without being affected by melancholy. All who come near the bed come away pale, speechless, thoughtful, carrying the sad picture of this corpse in their mind's eye, and incapable of merriment and entertainment until other objects have wholly effaced it." [15]

Thus the preachers evoked the spectacle of the dying. But they did not stop there; they wanted to turn the horrified believer's gaze to the grave itself, that he might witness the operation of death. "Let us go into the grave ourselves, and become spectators of what takes place there. . . . What discourse can really portray what you will see there with your own eyes? Hardly is the body of this person who was so glowing with health and so well proportioned enclosed in the tomb, than a prodigious quantity of worms and other insects, engendered in this corpse, begin to feed on the flesh in which they were born. You would see some devouring the eyes, others issuing from the nostrils, others twisting in the mouth, in the breast, coming in and going out of the opened chest; while the hair drops from the head, and the nose, lips, and cheeks fall away piecemeal; what is here is no more than a dunghill, a cesspool, a horrible heap of decay and corruption." [16]

Death is thus something very terrible, as the clergy ceaselessly repeated to the faithful. "It is more terrible than we imagine to see ourselves stretched out on a bed, cross in hand, awaiting the moment of death and the execution of the sentence pronounced against all men; to see that not only those who surround us but all creatures together are powerless to save us, to feel death slowly gripping our bodies, to sense the prostration which precedes it, and finally to find ourselves perishing and being destroyed as far as the world is concerned." [17] The threat of death hangs over us every day at every moment; preachers took great care to remind the faithful of the fact. "We shall see you, perhaps in a few days' time, stretched in a coffin, meditating before your corpse on the vanity of the things of this world, and learning from your example to despise what you have loved." [18]

We are far away, indeed, from that eternity which confounds everything, space and time; the universe has narrowed strangely; there remains only a suffering soul which fears death. What, actually, does it fear? Something terrifying: agony, burial, the grave, something it cannot exactly define. It feels itself dying; it would like to live. But is this dying man who fears death already a believer? Not yet. If, by directing his thoughts to over-distant horizons, he were to forget himself and fail to think of that fateful moment which would put an end to his illusions, it might also happen that, seized with terror at the thought of the destruction of his labors and haunted by the picture of a corpse, he might forget God.

Death is to be feared, but in a "salutary" manner, in a Christian manner. There are "fears which only alarm but do not change the heart," says Duguet.[19] In the imagination of the dying man, all kinds of specters may present themselves. Such primitive images must be driven away and replaced by others which faith can endorse.

"It is true," we read in Houdry's *Bibliothèque des Prédicateurs,* "that people are worried, and that they are mistaken, when they take fright at the notions of abandonment, need, solitude, and destruction which enter into the idea of death. But here is where it is certain that we are not mistaken, when we fear the judgment of God, which follows death; for it is certain that that judgment must needs be terrible for a conscience which feels itself laden with sin; and where is the man who is not in that condition, if he takes but a little thought about his past life?"[20] What we should fear, therefore, is hell, and the last judgment, and not really death itself. Or better, the fear of death must change its object; there must be a transposition of sentiment, and the primitive sentiment must assume a moral character. A man should be afraid not of death but of abiding in hell. His natural terrors should be turned into repentance and remorse.

"Hundreds upon hundreds of persons were converted by looking upon the decaying corpses of certain persons of distinction, who had been the idols of their times, either on account of their power or on account of their heroic deeds; or of some young persons famous for their beauty and the number of their admirers." [21] At such moments, remose awakens in the sinner's soul. "At the sight of such a spectacle, he will experience a prodigious change; he will begin to hear the voice of his conscience once more and recover from his torpor. The thought of death will make him realize that the death about to descend upon him will break the earthen vessel with which his soul is linked; that his soul is on the point of being conducted, naked and without other following than that of his good or bad actions, into the presence of an inflexible judge who will pronounce a verdict from which there is no appeal; that it will be delivered to the ministers of his justice, and buried in hell, where there will be inexpressible torments and gnashing of teeth." [22]

The terrors of the dying are thus based on a vision of eternity, an atrocious eternity, of infinite torments and unimaginable suffering. "What torment to burn always with an equal sense of pain, and without the fires ever being extinguished or dying down! Alas, twenty-four hours of headache, or a day of somewhat harder work than usual, appears to us so long and tedious; what will it be to burn eternally!" Before this eternity of suffering, the human being feels lost. "Oh, the greatness, the immensity, the multitude of the tortures of hell grips us with horror; but their eternity confounds my thoughts, freezes my blood and almost deprives me of speech." [23] For how should one, if only for a moment, represent to oneself the meaning of an eternity spent in hell? "A damned soul will have suffered in those blazing prisons during an unimaginable span of time, and that will be only a quarter-hour of eternity. Time will have ruined the houses which you raised, destroyed the cities which gave you birth, overthrown the countries where you lived; the end of time will have buried the whole universe in its own ashes, and as many millions of centuries will have gone by as there were moments in the duration of the world, and yet nothing will have gone by of that frightful eternity." [24]

Thus the dying man knows what he fears. Man fears death, but his terror is ill-defined; it is a sentiment without any precise object. It is a simple, "I don't want to die, I want to live; I'm afraid of dying, death is something terrible." But what is he afraid of? The Church will tell him. It will be able to interpret the confused voices and define the horror. "Death, the mere notion of which makes us shudder, is not really to be feared, by our own admission, save on account of the second death which precipitates sinners into the eternal abysses of hell," says the Pastor of Gap. Thus the dying fear death "because of the reckoning which they will have to make" [25] to God. They remember their sins. Now it is God who speaks, the pitiless judge who accuses. Fearing hell, they fear death.

Born of all the anguish of the dying, the image of hell is enriched with all the sufferings imagined by man. "We have seen, it is true, barbarous instruments and frightful machines designed to make men suffer; we have seen wheels; we have seen horrible fires; we have seen burning oils; but none of this approaches the pains of hell." [26] Or again, "If a man trembles on seeing the saw, the razors and the other instruments which will be used to cut off his arm or his leg, and is half dead with fright; if, during the operation, he utters cries which would melt rocks, what will it be, alas, when he suffers the most violent of all pains, when all the wrath of God bursts upon him!" [27]

The believer thus learns to define his fears. The confused sentiment aroused by the prospect of the natural death is replaced by reasoned fears of a second death, more terrible than the first. The fires of hell enlighten the opaque darkness of the grave; and death, henceforth of divine institution, is the punishment of sin.

THE DECLINE IN THE BELIEF IN HELL

The Unbeliever in the Presence of Death

"Neither the sun nor death may be gazed at steadily," observes La Rochefoucauld. The eighteenth-century clergy were not unaware of the fact and took care to remind their hearers, each of whom "promises himself some sort of immortality on earth," [28] that they were mortal. A truism, perhaps, but did they think about it? "You know it, wretch!" cries the Pastor of Gap. "And how do you show that you know it? Is it not, on the contrary, the thing which you seem to know absolutely nothing about, and on which you have least reflected? Dying is a word whose meaning seems to be unknown to you. You say, 'we have to die,' rather as some birds mechanically repeat certain words. You say, 'we have to die,' and you think of nothing less than of dying; you say, 'we have to die,' and you think only of living, and you live as though you would not have to die!" [29]

Life might have become secularized, but death remained a mystery. The "practical science of death" [30] remained a sacred science; only faith promised certainties. "Jesus Christ teaches us what will be the state of men after death; he tells us that the just will enjoy eternal happiness, and that sinners will be condemned to eternal sufferings." By contrast, none of the ungodly says, "I will teach you what will be the condition of men after death; their souls will surely be destroyed, or will subsist in this or that manner, quite different from that described in the Gospels." [31]

Faced with death, the worldly hesitated. There remained a "maybe," which, in hearts "ill-cured of faith," might revive former anxieties. "Alas, my very dear brothers," says another apologist in the latter part of the eighteenth century, "even were there only a mere *maybe* on the subject, it should make you quail. Maybe I shall burn in eternal fire, but maybe, too, this will not come to pass. . . . You have to be, I shall not say unreasonable, but utterly at enmity with yourself, to base a matter of so great importance on a *maybe!*" [32]

The Church, contrasting the certainties of life with the uncertainties of the hereafter, was often to prove victorious over the unbeliever, who hesitated and was troubled on the point of death. "Ungodly men," says Massillon, "resolute in their ungodliness, are rare." Of "all those who daily boast to us of their doubts and disbelief, and make so deplorable a show of it, there is perhaps not one upon whose heart faith has not preserved some claim, and who does not secretly continue to fear the God whom he affects not to recognize." [33] Thus they remained believing despite themselves, and feared hell while jeering at the clergy.

"And indeed, Christians, may this strengthen us in our faith in the judgments of God," says Abbé Molinier; "the ungodly man believes without realizing that he believes . . . or wanting to. He has made a thousand attempts, and perhaps a thousand investigations, to avoid believing in divine vengeance and to erase all such thoughts from his mind. He has therefore treated the doctrine of the judgment of God as the product of childish fancies, of misleading instruction, of fables told by priests with an axe to grind, and listened to by the ignorant. But this belief, which does not come to man from without, or from other men, but from himself, from the bottom of a soul that is naturally Christian on this point, . . . this doctrine, I say, remains in the ungodly man . . . and it will reemerge of itself in due course." [34]

The unbeliever, then, who had put on such a bold front toward God or at the least had accounted him "for nothing in the events of life," [35] would find his former anxieties reawakening in the presence of death. "For if a fatal disease strikes him, . . . run to his bed of pain, and you will find this so-called unbeliever persuaded. . . . He turns to the God of his fathers and fears the judgments which he previously affected to disbelieve. . . . This sinner, formerly so resolute, so proud in his feigned unbelief, so far above all vulgar fears, now becomes weaker, more fearful, more credulous than the most uneducated soul; his fears are more excessive, his very religion more superstitious, his religious practices more crude, more unrefined, more extravagant than those of the common folk; and since such excess is never far removed from the opposite extreme, we see him swing in an instant from ungodliness to superstition; from the resoluteness of the philosopher to the weakness of the ignorant and the unlettered." [36]

If there are "religious hypocrites," says Père Griffet, "there are also hypocrites of disbelief. . . . We see such hypocrites of disbelief every day; they appear resolute and assured in their irreligion; the threats of hell do not disconcert them, the fear of the judgment to come does not alarm them; they say so, they affirm it; but don't be so sure of their sincerity. . . ." [37] As Bayle had said earlier, one must often discount a part of what the unbeliever affirms when he denies the faith. "It is fairly obvious that those who affect in social gatherings to combat the most common truths of religion are saying more on the subject than they think." They are found objecting to "truths which they have learned in their childhood concerning the divinity, paradise and hell; but it is not a dead faith, it is only a fire smoldering under the ashes. They feel its effect as soon as they look into themselves, and principally at the sight of some danger." [38]

The vision of hell triumphs over argument; people are afraid without admitting it to themselves. "It is more a matter of forgetfulness in their case than of contempt of hell," says Abbé Cambacérès, "and it may even be asserted that fear of hell, for most of them, is the secret which they are most fearful of betraying and least capable of keeping." [39] The worldly man, so sure of himself in other ways, loses his assurance in the face of death. "He puts on an air of courage, and in secret he trembles," says Massillon. This ungodly man is "a braggart who boasts of fearing nothing and who doesn't tell us all that goes on in his heart." [40]

The Church, then, must revive this fire which is only barely damped down and ensure its own triumph by arousing in the dying the fear of the hereafter. "When you are under the threat of imminent death, stretched out on your bed of sickness, and the prospect of the grave forces you to call upon us to assist your soul, that is when our ministry triumphs," [41] says a preacher of the period, speaking to the worldly. The efforts of the ungodly to do without the faith are doomed to failure. "Why don't you carry your generous intrepidity to the end?" the minister of God asks the dying. "Why do you tremble at the approach of death? What makes you now repudiate your arguments and your past conduct?" [42] Why, then, have they vaunted their disbelief, their rationalism? "That," says Abbé Molinier, "is the usual end of the libertine who finds he is dying. Much good did it do him to put on such a show of courage! That is the end of the freethinker. Much good did all his cleverness and arguing do him!" [43]

But why should these "hypocrites of unbelief" be so anxious to show themselves braver than they were? Why these efforts, so often repeated, to prove to themselves and to others that they were not believers? Because, apparently, "they fear to be taken for cowards if they seem to subscribe to a religion which teaches the fear of God; as though courage consisted in being brave against God himself. . . . The same desire which prompts a man to appear bigger or stronger than he is in fact will cause him to adopt and repeat bold statements, pronounced in an offhand manner." [44] To convert them, their former fears must be revived. But while those who had put on airs found themselves forced to concede that they had put too much faith in their own strength, are there not others who would start all over again and attempt to prove to themselves and others that they were above "vulgar fears"?

In a "Memoir on the State of China," dated 1696, we find a curious report. It concerns a Chinese officer whom the Jesuit missionaries had sought to inspire with the fear of hell. His answer is instructive. "It would be shameful for an old officer like myself to be afraid," he tells them. "From the moment that I became a soldier, I undertook not to fear anything. . . . And after all, what reason have I to be afraid? I have not harmed anyone, I serve my friends, I am faithful to the Emperor; and if formerly I was subject to the usual disorders of youth, I am now quite temperate in my pleasures." Thus spoke our officer, but, "falling asleep, he had such horrible representations of hell," that, "upon waking, he found himself a Christian." [45]

The Church would thus have triumphed. But what did the worldly think upon reading the story? What if, among those who lauded bravery and despised cowardice and at the same time jeered at the clergy and scoffed at God and hell, there should be some who dared, "even on their deathbed, to refuse the help of the Church, to run all the risks of a disbelief full of uncertainty, and to dispute God's quality as sovereign judge to the very brink of hell?" Would they not enjoy a certain prestige, and would not the worldly show respect for those who thus died "in the full and complete conviction of the falsity of the teachings of religion," [46] and preserved their swagger to the end?

"Nothing is more cowardly than to brave God," says Pascal.[47] The worldly were often of a different opinion. An apologist writing in the latter part of the eighteenth century deplores the growing number of "those foolhardy persons who are believed to have died as philosophers because they defied the Divinity itself, and lost their eternal happiness. This unhappy century is rich in such shameful examples, to the point where even silly little women take pride in dying as unbelievers, that is, without hope, without fear, without God." [48] The living would then take courage from the example of the dying. "I see them all," says Abbé de Boulogne, "those heroes of worldly wisdom, encouraging, emboldening one another to cross the fatal passage without fear, instituting among themselves a lamentable emulation of those who will put on the best face at the edge of the abyss, and exulting whenever, for the honor of their system, one of their number dies, they say, as a sage." [49]

The Church had challenged the unbeliever; it awaited him on his deathbed. There, face to face with death, he must reply whether there was a God or not and whether hell was anything more than a fantasy.

In this confrontation, the bourgeois often maintained a prudent reserve. He witnessed the spectacle, but without committing himself too far. Which of the two would be victorious, the Church or the unbeliever? This, in miniature, was the great struggle of the period, the struggle between the dying man alone, face to face with the infinite, and a Church calling him to itself. If the dying man triumphed, the bourgeois used the fact as an argument against faith; if the Church triumphed, he nonetheless continued to develop and consolidate his worldly positions, since the fear of death alone could not suffice, as we shall see, to revive faith in its integrity and to create Christians.

Love and Fear

It is "by loving simply and abandoning oneself without self-seeking to the loved one" that one ceases to fear. "That is what makes death sweet and precious. When a man is dead to himself, the death of the body is no more than the consummation of the work of grace," writes Fénelon.[50] Fénelon would have wanted to make those "cowardly, self-seeking" Christians, of whom there were so many in a period of declining faith, a type of hero, mystical heroes who, loving God, would brave the torments of hell. "But disinterested love seems to be a source of illusion and abominable impiety," he writes again.[51]

The Church, indeed, is wary of those who think they can soar above the human condition. "The love of God has its crosses, its labors, its constraints," says the Bishop of Chartres. "It also has its rest, its freedom, its innocent joys. . . . But never does it throw off the yoke of the common laws and practices of Christianity; never does it carry experience beyond the frontiers set for it by faith." [52] An overrarefied religious experience loses its substance. Thus "the motives of love will vanish one after another; and by dint of seeking to refine love, we shall find it slipping between our fingers." And there will remain, finally, only a "false generosity" and an "extravagant disinterestedness" which will prevent the soul from "asking anything for itself." At this point the soul has only a "confused and general view of God, without distinctions of perfections or attributes," [53] and man ceases to be human and becomes a sort of false divinity. "God alone can love disinterestedly, because he suffices to himself, and has nothing to hope for from the object which he loves outside himself." [54]

Fénelon was thus guilty of a heresy of the sentiments; he was adulterating Catholic emotiveness by overstressing one aspect. A religion cannot consist solely of lofty sentiments; the whole personality must be involved, and only thus can faith conquer the human heart and dominate it entirely. Then the sentiments must be tempered so that they may form a whole, entering into that emotive complex, that organization of sentiment, which characterizes the Catholic. A particular sentiment may shock us; it may be too crude, too brutal, for instance, the fear of hell, the selfish attitude which never treats God as more than a means. Nevertheless, it is necessary that the Catholic should fear and that he should want something for himself. His spirit must be involved, but so must his flesh; to love God properly, we have to see that it is to our own advantage to do so. God "is satisfied that the thought of our own advantage should enter into our sentiments in his regard." [55]

Noble sentiments are not always the truest ones. Fear of hell, which certainly has nothing particularly exalted about it, is something real and substantial, something clear and well defined; a man knows what he feels, and there is no mistake about it. Disinterested love is much less clear-cut, and a man sometimes imagines that he feels something which he does not feel at all. "The earth is covered with their canticles, scoffing at hell and damnation," says Bossuet, referring to the Quietists. But "they do not understand themselves, they do not realize what they are saying; after experiencing but the slightest pains they imagine that they can endure those of hell." [56]

Thus we must fear God and not despise hell, as the clergy never wearied of repeating in the pulpit. "Whatever the ungodly may say to decry the fear of God," we read in Houdry's *Bibliothèque des Prédicateurs,* "the truth is that God himself owes to it his glory; grace, its victories; religion, its altars; virtue, its merits; and all sinners, their salvation and conversion." [57] But to fear God, and to fear him always, we must often think of death. That is why, too, the philosophers are mistaken in trying to teach us to regard death with indifference. "Nothing," says Nicole, "is more unavailing than the efforts of pagan philosophers and those who, like Montaigne, argue like pagans, to deliver men from the fear of death. Far from considering the general fear of death as a fault to be uprooted, the indifference with which they treat it must be regarded as one of their greatest errors, which we should seek to eliminate by a salutary fear of death." [58] Christians, therefore, will think of death in fear and trembling, and the Church, "led by the light of the Holy Spirit, has nothing more closely at heart than this thought; . . . it makes their salvation dependent upon it." [59]

"Persuaded that the fear of penalties alone suffices to change hearts," we read in an account sent to the *Nouvelles Ecclésiastiques* from Amiens in 1736, the Jesuits "have greatly insisted on this point. They have made such efforts to strike terror in souls through their sermons on hell, that these repeated discourses, delivered with extraordinary fire and vehemence, have unhinged several minds in the city, and the usual remedies have proved unavailing to restore them." And how effective was this method? After the departure of the Jesuit Fathers, "we find in the city the same luxury, the same worldliness, the same passions. The edifice suddenly put up by these new architects collapsed as quickly as it was built, because it was built on sand." [60]

It is, therefore, an error, as the Bishop of Angers points out, "to take the first tremors of a frightened conscience for conversion itself. Nothing is more directly contrary to the idea which the Church has always formed of Christian life than these cycles and alternations of relapses and spurious repentance, of death and of life." [61]

For the eighteenth-century bourgeois, the conflict often took place not in the clear light of day, as did the arguments between faith and unbelief, but in the regions of the soul where light penetrates but slowly. To win this battle, the clergy evoked sentiments of fear intended to reawaken emotions long suppressed. But would the fear of hell suffice to teach the bourgeois to live once more by faith and to reawaken in him that complex of sentiments—of charity, repentance, love of God—which previously had made him a believer?

The curious question whether fear alone sufficed to make a man Christian and agreeable to God was debated over and over again, and opinions were sharply divided. "A servile fear of penalties suffices to justify the sinner. It rules out the will to sin. It makes us children of God. These are propositions put forward by several new theologians," writes Du Pin.[62] This doctrine was known as attritionism, and the Jansenists frequently accused the Jesuits of adopting a theory which was "a summary of the whole ethics of the Casuists" [63] and which, they maintained, offended against the very foundations of Christianity.

Some sinners, says Mésenguy, "seized with horror at the sight of the eternal torments which faith presents to them, renounce the external action of sin through this sole motive; their hearts are those of slaves." [64] The Jesuits, especially, were regarded as having made slaves of the children of God by claiming, to quote Arnauld, that "attrition conceived through the sole fear of hell, without any love or the beginning of love, suffices to obtain for men, in the sacrament, the remission of their sins, however heinous, and to fit them to enjoy the ineffable blessings of eternal felicity which God says he has prepared for those who love him." This would mean that Jesus Christ "shed his blood to lift from men's necks the heavy yoke of love, by instituting the sacraments through which the world could be saved easily, delivered from the annoying obligation of loving God. This would include even those most caught up in the love of the world and those whose life consists of a continuous succession of confessions and crimes, for which they never feel any other sorrow than that afforded by the fear of eternally burning which, according to the Fathers, can only hold back the hand but not heal the heart." [65]

But the Jesuits were not the only ones to preach attritionism. We read in the *Nouvelles Ecclésiastiques* of 1773, "Everyone knows of the opposition of the fanatics of the Sorbonne, supported by the Archbishop of Paris, to that elementary truth of Christianity, that attrition arising from the sole fear of hell is incapable of setting aside the will to sin." [66] This new theology, which was regarded by many as offending against the most elementary truths of Christianity, should perhaps be taken as dictated by changed attitudes and a ratification, on the doctrinal level, of a process which had taken place in individual consciences.

The eighteenth-century believer was no longer capable of combining in his heart the different emotions which faith must arouse, and by isolating this or that sentiment he distorted the whole. It was too much to ask him to fear hell and at the same time to love God. Sometimes he loved God without fearing the devil; most of the time it was the reverse. The Jesuits, though not always, put up with the situation; others grew indignant. "For make no mistake, my brothers," says a preacher of the time, "fear is salutary, but it is not sufficient. What would you have thought of the penitent woman in the Gospels if, as she cast herself at the feet of the Saviour, you had heard her utter these words: 'Lord, I come to implore your pardon for my hideous profligacy. . . . But I don't want to deceive you; the reason I humiliate myself before you like this is not that I love you; I am quite indifferent to you and your gifts; but you have painted the torments of hell for us in such frightful colors that I am appalled; and it is this fear which moves me, and not your love at all!'?" [67] Fear without love "is but a servile fear, which is not even sufficient to save you." [68]

But the question arises whether the worldly remembered this.

"I blush to tell what I have witnessed myself on this point," says the Pastor of Gap, referring to the ignorance of the faithful in matters of religion. "People who confessed certain heinous sins solely out of fear of burning in hell . . . admitted to me that, if the pains of hell had consisted only in being deprived of the vision of God, they would never have confessed these crimes and would have continued to commit them." [69]

But, as Du Pin writes, "however much you subtilize and, as it were, haggle with God, he will always love only those who love him sincerely." [70] But how many, at that price, might still hope to be saved? The Jansenists, it is true, far from fearing such a consequence, accused the Jesuits precisely of making heaven too easy of access: After reading certain passages in which the attritionists present their theories, "who will not exclaim," one Jansenist writes, "that there are not a few elect, as Jesus Christ said, but on the contrary a very large number; and that the gate to life is very wide! For is there a single sinner in the Christian world who does not fear hell, and is not sorry to have offended God, not because God is sovereignly good and sovereignly deserving of love, but because he is terrible in his vengeance upon sin?" [71]

God appeared to have become a specter, the specter of death. He had lost everything save hell. Therefore, so the theory ran, souls must be frightened into returning to God. "Although grace has different ways of leading back sinners," says a preacher of the period, "it nevertheless appears that the most effective is that of fear; man is too ungrateful to turn to the Lord only on account of the blessings he receives from him; too carnal to let himself be guided only by the hope of invisible possessions; too much a slave to his senses to detach himself from them through love of justice alone. . . . Woe, then, to those men who, unwilling to think of what disquiets them, dismiss from their thoughts the terrifying idea of an avenging God; let them know that only fearful souls will have cause for hope on the last day." [72]

Other theologians, it is true, grieved at being reduced to such methods. "Is it then necessary, oh my God, that we should daily call the terror of your judgments to the aid of our cowardice and weakness? Is it necessary that gratitude alone and love should make only fleeting impressions on our souls? Must we constantly steady our souls by fear? Oh shame, oh suffering! Is it then possible that a God who pardons and loves does not move us as palpably as a God who crushes and punishes?" [73]

Was it not possible, in order to convert sinners, to put more stress on the joys awaiting the just than on the pains awaiting the wicked? "I do not know why we are always told about the sufferings which the damned will experience in their bodies, whereas we are never told a word about the sublime sentiments which the elect must naturally experience," writes Caraccioli, an apologist of the second half of the eighteenth century, and to make up for the omission he attempts a description of the joys bestowed on those whom God has pardoned.[74] But however glowing the description, hell seems to have been a surer means than paradise. "Fear of eternal punishment seems, indeed, the strongest motive for resisting the attraction of vain pleasures. The hope of rewards promised for virtue may attach men to justice; but that hope draws all its strength from the love of heavenly benefits; and such love is always weak in hearts carried away by the violence of the passions." [75]

Fear of hell thus appeared necessary to keep the believer on the right path. It is true, as Père Elisée remarks, that this sentiment "does not principally affect virtuous souls"; nevertheless, he immediately follows this remark—and the admission is instructive—by saying that "there are few such noble souls whom love of order and gratitude cause to cleave to duty; most men are more moved by fear of the future than by any other motive." [76]

The bourgeois who remained a believer, or returned to the faith, did so almost in spite of himself. He did not want to have to admit it. When he said, "I believe," he was saying that he was afraid. And how should it have been otherwise, since he no longer believed, except with that part of his soul which he considered, and rightly so, as the least noble? The fear of hell, last remnant among the worldly of a constantly shrinking religious experience, lacking greatness or nobility, frequently contributed to discrediting a faith which it was supposed to revive.

Hell, a Literary Fiction

"If the thought of hell does not convert us, if the prospect of those torments, of that eternity, of that eternal repentance does not detach us from sin and from the vain pleasures of life, we are lost; these truths have made the martyrs; they have peopled the deserts; even today they still fill the monasteries with saintly religious." [77] A believing Christian could not think without horror of the eternal torments awaiting the sinner in the hereafter. "If our faith, my brothers, were far more alive than it is, the image of the last judgment would produce in us the most salutary effects. . . . We should be insensible to all the rest; we should take every possible care to win our Judge's favor and to be able to appear one day with confidence before his judgment seat." [78]

But how many Christians live in the fear of the Lord? "Unfathomable mystery! Mystery more astonishing than hell itself! . . . There is a hell, and there are sinners; there is an eternal hell, Christians know it, and this eternal hell is full of Christians! I cannot comprehend it; these are contradictions which experience alone can explain." [79]

The clergy neglected no device in the pulpit to portray the torments of hell in the most vivid colors, in the most harrowing detail, in order to strike terror in the souls of their hearers. "This is what faith teaches us: an eternal fire, a fire which acts on the spirit as on the flesh, a fire which burns without consuming; that is what we have to fear. But what astonishes me is that so moving a truth should move us so little. . . . Is it stupidity? Is it heedlessness? Is it madness? Is it an enchantment? Do we believe this fundamental point of Christianity, or do we not? If we believe, where is our wisdom? If we do not believe, where is our religion?" [80] The answer might be that it was believed at some moments and forgotten at others. But what could the clergy do to prevent these impressions from being effaced and everyday life from regaining the upper hand? Heighten the tone, pile on horrors, stir up emotions to the point of paroxysm.

"Oh death, lend to my words that terrifying note which you impart to all whom you rob of father or children, of husband or wife, of parents or friends, that I may impress my hearers with a salutary terror!" [81] Drawing upon the thought of death, preachers sought to make their hearers tremble; they vied with one another in anticipating the horrors awaiting the damned in hell, and, after giving free rein to their imagination, they told their hearers that this was but a pale similitude of the reality. "The most terrifying description of hell, drawn according to men's imagination, is but a feeble image of the wrath of God, a shadow compared with the reality." [82] Another contemporary preacher writes, "Imagine to yourselves a vast and immense subterranean area, in the midst of which is a pool of fire and blazing sulphur. That is where the Lord, bent on vengeance, causes inexhaustible springs of pitch and sulphur to flow!" [83]

The object, however, was not merely to depict scenes of horror, but also to make men feel that the moment was approaching, or already upon them, when the abyss would open before their feet. "Can you imagine anything worse than this hell of which I have given you such a terrifying description, yet a very pale one compared with the reality? . . . Do you not tremble at the danger which threatens you? For what would become of most of you, dear parishioners, if you were judged at this moment, as I speak to you? What has become of all who died before you in the self-same dispositions in which you are now? How many among your relatives and friends, your fathers and mothers, now burn in hell for living exactly as you live now!" [84]

Strong stimuli must be used to move sinners; the congregation, as they listened to the sermon, must be made to feel something of the sensation of burning; they must already feel themselves in hell and cry mercy. But it seems that all the oratorical arts of the clergy of the period could not suffice. "We open the eyes of their faith to the abysses of hell ready to swallow them up; we threaten, we blaze, we thunder," says one such preacher, "and what do we see? Insensible hearers, whom even the most interesting points of religion cannot arouse and who fall asleep to the sound of anathemas!" [85] "Yes, Lord," cries Cambacérès, "you see what your word has become in our mouths; no one fears it." [86]

The worldly, then, apparently no longer feared the last judgment. "The picture of this great spectacle, which formerly was able . . . to subject the whole universe to the yoke of the Cross, this terrifying picture is barely calculated to alarm any but the timid and unlettered. . . . The only result we usually get from such discourses is to have people ask, as they leave, whether things will really happen as we have said." [87] Laymen debated and raised all kinds of awkward questions. "If a minister of the living God raises his voice to announce divine judgments and vengeance, if he opens the gates of the abyss, . . . these sacred truths everywhere encounter hearts steeled against their salutary impressions; and all the benefit people derive from them is to philosophize coldly about the reality of eternal pains." [88]

While the preacher painted his terrifying picture of the torments of hell, the worldly debated whether he was not going rather too far. Through discussion and thorough analysis, they guarded themselves against the sense of fear. Through discussion of the danger, they took heart; they might even be said to have become curious, to have drawn closer to the specter of death, to have prodded it to find out whether there was any cause for fright . . . and they were reassured. One gets used to everything, even terror. And in the end, the most harrowing description of hell came to appear as no more than a blood-and-thunder show to be assessed on its merits.

"The Christian discourse has become a show," La Bruyère had said earlier. Among the listeners were people "sacrilegious enough to make no distinction between the sacred and profane," and people who "come to show off their taste, instead of learning to rule their hearts." [89] What use, then, would it be to lead the congregation "to the brink of a hell which awaits them and prepares to receive them?" [90] "We announce to them the most terrible truths, and they are concerned only with the amenities of language. . . . And if the word of God still bears any fruit, it is only among the humble and docile populace," says another contemporary preacher.[91] Thus, in the eyes of the laity, preachers became actors who played their parts well or badly, according to whether they moved their audiences or bored them. "We find ourselves forced to use the whole apparatus of ostentatious eloquence. . . . We are forced to become orators. What a title! We are no longer permitted to be apostles." [92]

Hell had become a literary fiction. This was a danger which the Church could not prevent. There is an emotional disbelief, as there is a rational disbelief, and it would be hard to say which is the more dangerous to faith. Sentiment may cease to be a reality of experience and be transferred to the realm of the imagination, and it becomes possible to enjoy even terror. It is a perversion of the religious sense, a tasting of the pains of hell without experiencing them, making sport of something real, making fun of God and the devil. Something of the religious sentiment, or at least of a sentiment of religious origin, may subsist, but it is sentiment without belief; it is hell become an image.

"Actually," La Harpe says, "heaven and hell are rather subjects for frequent reflection and meditation than for long descriptions; if one goes in for the latter, it is very hard to avoid rhetoric, which should be avoided above all things, especially in the pulpit." [93] A rhetorical style runs the risk of producing mere fiction, and indeed poor fiction. This was what the worldly would not forgive in their clergy.

"Today, oh my God," we read in Champion de Pontallier's *Trésor du chrétien,* "belief in your judgments no longer frightens anyone, and the fearful descriptions which your ministers give of it often do no more than provide matter for impious jeering, instead of producing terror and consternation in consciences." [94] And it is no longer simply "countless foolhardy young people" who scoff at the "threats of eternal fires, which the justice of God kindles in hell." Even those "who are prepared to listen to the truths of the Gospel become impatient when one speaks to them of hell." [95] "Some false delicacy has seized our minds," says a contemporary preacher. "We are obliged to preach the most austere truths of the Gospel; we would not be pardoned the slightest mitigation of doctrine; but if we speak of hell-fire, then from that moment we are no longer worthy of attention, and we are regarded as playing on the gullibility of our listeners." [96]

Thus the clergy, instead of reviving the secret fears often harbored by the worldly concerning death, had diminished them, by displaying them in broad daylight and translating them through rhetorical devices. Thanks to them, one might almost say, there often took place a form of catharsis of the heart, which they had delivered from certain fears precisely by attempting to awaken them too rudely.

But such considerations only partially explain the kind of emotive disbelief which enabled laymen to regard with indifference or to ridicule "those great truths which formerly caused even the most independent-minded to tremble." [97] For radical changes had taken place in the consciences of the faithful themselves, corrupting and disintegrating the religious experience.

The feelings which Christians experienced in the face of death were of many different kinds, from pure contemplation of eternity and disinterested love of God to carnal terror in the face of hell. But as time passed, the oppositions involved in the Christian faith became increasingly evident and affected its substance.

"Man was created to live in an eternal solitude with God alone," writes Nicole. "Hence to prepare oneself for death," he continues, "is to accustom oneself to this solitude with God." [98] But in the believer concerned exclusively to escape hell, is it still possible to recognize the man who is preparing himself for eternal solitude with God?

"The finite is annihilated in the presence of the infinite, and becomes pure nothingness. Thus it is with our mind in the presence of God," writes Pascal.[99] But the cries of the damned disturb the silence of the infinite spaces, in which man communes with God alone, and the vision of eternity is lost when it is too carelessly combined with images of hell and the fears of a soul in torment.

Yet apparently fear of hell could not be dispensed with, and the worldly tended to be more afraid of the devil than desirous of the vision of God. But then there took place what the preachers had not foreseen; the fear of hell, a sentiment so solidly rooted and altogether unrelated to the more refined emotions "in which, however, imagination always plays a large part" [100] or to those ideas "contrary to genuine and solid piety," [101] in time came to take on a fictional character. Some, then, wondered whether they had not taken a wrong turning in constantly stressing the "sempiternal roasters" and went so far as to want to abolish hell.

"Fear of hell-fire has been unable to produce what should be the effect only of the love of God," says a writer of the period, who would have heaven open to all men, so that the fear of death might be banished and, delivered from "servile fear of eternal torments," we should have toward God only "filial fear filled with love and thanksgiving." [102] But would many still want to know this God deprived of his hell? "Alas, how many there are who would be quite willing to be quit of Christ as their Redeemer," exclaims Abbé Boileau, "and who would give up the means of salvation which he offers them, if he were to give up his right to punish them!" [103]

Faith could not do without hell. "A religion which offered sure rewards in another world would find its devotees disappearing by the thousands," [104] says Montesquieu. There were "clashes" of sentiment, which, more than all the contradictions which reason could reveal in the sphere of dogma, helped to shake the faith of those who were no longer capable of believing without questioning. Men had established themselves in this world, and human life had organized itself increasingly outside religion. But all religious sentiments were not at first equally affected by the development of what Nicole calls "human views";[105] some were better able than others to withstand the attacks of secular life. Thus, if the worldly man could love the divinity with a "principal and dominant passion" which caused him to "prefer God to all creatures, and despise temporal things," [106] he might still, for a certain time, experience the fears of hell, which were more readily identified with the interest he must necessarily take in his own fate and with his anxieties concerning the hereafter.

But could the Church reawaken the faith of former days in consciences by reviving ancient fears and anxieties? And could such souls, hesitating still before the unknown and uncertain what road to take, through prudence become once more what they were no longer able to become out of a spirit of abandonment; that is, Christians? "Mr. Pascal's famous argument," Montesquieu had said, "is cogent enough to inspire us with fear, but not to give us faith." [107] By singing the triumph of death, the Church was powerless to prevent the "main part of life" from developing increasingly outside faith, which, existing for many only in the form of fears—last vestiges of a religious sentiment—

now appeared as one of those unfortunate prejudices to be shaken off.

Death and the Upright Man

"Life can be judged by no more false a rule than death," says Vauvenargues. "The thought of death deceives us, for it makes us forget to live. . . . To achieve great things, we must live as though we were never going to die." [108] What could be more contrary to the mind of the Church? "The conscience of the dying slanders their life." [109] What would become, then, of the sinner on his deathbed, whose image the Church evoked to convert unbelievers? It is true that Vauvenargues was careful to add that he was referring to "the thought of death, without the viewpoint of religion." [110] But what is death without faith? "Death without the light and the consolations of religion," says the Archbishop of Lyons, "is a horrible thing, a shameful and cruel torment, a bottomless abyss, a misfortune without remedy, the fatal reef of human wisdom." [111] If humans imagined that they could interpret life according to their own standards, then the meaning of death seemed bound to elude them forever. "God, the necessarily eternal, immutable, independent Being, wished his creatures to render continual homage to his eternity, his independence, his immutability; and death is that homage," says an apologist. "Yes," he goes on, "in every part of the universe, and at every moment, millions of individuals of all kinds die to honor the greatness of the sovereign Being, and to instruct us that he alone is indefectible, and that his times endure eternally." [112] But now it seemed that the laity wanted to conceive of death without God, without heaven, and without hell, as a human fact; and it seemed that life alone made death intelligible to man.

It would nevertheless be false to say that the worldly, in thinking of death, had substituted for the ancient religious view a concept of a secular character. The enlightened layman might admit his ignorance and sometimes his anxiety. "There is a subject concerning which man, having naturally only little and very inadequate information, has always had much anxiety: that is his condition at the end of this life. Who can reassure me on this point?" [113] The layman who put this question was a highly educated man, very sure of himself, and those who shared his views sometimes turned to religion for an answer they could not find elsewhere; on the other hand, they might also go on as before, leaving the question unanswered, so that their life no longer depended on what they thought of death.

"Where are the men who think of death, who regard it as really incorporated in them, as something that will soon erase their features, destroy their bodies, bring to nothing their plans, their riches, their honors?" asks a Catholic apologist. [114] The worldly, apparently, were no longer merely questioning the Church's answers on the problem of death, but setting the problem aside altogether. "Since death is as natural as life, why fear it so much? It is not to the wicked, to scoundrels that I speak. . . . But I should like to arm decent people against the chimeras of suffering and anguish of that last part of life. . . . Men fear death as children fear the dark, and only because their imagination has been frightened by phantoms as insubstantial as they are terrible," we read in the *Encyclopédie*. [115]

Thus respectable folk have nothing to fear from death, and if those who are not virtuous fear it, that is their own fault. There is a very simple cure for the fear of death, says Abbé de Bonnaire: "Be virtuous, I shall tell them, or endeavor sincerely to become it. You will no longer fear death, or you will fear it with a fear mixed with the sweetest hope." [116] Thus all would be well, and it would be a mistake to fear death. "To worry, to be constantly alarmed about the uncertainty of our last hour, is to arrive at the end of life like a murderer walking to the scaffold," says a writer of the period. "If there is anything painful about death," he continues, "it is rather the fact of others dying that should cause us sorrow, than the fact of dying ourselves. . . . The only real misfortune is the loss of persons dear to us." But there is a way to console ourselves. A "provident nature" causes "time to assuage the pain of the first access of grief, changing it into a kind of sweetness which might almost be called pleasurable." [117]

In any case, the respectable citizen usually left children to continue his work. "The man who is completing his career takes leave of life the more sweetly in that he leaves to an *alter ego* the prospect of a more gracious future. The goods of the father naturally devolve upon the son, through whom the family is continued, and possession is not interrupted. These hereditary possessions, easier to preserve than to acquire, make the work of the new head of the family less hard and more productive; and his mind, less bent under the weight of physical needs, takes freer flight, performs its duties better, uses its rights better . . . and enjoys its good fortune more, a good fortune consolidated and developed from age to age." [118]

Thus the vision of death was gradually losing its terror, with a corresponding effect on the character of life itself. "Men take wives, women take husbands; people eat, drink, buy, sell, plant, build; that, up to the hour of death, makes up most of the preoccupations of what are called men of the world," [119] we read in *La Religion Chrétienne méditée dans le véritable Esprit de ses Maximes*. And "what is the life of most men, if not a continuous and deliberate distraction from death and its frightful consequences?" [120] The bourgeois had a different approach to life, since he no longer wanted to hear of the "sad, uncomfortable, preconceived notion of the fear of death." [121] "Three things," we read, "are necessary to man's happiness: good health, good sense, and a good conscience." [122] And these three things are within the reach of every man of the world. Since he knows how to be happy in this world, he will know how to be happy in the next . . . if it exists at all. "Every reasonable man desires and seeks happiness; he knows what procures it for him here below, and ensures it to him after his death; therefore, he has nothing to fear, and, assured of happiness on every side, he will, it is hoped, survive in the hereafter." [123]

Of this attitude, Pascal writes, "Their neglect in a matter which vitally concerns themselves, their eternal destiny, their all, irritates me more than it moves me; it astonishes and appalls me; I find something monstrous in it." [124] "It is a monstrous thing to see," he writes again, "in the same heart and at the same time, this concern for the most trivial of matters and this lack of concern for the greatest. It is an incomprehensible form of bewitch-

ment and a supernatural torpor which is a proof of an all-powerful force that causes it." [125] Pascal's man, on the one hand, and
the respectable bourgeois, the contemporary of Voltaire and
Rousseau, on the other, were no longer able to understand each
other. When they spoke of death, they were not speaking of the
same thing. One *believed* in death, as he believed in God and
hell, or, better, it was because he believed in death that he had
faith. For the other death had ceased to be an object of faith; it
had become a fact and ceased to be a mystery. Death sometimes
still struck terror into souls, but almost by accident; it was no
longer at home in a world without mystery. But what would
then become of faith? Could it still subsist without the concept of
mystery and death, a concept basic to all mysteries, whether
that of God, of divine love, of sin, or of hell?

7 · THE IDEA OF GOD

OLD AND NEW CONCEPTS OF GOD

"We can never fear hell too much, or desire paradise too much, that is, have too much religion either for our own happiness or for the happiness of society; thus the greater or lesser degree of religion of each man consists particularly in the more or less strong habit of fear of the pains of the future life, and the more or less strong habit of hope in immense and eternal joys."[1] The good Abbé Saint-Pierre was defining the religion that ultimately remained to the worldly. To the extent that they believed that God existed, the divinity would be for them "the one who punishes sins and rewards charitable works," which constituted "the essential part of religion." A greatly oversimplified concept, which would not seem to require much exegesis. God was justice itself, and because he was just, he would punish people only for their deliberate faults. He would be absolutely impartial and would take care not to have preferences. Finally, his judgment would not be excessively severe, for he was always good and merciful.

All this would seem to leave no room for discussion; yet the lengthy controversies which took place among theologians and which long disturbed the peace of the Church prove that this was not the case at all. If the all too comprehensible divinity of Abbé Saint-Pierre finally outlived the "infinitely incomprehensible" God of Pascal, that victory was not achieved without a series of violent struggles, which shook the foundations of the faith.

The man of the world, subsequently assessing the disputes which had arisen between Jansenists and Jesuits, was to speak of them with some contempt, judging that the whole discussion turned on "so essentially boring a subject." And yet the *Unigenitus* Bull, over which the fiercest battles were fought and which, according to Duclos, "was only an exercise for idle schools," [2] was in fact, as a Jansenist writer put it, "one of the most important events to take place in the Church. . . . What does it not cover? And what does it not influence? The Bull has become central to everything." [3]

What, precisely, was the issue? The one hundred and one Propositions drawn from Père Quesnel's *Réflexions morales* and condemned by the Church, are not easy to summarize; they touched on nearly every aspect of theology. But if we go to the bottom of the conflicts surrounding the Bull, we find that the central issue was really the tragedy of a dying deity, of a God whose champions were trying to save him and who was becoming progressively more incomprehensible to the worldly as time passed and the concept of mystery faded.

"The history of the Church should, properly speaking, be described as the history of truth," [4] says Pascal. As such, it was presumed to be independent of what was thought and felt by the faithful who, being unstable in their views, often altered it according to their feeble lights and their specific needs. The Church, in this view, would always preserve the image of the true God, whatever idols were substituted for it by minds swayed by whim and incapable of conceiving of undiluted truth; and the faithful, in listening to the voices of their pastors and submitting to the authority of the Church, would always find the same immutable image of the eternal God. But some eighteenth-century theologians, adducing texts and ancient traditions, were to claim that the image of God had been retouched or even that another image had been substituted for it, bearing little resemblance to the true God. They refused to adore this new divinity and proposed to maintain an unshakable fidelity to the God they had always known.

These struggles turned not on beliefs, on those multiple transformations which minds necessarily impose on the object of faith,
but on faith itself. What was questioned was no longer faulty
interpretations but the text itself, since two versions presented
themselves which appeared to contradict one another in every
particular. The worldly frequently questioned their pastors to
find out how they should believe, raising any number of difficulties in accepting what the Church proposed to them; but the
supposition was always that there was agreement on what should
be believed and that the object of faith in itself was certain. The
Church showed them the image of the true God, and they replied,
without disputing that this was the God of the Christians, that
they were not sure whether this God was still theirs; but when
they saw the theologians argue among themselves, they realized
that the identity of the true God of the Christians was not in
fact clear. There were two divinities, both claiming that title and
appearing to accuse one another of having usurped the throne of
the Almighty.

"Pride and dissoluteness," writes Nicole, "tend equally to withdraw man from the power and from the wisdom of God, just
as sound piety tends to subject him increasingly to the one and
to the other." [5] The true Christian would love his dependence.
"Our glory is to be in God's hands," he would say, "and our righteousness consists in depending upon him and loving that dependence." [6] Hence there is "no more terrible punishment than to
be thrown back on oneself." [7] Whereas the "proud man would
like to dispense with" God's assistance "and owe him nothing, the
joy of the truly humble man is to owe him everything, and attribute nothing to himself." [8] For "the less we merit on our own,
the more we owe to God. The treasure we find in our poverty
and the rich substance of Christian humility consists in being unable to glory in anything, so that we may give all glory to God,
and eternally sing only the praises of his eternal mercies." [9]

Thus the Christian soul needs a God before whom it can humble itself; it seeks the triumph of God in its own abasement, for
the soul penetrated "by true humility . . . desires in all things
that the Creator should be glorified, and that the creature should
be obscured and annihilated." [10] This soul, humbling itself before

the Almighty, would want to keep nothing for itself. Everything of its own would estrange it from God. It would feel it to be some kind of infidelity to God to belong to itself, to be able to be free; it would feel that what it acquired by its own powers would in some way have been taken away from God. Hence it would desire to be saved by God alone. "The helplessness of nature in the matter of salvation is not the despair of the Christian, but the triumph of the grace of Jesus Christ. Oh blessed helplessness, which forces us to await everything of him without whom we can do nothing!" [11]

The man who loves his helplessness wants to owe nothing to himself. To be free, for him, is to feel abandoned by God. So he wants God always to act in him. "And far from fearing to be moved in this way, he desires it, he asks it, to the point of praying that God may force his rebellious will, fearing nothing so much as to be left to his own resources, for he finds in his own heart nothing but falsehood and sin." [12] The Jansenist, one might say, was jealous on God's behalf at his own expense. May God be magnified, and may his grandeur be nurtured from all that is in me, from the substance of my being! I want no freedom in relation to God, I want to reserve nothing for myself! The Christian must not bargain with God. A God who is not everything for him is nothing.

Thus the Jansenists defended the "cause of God" [13] against the creature. Man, they said, was being set up "in competition with God." [14] Man would be free, but God would not be all-powerful. A great trial had been initiated, the Jansenists maintained: the trial of God. "No, God will not abandon us. It is his cause that we have the joy to defend. Let us defend it to our last breath. Let us consider ourselves fortunate to have been chosen to defend the interests of the Lord." [15]

The Jansenists were championing their God, the God of old. "We combat those who would take from us the heritage of our fathers," they said.[16] For the all-powerful God adored by Christians, some were attempting, they said, to substitute a new God, more willing to condone human pride, the Jesuits' God, who, "using a thousand stratagems" with men, allows them to act according to their whim. "Weak, helpless, not daring to use his power to change hearts for fear of violating men's freedom," he watches for "opportune moments to . . . bestow his graces." [17] "Having no means infallible enough in themselves to make his creatures obey him," he is "obliged to consult their free will, to see if they are willing to lend themselves to his designs, to consider whether they are prepared to grant or to refuse success to his graces." [18] "These are the sorry politics of a weak-kneed being," said the Jansenists, "reduced to consulting the wishes of his creatures to determine the time and circumstances when they would be prepared to accomplish his designs!" [19]

But if the Jansenists despised the God of the Jesuits who dared not give proof of his power, the Jesuits in their turn had no difficulty in finding arguments in support of the God they worshiped or in showing up the weaknesses of the other. The Jansenists' God, they said, was "neither holy, nor just nor merciful." [20] According to a Jesuit preacher, this divinity was "a pitiless and barbarous tyrant, a God who would be deserving of all my hatred." And yet, he continues, this is the God whom the Jansenists command us to love, and "they insist emphatically on the obligation of the great commandment." [21] But how should their God be loved? "To love God! Oh, how can I, when Quesnel depicts him for me with the most odious features, most capable of making me hate him? Personally, I understand nothing of your language. Every one of you is always talking about the love of God. To judge by Quesnel, the love of God is the sole virtue which honors that sovereign Being, the only one he understands, the only one he rewards. . . . Anyone who acts for any other motive runs in vain, and there is neither God nor religion where there is no love of God. That's very fine. But what happens? What happens, after this fine statement, is that this God, the love of whom is the only licit virtue, and even the fear of whom is reproved by Quesnel, is according to him nevertheless a tyrant, who commands impossible things and who, not content with commanding them, proceeds to damn pitilessly those who have not carried them out. Seriously, is this a God one can love?" [22]

The Jansenists' God, according to the Jesuits, compromised the divinity whom they claimed to defend and furnished ammunition to unbelievers. "A libertine perceives in him, with satisfaction, and considers, with malignity, a God whom he can neither believe nor love, because he is portrayed with the features of a cruel and wicked master . . . who orders all men to believe in him, and provides them with far more tangible reasons for despair than for confidence; . . . who eternally rewards favorites without genuine merits, for alien virtues and a forced perseverance, while he eternally punishes men whom he is pleased not to love, not for misusing the freedom which they do not possess or resisting a grace which they have not received, but for the abandonment in which he leaves them and the gratuitous hatred which he bears them. . . ." [23]

Thus the Jansenists, who had "affected to preach the love of God," were really, according to this view, "doing their best to stifle it." [24] As the Bishop of Lodève put it, "how revolting is this object presented to the faith of believers! A cruel and barbarous God, whose hand fashions a dark and burning abyss in the bowels of the earth, into which he ruthlessly plunges most of his creatures to whom he has refused—indeed, for whom he never prepared and to whom he never gave—any of the means needed to prevent so deplorable a fate!" [25]

How did the Jansenists justify a God who, in the eyes of their foes, was "the most cruel of all masters?" [26] "Were I not a Christian," writes Arnauld, "and since I am only too keenly subject to the impulses of human pride, I would not lack the temerity to find fault with action on God's part which seems to us incomprehensible, and at first sight so little adapted to our notion of his goodness and righteousness. But I stop myself as soon as I remember that God's nature being infinitely above my own intellect, and he alone being able to understand himself, it would be great folly to want to judge of the equity of his conduct by the vanity of my thoughts, rather than by what it has pleased him to reveal to us himself in his Scriptures." [27]

God's justice, then, should not be judged by human standards. "God is essentially incomprehensible to anyone who is not God," writes Mésenguy. "If divine justice could be understood by us, it would no longer be divine justice." [28] And the pious soul of the Jansenist could love this infinitely incomprehensible God, humbling himself before him with a passion nurtured by all the sacrifices which he had made to him and all the mortifications which God had inflicted on him. He knew that there were "terrible truths," but taking the view that "what is terrible in them must vanquish our pride, and keep us in a just dependence in regard to God," [29] he could, equally removed from despair and presumption, "walk between fear and hope" [30] and love God without questioning him. Did the God he loved want him? Of this he must remain in ignorance. "The condition of the voyager, which is that of this life, and which ends only in death, rules out all absolute certainty of predestination or reprobation." [31] But not daring to question the one he loved, he was enraptured and sought the infinite in the face of mystery.

"Religion rightly understood casts us down and raises us up, humbles us and consoles us," says a Jansenist writer.[32] Abasement and elevation, fear and hope, abandon and anxious heart-searching, troubled questioning and confidence, from these coflicting and irreconcilable sentiments sprang the Jansenist's great passion for his God. He could not love a God who did not desire to possess him wholly; he could not believe in a heaven that was open to everyone. "People want to be Christians too cheaply," says Quesnel, "and consequently they are not Christians at all. Salvation has to cost, it has to cost everything, at least as far as the disposition of the heart is concerned." [33] To love God must be a costly business, and there would no longer be anything divine about a God who let himself be loved too easily.

The Jansenists could not love the new God, who "gives grace abundantly to everyone." [34] He was too welcoming and too accessible for the Jansenist soul to continue to love him alone. How would they recognize in this God the God of the early Christians who "subjected themselves to painful and continuous works of a sincere penitence"? [35] Before this God, become too human, whose ever welcoming smile seemed to expunge the memory of the terrors he had formerly spread abroad, how would man's soul enter once more "into a profound abasement under the hand of God, and into supreme contempt of self," judging "God worthy of all honor, all praise, all thanksgiving" and itself "deserving of every kind of contempt, humiliation and abasement"? [36] And how should it find, in this heaven with its wide-open doors, that "infinite good" for which it hoped, as Pascal put it, with a hope mingling effective enjoyment and fear? "Where are the blind, the deaf, the dumb, the lame? Where are the caves inhabited by dragons, the mountains to which wild beasts repair? Everywhere I seek that path which will be called the holy road, along which the impure man will not pass; but I see no path which is not common to all men." [37]

THE CONSTITUTIONAL GOD

"Every day you say: 'I believe in one God, the Father Almighty, maker of heaven and earth, and of all things visible and invisible,' and it is because you believe it that you address God to ask him to touch your hearts, to change them, even to force your rebellious wills. For is God the God of bodies only? Is he not also the God of minds? Is he not powerful enough to make free and reasonable beings act freely? Yes, in the order of grace, as in that of nature; in the spiritual and invisible world, as in the material and visible world, his empire, you know, my brothers, is a sovereign empire. He gives death, and he gives life; he casts down, and he lifts up; he leads down into the pit, and he saves from it." [38] God must be recognized as possessing limitless and utterly undivided power. The Jansenists' great grievance against the Jesuits was that "They do not hesitate to limit God's power in relation to the spiritual world. They associate with him in the government of this world another powerful principle . . . . free will." [39]

Thus "free will receives sovereign honor," [40] and God no longer governs the world alone; he must take into account another power, free will, the power of man. "As soon as you admit of a balance of strength or of power, you place the creature on a level with God in the power which he exercises through his grace. . . . These are two sovereigns . . . treating with one another as equals, fighting each other with equal forces." [41] Thus there is a duarchy in the world, God and man, each with his own sphere. "They have assigned to God his portion and to man his. And they have separated them from each other so completely that nothing can be added to one that is not taken from the other." [42]

In the government of this world, then, there is a kind of distinction of powers, an orderly division determining the exercise of power. "According to Molina, we always have to come back to a division between God and man. Strange division! Where after putting on one side what belongs to God and not to man, we put on the other what belongs to man to the exclusion of God!" [43] But in that case, was not man the equal of God? Was he not God himself? "If man were to share with God, if to him were due the least glory which did not belong to God more than to him, . . . man would be a god, and would be able to glory not in the true God, but outside God. He would glorify himself . . . in what he had not received."

The Jansenists could not accept the position that "man's glory" might be established "at the expense of God's," that man might be placed "in competition with God." [44] Their God "cannot suffer that anyone should dare place limits on his power." [45] He wishes to rule alone. "No one shares with God," [46] was the Jansenists' contention. "For if God is not all-powerful over all creatures, both spiritual and material, we no longer conceive of anything infinite about God; he is not God." [47]

A curious parallel might be drawn between the changes which were taking place on the religious level and those which were to take place on the political level. The Jansenists' God was an absolute monarch, and his subjects were in no wise qualified to ask him for an accounting. The new God, by contrast, resembled a king who had come to terms with his subjects and was seeking an arrangement which would reconcile his rights with those of his people. To retain his dominion, he had to make concessions. His creature was important; he would therefore leave mankind some share of freedom and would have to abide by certain rules and justify his decisions; finally, he would have to show himself good and kindly to win the hearts of human beings, who otherwise might object that he was making too much of his power and accuse him of despotism.

"The Lord is merciful to whomsoever he is pleased to show

mercy; he enriches with his gifts those whom he is pleased to enrich because he is all-powerful and none is entitled to ask him to explain his deeds." [48] That was precisely what the worldly could no longer accept, and, appearing before the throne of the Most High, in a sort of reversal of roles, they might be depicted as asking a reckoning of him who was to judge them. "You will allow me, Lord," they might say, "to file suit against you. . . . I ask you, did I forsake you first? Did you not condemn me first, before any fault on my part? Were you not my enemy without my having been yours?" [49] Or again, the damned soul would make objections of the following kind: "Had you wished to save me, and touched me with your grace, I should not have resisted, and should have kept your law. So you condemn me because it is your pleasure to condemn me." [50]

Of course, God would not have to answer. But a preacher of the period imagines how he might justify himself. The wrathful judge tells the reprobate sinner: "Now that the designs of my Providence have been made manifest to you, come, I am ready to give you an accounting of my conduct, I am ready to enter into discussion with you; accuse me, if you dare, of injustice, of indifference toward you." This preamble, making it clear that God does not seek to avoid discussion, is followed by a development of the arguments used by the Jesuit Fathers. In conclusion, the deity tells his questioner, "You see, it was entirely up to you to save yourself; you could have done so through the aids given you in my Church. Such external aids, of course, would have been unavailing for salvation without a strong and powerful interior grace; but you were told a thousand times, on my behalf, that this interior grace was the result of prayer; that he who wishes and is not able, has only to pray, and he will be able." [51] In other words, our sinner was wrong in falling back on the argument of "refusal of grace." "A man can be a heretic all his life," says the same preacher, "but not after death." [52]

God parleys with his children, as the king-patriarch does with his. Indeed, we might say that before the French demanded a charter from their sovereign, French Catholics had demanded one of their God. It was understood that God must be just, that he had certain obligations toward men, and that certain reciprocal relations had to be established between creature and Creator. God should no longer make distinctions showing himself inflexible to the many while reserving his favors for the elect alone. Everyone must be able to share equally in God's blessings; otherwise, there would be no justice in this world or in the next. "Would such odious partiality be fitting, my God, for a heart as bountiful and as just as yours! What a way of urging us to love you, and to make us cherish the great precept of that love, to attribute to you the sentiments of a tyrant!" [53]

Thus, God must love all men, without distinction. "Whoever we are, we are born agreeable in God's eyes; it suffices to be the masterpiece of his hands, and to be an object dear to his heart." Nevertheless, the author of these words did not wish to deprive God of all right to certain preferences. "God's love for men," he says, "has degrees; all are equally dear to him, but all are not equally his favorites." [54] Thus certain concessions are made to God, but without letting him be too unjust. The same, in any case, applied to kings. "A king is not bound by all the laws of justice which are binding upon individuals," writes an apologist of the late eighteenth century. "Often he is judge in his own cause, for example; it is not so in the case of his subjects; will it then be concluded that a king is unjust?" [55] Like kings, God may thus preserve certain prerogatives. We might even go farther and say that "when God makes gifts to his creatures, he is free to distribute them as he wishes"; or again, "God, the absolute master of his gifts, whether in the order of nature or in that of grace, may, without injustice, introduce any inequality he wishes in the distribution of such gifts." [56] The worldly-minded, however, were less and less inclined to have it so, either in the secular or in the religious sphere; they wanted a justice equal for all, and with no exceptions for anyone.

The religious conscience wanted no more privileges; it asked for justice. It seemed that a new covenant was being concluded between God and man, by virtue of which the deity would have to fulfill certain obligations which might no longer be disregarded. "This means that grace is no longer a grace but a debt. Thus God no longer distinguishes between one man and another by helping one and not another, by giving one what he asks and not giving it to the other." [57] The Jansenists' God had no obligation toward anyone. "Let us not fear to say it, my very dear brothers: grace is never owed to anyone; God is the absolute master of his gifts; he distributes them to whomsoever he wills, and in the manner he wills, with a sovereign independence." [58] The new deity might no longer dispose of his gifts so freely. "Faith, and the use, increase, and reward of faith, are all a gift of your pure liberality," Quesnel had said in one of the one hundred and one Propositions condemned in *Unigenitus*. "Yes," replies one of his numerous adversaries, "we have everything from God, and we owe him even our merits, but because those merits which we owe him are the effect of his grace, God owes them a recompense; and this recompense which is their due as a matter of divine justice is thus no longer a gift of God's pure liberality." [59]

The new covenant thus appeared to be neither more nor less than a "conditional contract, formed between God and man, through which God promises eternal life to those who make good use of the manifold grace which he gives them. . . . If you do thus and so, I shall give you this or that reward," [60] God tells his creatures. Man, in fulfilling his obligations, expected God to honor his. There was not, of course, too much insistence on the binding character of what God owed to man or, if you prefer, to himself. While the theologians might still debate the problem, for the worldly-minded it seemed to have been resolved once and for all. The worldly were unable to see why God should not give men their due if men, on their part, fulfilled their obligations.

A new man had emerged. He was demanding his rights; he was conscious of his importance. As he was before men, so would he be before God. What he had acquired materially or morally was his own, his very own, and neither king nor God might dispute its possession with him. He loved his God as he loved his king, but on condition that both respected his rights. The Molinists, said the Jansenists, "want assurances from God, failing which they do not conceive that he can be trusted. They want to treat with God, not as with a father and a friend, but as with an enemy, or at least a stranger, with whom one is careful to secure every guarantee." [61] The new man was cautious, and before embarking on so serious a matter as that of his salvation he wanted guarantees; he was not willing to have labored for nothing and to have undergone so many privations without certainty of reward.

Thus the new man, wishing to enjoy his independence, needed a God with limited powers, a God whose authority was regulated by fundamental laws, so that the sinner, when summoned before the throne at the last judgment, might plead his cause, documents in hand. Everything must proceed according to the rules. While he knew his duties, he did not forget that he also had rights, which he wanted to have respected. He wanted what might be termed a declaration of rights which would be of equal validity for all. Such a declaration would be posted on the gates of paradise at the last judgment.

Imperceptibly, a charter, a constitution, was being substituted for God, and human destinies would be ordered in a manner to ensure that the creature might know exactly where he stood in the matter of his salvation. There was to be no more secret diplomacy; everything was to be done in broad daylight, so that people might know what to expect and be able to make their arrangements accordingly. All was simple and well ordered in a world without mystery. "Our salvation is our own handiwork, without the aid of grace; it is a recompense, and not the effect of chance, like the number in a lottery, on which neither our desires nor our efforts have any effect." [62] The great unknown, the terrible secret which had formerly filled the hearts of the faithful with dread, had vanished; God and man had talked things out, and the result of these explanations was perfect order. Man would act; once he died, God would draw up the balance sheet of his actions; and the conclusion would be a judgment duly executed, in accordance with laws comprehensible to all, and kept, regardless, by respectable folk, even without having to fear God.

THE GOD OF THE BOURGEOIS

To owe everything to God, without God's owing us anything . . . that, for the Jansenists, was the very foundation of Christian piety. "God owes men nothing; that is the great principle, the consummation of everything." [63] But the new man, conscious of his rights, could not accept this. Grace, for him, was not a gratuitous gift bestowed upon man and sometimes refused; it was a form of tribute which God regularly paid to his creature. That would put an altogether different construction on matters, for man, in that case, would be "no longer weak; and God no longer strong." [64] Or rather, man would have established "his own God. For our real God is the one on whom it depends whether we avoid evil or do good." [65]

Thus "they take from us our God and leave us with man as a god," was the Jansenists' charge. Man was lifting himself against God and seeking to be free. "Oh, arrogant freedom of the children of Adam! Oh monstrous idol! Whence did you conceive the thought of such an outrage as to raise yourselves against the Almighty? . . . You usurp everything—power, and sovereign dominion, and scepter, and crown, and adoration. . . . Ah, that indeed is you, human freedom! That is you! And it is you we see lifting yourself up today above everything that is divine and that is adored, to the point of seating yourself in God's temple and wishing to pass for God yourself!" [66]

But what was this unimaginable catastrophe which was supposed to have suddenly rocked the foundations of the Christian universe? It was the Bull, *Unigenitus*. "May God's sovereign dominion and his almighty power over our hearts no longer be disputed; may men consider themselves happy to have been redeemed by the blood of Jesus Christ; may they love to live under the holy rule of grace; may they realize its value, its gratuitousness, its efficacy; may they know that this grace, which causes us to pass from darkness to light, from death to life, is nothing else but the inspiration of holy love. Will there remain a single believer who will not say anathema to the Bull? It is clear that the *Unigenitus* constitution is the enemy of those precious truths, and that it takes from religion its most august prerogatives." [67] For if God is "stripped of his sovereign power over man," what remains of the Christian? Man, then, "no longer awaits from God the decision of his fate for eternity; humility is destroyed; . . . and the grounds for hope are shifted.

. . ." [68] It is no longer in God "that we must essentially place our trust, but in ourselves. Prayer, thanksgiving, sentiments of humility—in a word, the interior worship which we owe to God, changes in character altogether." [69] Thus the sources of piety would be dried up, and Christian humility would be "transformed into a vain confidence in man's own powers." [70] Having become absolute master of his eternal destiny, independent of God, man would have ceased to be a Christian.

Molinism, it was charged, was "truly a new gospel, a new faith, a complete and organized system of religion." [71] Thus "there are now in the bosom of the Catholic Church two bodies of doctrine, and two systems of religion, diametrically opposed and absolutely irreconcilable." [72] The struggle, as we said before, was between two divinities, the old and the new, who could not possibly be reconciled. The final victory would rest with the God of the Jesuits, more welcoming and more accessible to men, but up to the last the Jansenists were to refuse him their allegiance. They refused to concede that the new God was the God whom Christians had always adored. Their God was the all-powerful Lord of a universe which he governed as a master; the new God allowed man to reign in his place and to be master in all that concerned his salvation. "Here, then, is a new king, installed by man's hands . . . and set up parallel with God; or, to speak more accurately, substituted for God in the government of this world." [73] "To have an accurate notion of Molinism, it is not enough, therefore, to say that Molina sets up a throne on which he places man at the side of God; it should be added that he causes God to descend from his throne so that man alone may reign in the kingdom of justice." [74]

Thus man constituted for himself "a sphere in which God has no part." [75] He was free in a world where everything was subject to God except the free will of the intelligent creature. God "can do all he wants in heaven and on earth, but to the exclusion of the decisions of the human heart." [76] "We know well that your hand made everything in this material world; that you feed even the birds of the air; that a hair cannot fall from our heads save at your command." But "in this spiritual and invisible world where the greatest marvels shine forth," God no longer spoke as master and lord: "You do not have the power over a heart that you possessed over a sea, over rivers, over rocks, over diseased eyes and limbs, over the dead; but man has it— man!" [77]

Now that man had constituted himself his own master, God no longer reigned save over nature, but the material kingdom would soon have its "constitution," too. The natural laws would rule the movement of the stars and of all that took place here below; and God, as a good constitutional monarch, would let the law prevail, taking care not to interfere in the course of events and to upset the perfect order which he had established. "Molinism and deism," the Jansenists maintained, were "twin brothers, differing scarcely more than in name and face, but with approximately the same origin, the same nature, the same principles, and the same effects." [78] Both, in their own ways, were seeking to temper, if not the divine power, then at least the exercise of that power or, as the Jansenists put it in speaking of Jesuit teachings, to "contract and restrain" [79] the rights of God.

Such, then, was the God of the worldly-minded, who would be grateful that he had organized the things of this world so that everything was in accordance with laws which they could understand, and that he did not interfere in their decisions when, as prudent and reasonable men, they wished to order their own destinies. "Certainly," says a Jansenist writer, "there is not the slightest trace of mystery here," [80] but then, the worldly were not anxious for mystery. They asked that between themselves and God everything should be clearly laid down, so that there might be no possibility of error and that everything might be organized in an orderly and foolproof manner. That, too, was why they could love this God who was moderate in all things, who never made too much of his power, realizing that he had to respect the laws and man's legitimate freedom.

Everything, then, was for the best in a world from which despotism and mystery had been banished. Man was able to live there, to attend to his business, convinced that everything that happened was perfectly regulated and that God could not be unjust. Yet there were times when man, though knowing himself master in a world which was now his own, started worrying again. That was when he thought of death and of what awaited him in the beyond. Even though God had been partially dethroned in favor of "nature" and of man, he had retained his function as judge, and on the last day, while abiding by rules and giving to each according to his deserts, his justice would be terrible.

"Indeed, my dear parishioners," says a preacher of the period, "if men tremble before other men, if they are surprised, dismayed to the point of changing color and losing their power of speech in the presence of an earthly judge, when they feel guilty of certain crimes, what fear, what terror will seize us when we are cited before the judgment seat of the thrice holy Lord, at whose coming the sun will be dimmed, the moon will give no light, the firmament of the heavens will rock, and men themselves will wither away with fear? . . . I see him, the avenging God, fury in his eyes, turning to face the reprobate. . . ."[81] For "when God hates," says another preacher, "he hates without measure, forced by the necessity of his being; an incomprehensible hatred, all the more formidable in that it takes the place of the most intense tenderness; and this is the final triumph of divine justice."[82]

But was God really as terrible as he was depicted? "God is good," the worldly-minded told themselves; "he is patient; he waits for the sinner; why should he have made man if he intended to damn him?"[83] The "frivolous notion that God would not want to damn so many Christians" had previously been denounced by the pious Nicole. "There is a delusion," he writes, "which is difficult to shed: people cannot imagine that God would be willing to have everyone perish. Sins which would terrify us if they were peculiar to ourselves alone cease to frighten us when they are shared. The sinner sleeps soundly when he finds himself surrounded by a multitude, as though God were obliged to spare him." That, incidentally, was one of the main reasons Nicole feared "that of all this crowd of Christians who gather in the churches, and in all those numerous cities where there is no one who does not profess the true religion, sometimes not a single adult is saved."[84] But the worldly could not believe this. They were exasperated by preachers "who announce only misery, terrible deaths, a God who is always dissatisfied, always punishing, always fulminating." "What justice, my God, is this, to throw twenty-nine out of thirty into the blazing flames?" [85]

But was there not also a danger in making God too good? "A God who does not punish is a God who is not adored," says a preacher of the period; "once he is no longer feared, he is no longer obeyed." [86] There had to be a God who would punish the wicked. "Will our century boast of having delivered us from the fear of an avenging God, that restraining force on evil, that powerful incentive to good?" [87] asks a contemporary preacher. And what would happen, then, to that "populace without education, without opinions, without ideas, barely held in a condition of order and dependence by fear of an avenging God, aided and supported by terror of human laws?" Would they be "flexible and docile to that voice of pure reason which is heard only in silence, and which will never speak loudly enough to reach them through the tumult and commotion aroused in them by the painful sense of their bondage, their poverty, their passions and their misfortunes"? [88]

Respectable folk would not want a God who was too readily disposed to indulge in a universal benevolence of which they generally approved. They wished the Deity to remember his responsibilities and to be severe where necessary. "There comes a point where goodness becomes weakness and even injustice," [89] says a contemporary preacher; and the pillars of society would be the first to suffer from it. "Rightly understood, God's justice is part and parcel of his goodness; if he never punished, this world would no longer be habitable; upright people would be the victims of the impunity granted to the wicked." [90] The bourgeoisie was thus soon to recognize that it was unable to do without a God who could be severe and a hell which served as the complement of the order of this world; in the constitutional regime which it extended to the whole universe, God was to be the executive power of the bourgeois conscience for the next world.

JANSENIST LAMENTATIONS

Such was the demise of the ancient deity, so alien to twentieth-century ideas and sentiments, and fallen into such profound oblivion that our generation would find it hard to believe that he had ever commanded men's allegiance. As a matter of fact, this was already the case by the end of the eighteenth century. Only a few pious Jansenists still acknowledged him and rendered him a last tribute. "No, no, my God," they said, "you do not want our hearts to be divided. You do not want our confidence to be placed partly in you, partly in ourselves. You, my God, you alone do everything in us!" [91] And rejecting the freedom which man had arrogated to himself, they begged God to take away all will of their own. "Oh my God, how long shall my own will play the tyrant over me? How long shall I be under the bondage of my own spirit? Come, then, oh my God, free me by subjecting me to yourself!" [92]

The God they adored was a jealous God, who did not tolerate any of the thousand infidelities which his successor, the "new" God, was perfectly prepared to take in his stride. "As soon as the love of God comes to a heart to rule in it, every other love must withdraw; it suffers no associate, it occupies all, fills all, possesses all; and what troubles the children of God is to have hearts so narrow to receive a love so vast." [93] Therefore, addressing this God who was being abandoned by his creature, they beseeched him to destroy in them all other love, so that they might be wholly his. "Inebriate me more and more with the wine of your love! Burn me utterly with the fire of your charity! Kindle this divine fire so strongly that it may extinguish all other fire, so that I may be consumed in you forever! Amen, amen, amen!" [94]

Even in the upheavals of the Revolution, there were some who remained faithful to this God adored by Pascal and Arnauld. How could they adore a God who, unable to require the supreme sacrifice, deceived man's heart, which was eager for humiliation and abasement? "Don't you see," they seemed to say to the worshipers of the new deity, "that by seeking to bridge the abysses which separate us from God, you drive away the God whom you wish to make more accessible to us? Don't you see that this God is shriveling daily, as he becomes more comprehensible, as he draws closer to human sentiment? Give us back our God, give us back our infinitely incomprehensible God, so that in him we may find once more the infinitely good, but mysterious and terrible being who filled our souls with anguish and love!"

But this God, the God of the terrible secret of predestination, had had his day. The Jansenists accused the Jesuits of having killed God, and they protested against those who, in order to reconcile men's hearts to religion, were silent on its difficulties and who spoke in circumlocutions. Our fathers "were more straightforward than we about truth," they would say. "It's a fact that no one would dare speak so firmly today. The reason is that we no longer have the same generous zeal for religion." [95] "Truths have become as a foreign language to most Christians," we read in one of Quesnel's propositions, condemned in *Unigenitus.* "And the manner in which they are preached is as an unknown language, so far is it from the simplicity of the Apostles, and beyond the understanding of the ordinary faithful. And people don't reflect that this decline is one of the most obvious signs that the Church was old, and of God's wrath against his children." [96] The Church, then, had grown old, and the philosophers were to praise its ministers who stripped theology of principles which seemed hard.

"How is it," asks a traditionalist, "that these men who think themselves enlightened do not realize that by trying to humanize religion, they have left nothing divine in it? By trying to lead us to God by a path which does not shock human wisdom, they deprive themselves of credibility." [97] Religion was too lacking, now, in those "truths which are as certain as they are impenetrable" and which caused the believer to feel that he was not a good Christian without "much adoration and submission, much prayer and humility, much confidence and abandonment to the infinite goodness of God." [98]

A God without mystery would not be God. He must be in-comprehensible if he was to be divine. But were not all Christians in agreement on this point? "Roman Catholics and Protestants," says Bayle, "fight about an infinity of articles of religion, but they agree on this point, that the mysteries of the Gospel are above reason." It would be an error to treat the "mystery of grace as something reconcilable with our weak reason." [99] Men must therefore love God without understanding him; all Christians agreed on this point. But there might be ambiguity in what they said. "We love God without understanding him" might mean either "we love him *although* we do not understand him" or "*because* we do not understand him."

When it is said that mystery is above reason, it is not yet clear what reality mystery represents in the religious conscious-ness or how it exists in and for man. "God is incomprehensible," the Christian might say, "and I love him." One might say, "When I love him, I confine myself to what is comprehensible in him, since I cannot love what I do not understand." Another might seek what was most incomprehensible in God in order to love him more perfectly. His love was directed to the mystery, to the mystery not only as transcending reason, but also as apparently conflicting with human sentiment and destroying all love. "Impious blasphemers, who seek only to make me hate God by persuading me that he hates me!" exclaim the Jansenists' opponents.[100] And the Jansenists might answer: "We love what man cannot love humanly; we love with a love which is itself a mystery, a love which contradicts all love, and we cannot love the infinite love which is God in any other way."

Both Jansenists and their opponents said that God was good; yet they could not agree on the meaning of the term. The Jansenists' God was good only for the one who loved him; "we believe," they might have said, "that he is good even though we cannot see it, or rather, even though from our worldly point of view the contrary seems to be the case." It was thus the Jansenist's love which made him believe in divine goodness, an infinite goodness that is infinitely far from us, for between God and man lay death, the wages of sin. Love, here below, could not conquer death, nor could death conquer love, and these two ever conflicting themes were united in the Jansenist's soul, awakening in him a nostalgia for the infinite so strong that he could love nothing else. And that was how it should be, according to this view. Never should the theme of infinite love sound in the dying man's ears without the accompaniment of discordant themes expressing the fear and horror of a soul reluctant to die; for otherwise, knowing that God was good, and seeing ourselves assured of his love, and loving him consequently with a very human love, we should no longer believe in God and in the mystery of his infinite goodness.

It is "useful for us," writes Pascal, "that God should be partly hidden and partly revealed." [101] In this view, the secret of the power which religion exercised on souls lay precisely in the mingling of darkness and light, certainty and uncertainty, fear and hope, in its capacity for bringing God closer to the soul of the believer and at the same time keeping him infinitely distant, so that, without repudiating the vision of death, the believer might perceive, yet ever doubt, his deliverance in some uncertain future and thus have faith in that mysterious world which, though his own, he might possess only through a miracle of grace.

The worldly, whose feelings about death were in any case very different from those of their fathers, were very far from taking such considerations into account. They wanted to be sure of the divine goodness and justice and to enjoy it unalloyed. Therefore, finding too many shadows in the former picture of religion, they were concerned to remodel it, disencumbering the divine goodness of everything that seemed merely to obscure it. But thinking thus to have found the true God who was good to everyone, they progressively ceased to be Christians and ended by losing their faith. The Jansenists were indignant at the smiling and affable idol which had been put up in place of their God. But in their endeavor to destroy the idol and to recall worldly-minded men to the purity of the faith, they succeeded only in creating unbelievers, who, in this struggle between two divinities, decided to believe neither and to abide by the teachings of the philosophers.

"Men being naturally Pelagians," says Arnauld, "they are

easily shocked by this humiliating doctrine which deprives them of all confidence in their free will and places them in so absolute a dependence upon God that they must base their hope . . . of salvation only on his mercy." [102] Pelagianism, we read again, "is so natural to man that it may be said that he bears it in his own heart." [103] Man wants to be his own master "because the love of independence which caused the first man to fall into sin thrust such deep roots in the hearts of his children that nothing is more unbearable for them than to depend on others. Thus each naturally desires his salvation to be in his own hands, and since this is what he wishes, he easily talks himself into believing it to be so." [104] In any case, whatever came "naturally" to man's mind would be contrary, so the Jansenists felt, to the doctrine of St. Augustine.

The contemporaries of Voltaire and Rousseau were little inclined to combat what was "natural" in man. That, too, was why the theologians of the old school despised the men of their generation who, being no longer able to adore mysteries transcending man and to cultivate sentiments repugnant to him, were prepared to love God only on condition that they understood him, and wished "by all too human ideas of his goodness" to change what was frightening and impenetrable in his designs. Their God loved only those who fought. "What an agreeable spectacle in God's eyes that a minister should be fighting bravely against the world and its maxims!" [105] The Jansenist's faith was but a form of combat; it was a supreme struggle waged against himself, when, seeking what was hardest in religion, he challenged reason and the human heart, despising those who, in religion, confined themselves to what was easily accessible.

But it was the tragic fate of the Jansenists that, in fighting for the cause of God, they helped to defeat it. Since a "hard and cruel God" appeared to the godless a contradiction in terms, they chose to abjure faith altogether. "Thus disbelief was born of the misuse of theology," says Abbé Yvon. [106] No longer able to love the Jansenists' God and perfectly capable of dispensing with that of the Jesuits, the respectable citizen was to find in a well-established moral code and a thoroughly ordered life what he could no longer find in that mysterious world which the two divinities had disputed and the vision of which, incidentally, was to be lost as time passed and the new man became more sure of himself.

8 · THE IDEA OF SIN

THE SINNER

Original Sin

"Our religion, I concede," says Père Charles Frey de Neuville, "is but a continual teaching of the infinite malice and fatal consequences of sin; in its aids, in its graces, it only preserves from sin." [1] Thus, whatever transformations had taken place in the concept of God, nothing essential, it seemed, had been changed in regard to sin. God still had his sinner; the sinner had his God; and each would find the other again at the last judgment. But as time passed and the number of respectable citizens increased, were there any sinners left? The question might appear, at first sight, quite extraordinary. For whatever the social order established by the respectable, there would always be some less respectable who would violate it. Yet would those who violated human laws continue to meet the definition of the real sinner? Since the idea of sin is essentially religious, the eighteenth century distorted it by reducing it progressively to no more than a moral concept, to the point where the sinner, like the former God, seemed to belong to a vanished world, the decay of one necessarily involving that of the other.

On the subject of predestination Bossuet says, "What appears most difficult in this matter is that, in a single cause, which is the common cause of all the children of Adam, there should be so prodigious a difference among men; that some should be gratuitously predestined to eternal life, and others eternally damned." [2] The Jansenist position, on the other hand, was "Who can complain that, from the same mass of mankind, infected by original sin and condemned to death, God should have chosen a part in which he would cause his grace to shine by saving it, leaving the rest in its corruption, to manifest his justice by punishing it?" Thus God was justified, for "however small the number of those to whom God is merciful, he does no injustice to anyone, all being sinful, and his justice punishing none that does not deserve it." [3] All difficulties were resolved, according to the Jansenists, as soon as the antecedents of the human race were taken into account. It ill became "exiles, men banished from paradise with Adam," [4] to ask God questions which amounted to so many recriminations. "Criminal children of a criminal father," [5] men had the fate they deserved, and that must suffice.

"The Church believes that children coming into the world are slaves of the devil, that he holds them in his thrall, and that they are under his tyranny," says Colbert, "which implies that original sin is a sin which kills the soul and merits death and eternal damnation." [6] Men, then, were born sinners and would naturally continue to sin, "for, in addition to the original sin with which they are born, they are so corrupt that they will not fail to add sins upon sins as soon as they make use of their reason, if they are left to their own devices." [7]

Men, then, could not do otherwise than sin. "It should not be surprising" that the children of Adam were "sinners and, being sinners, perish. What should be surprising, on the contrary, and a cause for exclaiming at the unexpected mercy of God, is that he finds it good to save them. And none being worthy of salvation, he communicates salvation to those whom he is pleased to save." [8] But, the unbeliever asked, "How is it that the most distant descendants are punished for the disobedience of the first man, and even guilty of this sin in which they had no part?" [9]

How indeed conceive it, and how explain that the newborn infant was a great sinner and guilty in the sight of God? "As certain as it is that children are in a state of sin," says Du Pin, "it is as difficult to say why, and how. It is certain that sin is an aversion from God and a conversion to the creature; infants, having neither knowledge nor will, can know neither God nor the creature, nor love either with an active love, at least with a perceptible and deliberate love. Some new philosophers attempt to explain this aversion from God by marks which, they claim, are formed in children's brains, similar to those formed in Adam's after his sin, which move the soul to evil." But this "scientific" explanation did not really satisfy Du Pin. "From this it would not follow," he says, "that the child with such disordered inclinations was guilty, since it would not depend on him not to have them, and since he did not give them any deliberate consent, had not God set his hatred upon these disordered inclinations, had he not imputed them to the child as deliberate, and in consequence resolved to deprive him of beatitude and perhaps to condemn him to torments, as faith teaches us that he has done." [10]

Indeed, if it was so natural to men to sin as the Jansenists maintained, could God hold it against them that they were sinners? "All the descendants of Adam are sick, but with a sickness that leads infallibly to eternal death." [11] To this an opponent of the Jansenists rejoined that an obviously deranged man or a man in a high fever would not be condemned to death were he found upon the highway with a gun in his hand; indeed, even were he to commit murder in that condition, he would not be held guilty, because he had not acted as a free agent. [12]

In the eyes of the Jesuits, the sinner as conceived by the Jansenists was a maleficent being indeed, but not responsible. He needed treatment rather than punishment. The world, according to this theory, was "a vast hospital" [13] filled with the sick, or an insane asylum, and even if the inmates did not deserve sympathy, it was quite wrong to be angry with them for a madness which was hereditary. They were not responsible for their actions, or at least their responsibility was greatly diminished. They should be pitied rather than condemned; they could not act otherwise than they did. "What justice would it be to make us expiate by the sword of the law crimes which our will was helpless to avoid?" [14]

Thus the problem of responsibility was raised. While the Jansenists would not admit any challenge to God's right to inflict on man "a penalty in the full sense of the term in consequence *merely* of original sin," [15] the Jesuits raised a number of questions concerning the conditions which must be met before God could impute to us our faults. Let us assume, for example, they said, that a man thought he was acting in conformity with justice and that he was mistaken. "Can you convince yourselves that a God so just and so good should punish him for all eternity for doing what he believed in conscience to be his duty? Could anything be more tyrannical? And were the Christian religion to give us such an idea of God, would it not be a greater insult to him than idolatry itself?" [16]

There were cases where a man who committed actions regarded as criminal in themselves could nevertheless not be said to be guilty. "A father who accidentally kills his son in a hunt is inconsolable. Nevertheless, he cannot say that he is guilty of homicide, or regard so deadly an accident as a crime, since it was not the result of any imprudence or any bad intention." Such might be the case of certain penitents. They might say, "I consider myself very unfortunate . . . to have done so many things which the divine law prohibits, but I do not think that I can really say that it was my fault." What could be the Jansenist's answer to a penitent in such dispositions? "The only reply which the Jansenist director could give him would be to urge him to compunction by reason of original sin; for that is what they constantly come back to. But do they not mock the faithful and religion itself by reducing the whole of the sinner's contrition to asking pardon for the sin of Adam?" [17]

The Jansenists felt that there should be no subtilizing in so grave a matter. "According to the Molinists," they said, "it is written in the eternal law that nothing is bad save those actions which free will has the sovereign or Molinian power to avoid. This clearly establishes a universal moral principle." They insisted, however, that "It is written in the eternal law that certain actions, such as, for example, lending one's hand to the iniquity of another, killing one's friend in order to enrich oneself from his spoils, and so forth, are evil in themselves." In vain would the man who had committed them seek excuses. "Not to have the freedom and stability to avoid these actions; to be so blind as to fail to see their iniquitousness, is not an excuse but a confirmation of a vitiated nature and a sullied soul." [18] It was always to the "vitiated nature" and "sullied soul" that one must return to judge rightly. The Christian should be ashamed to appear before God; he should ask pardon of God for being what he is.

But is it our fault, asked the arrogant creature, if we do not cut a better figure before God, if we are "sick"? It has to be our fault, the Jansenist replied. By excusing the creature, we accused God. "If we do not accept the doctrine of original sin, God must appear to us as a strange, unjust and cruel being, who takes pleasure in the misery of innocent creatures, the work of his hands." [19] For how otherwise should we explain our profound wretchedness; how explain that man should have fallen "into this blindness and this strange darkness which fills his mind; into this extraordinary powerlessness to do good and this violent inclination to do evil; into this perpetual warfare which he continually experiences in himself and against himself; into this cruel tyranny of the passions, which involve him in so many excesses and disorders; into this shameful necessity of blushing for the most natural actions, even when they are licit; and finally, into this infinity of pains and torments which afflict this mortal and wretched body, from the first tears of its birth to the last sighs of its life"? [20] We have to be guilty in order to exonerate God, and we have to be very guilty for the world to be what it is.

Man, then, was unhappy because he was guilty. To his misery, he added repentance and thereby justified God. For while deeply aware of his wretchedness, he loved God, and by accusing himself of a monstrous crime, he glorified the divinity. God would heal his afflictions if that was the divine will or add to his miseries here below pains of eternal duration. "We are sick people who must be healed and sinners who must be punished." [21] Would this individual be among those whom the celestial physician would heal or among those whom the ruthless judge would punish? God would decide. As for man, he was conscious of his guilt and implored divine grace.

But guilty of what, and in what way? A crime had been committed, our common crime, was the Jansenist's reply. Man was guilty, man as he was born anew in each one of us. "Man is born unjust and unhappy, and it was not thus that he issued forth from the hands of a God who is infinite goodness and essential holiness; he must therefore himself have woven the web of his injustices and misfortunes. But when and how did he become guilty? The question is one which human philosophy is incapable of resolving." [22] Religion alone could provide an answer to man's question; it would indicate "the precise moment when he was stripped of righteousness." [23]

Thus the Christian, knowing his origins, would be able to say why he was a sinner. But the very thing revealed by religion—and which ought to explain everything—was itself a mystery, the most incomprehensible of all. "The transmission of sin"—Pascal is referring to original sin—"seems to us not only impossible, it even seems very unjust; for what could be more contrary to the rules of our sorry justice than the eternal damnation of a child incapable of will power for a sin in which he seems to have played so small a part, and which was committed six thousand years before he was born? Nothing, to be sure, is more a shock to us than such a doctrine, and yet without this mystery, which is the most incomprehensible of all, we should be incomprehensible to ourselves." [24]

Man, then, finding himself incomprehensible and a "paradox" to himself and thinking to have found the answer to his question in an event reputed to have taken place at a specified date and in a place which he could indicate with certainty, had merely displaced the mystery and substituted one paradox for another. "Reason, at sight of the misfortunes with which man is overwhelmed from his entry into the world, and of the depravity of his mind and heart, cannot dissimulate from itself that we are all born in disorder and corruption," says Pelvert. "But that these misfortunes and this corruption come from the sin of Adam, transmitted to us; that this sin, although voluntary in its principle, should be so little voluntary in its propagation; that no one can escape it or protect himself from its terrible effects; and that it nevertheless renders us culpable, unrighteous, and deserving of punishment—that is what the human reason does not understand at all, what it has never understood, and what it will not understand save in eternity, when God, drawing aside the veil which conceals the interior of this mystery, will cause us to see the truth, the reason, and the justice in the source itself." [25]

The logic of religion thus moved from one unknown quantity to another; for one unknown quantity, man, there must be substituted another. But a new type of man began to judge the things of this world differently. He no longer had that sense of his deep corruption and, having ceased to be incomprehensible to himself, found the great mystery of his destiny, the most incomprehensible of all, vanishing little by little. Man, then, felt himself rehabilitated in the sight of a God who, far from being angry with him for being what he was and having necessarily to be just and to love equally all the creatures whom he had made in his image, could no longer hold man's ancestry against him.

The Child of Adam and the Respectable Citizen

The Jansenist was intimately persuaded of the utter hideousness of man, a hideousness manifested not only in certain uncouth and indecent gestures, but also in his habitual bearing. Sin had made man ugly; he was born uncouth, and his unsightliness was part and parcel of his mode of being. In order to realize this and never forget it, we have to see in the newborn infant, before any actual sin, the sinner entering upon the scene. "He is a child of Adam; therein lies his crime. That is why he is born in ignorance and weakness; that is why his heart is the source of all kinds of evil desires; all he lacks is the strength to declare them." [26] To know what God must think of us, therefore, we should first learn to see how unsightly we are. Only after being profoundly penetrated by the realization of our original corruption should we put to ourselves the question how some are saved and adore the infinite grace of God.

Gradually, however, men came to consider themselves less ugly and, reassured, dared look God in the face. The Jesuits, so the Jansenists maintained, had contributed greatly to giving man a better opinion of himself. "The school of Molina," writes Arnauld, "does its best to minimize the corruption of nature and its powerlessness to do good." [27] "There is never any question of the corruption of human nature by sin, but only of its degradation," we read in a dissertation by a Jesuit Father.[28] Not that the Jesuits openly denied original sin and its consequences, but, said the Jansenists, "if they have been obliged to preserve the name of original sin and that of the grace of Jesus Christ, they have, like Pelagius, destroyed the whole reality of both." [29] "They say that there is original sin; but as soon as we go into the detail of their teaching, we realize . . . that they teach it precisely as though they were saying that there was no original sin." [30] Thus, "preferring the darkness of Pelagianism to the light of the Gospels," they failed "to understand the deplorable condition into which man has fallen through sin." [31] The Jesuits, according to this view, were very much akin "to our self-styled philosophers," the only difference being that "the Fathers preserve the name of original sin, whereas our philosophers do not," all "agreeing to assert that human nature is not corrupted and vitiated, and that all that is in it is good." [32] As proof, the Jansenists cited, among others, the opinions of Père Berruyer. "Original sin, according to this innovator," we read, "is merely a degradation, a deprivation, a pure loss of supernatural justice, an imperfect state, and not a state of sickness and iniquity, rendering us truly sinners and criminals in the sight of God." [33]

Gradually man regained his self-confidence. He was no longer the sick man whom sin had "corrupted, rotting all his substance," [34] who, though suffering always and in every particular, of a disease which God alone could cure, felt guilty of his sickness, a shameful sickness which had disfigured him forever. He was now a convalescent, who felt his health improving daily and who therefore no longer forbade himself decent and licit pleasures. "Let us realize," Arnauld had said, "that our human nature is that of the woman in the Gospels, possessed by the devil, and so bent to the earth by her attachment to herself and to creatures that she finds it absolutely impossible to look up and to raise her heart toward God unless the divine physician calls her to himself, through an altogether gratuitous mercy, delivering her, raising her, giving her the means of glorifying God by her deliverance." [35]

But would this man who was regaining his strength long remain in need of his celestial physician? If he listened to the Jansenists, his position, short of divine intervention, must have seemed desperate to him. "What hope remains to this desperately ill man, whose illness is aggravated and envenomed by the remedies? None, indeed, neither in nature nor in himself. Only God can raise these dead men; sunder the chains of these captives, laboring under the bondage of sin; give sight to these blind men; heal these corrupt wills by taking from them their vicious self-love, which can produce only evil fruits, and inspire in them his divine love by the infusion of his own spirit." What could man hope of himself? Disease had invaded his whole being, affecting everything in him. "Let us then recognize that man's heart is poisoned from birth, and that he is filled with a subtle poison which spreads through all his actions, and which is none other than pride and self-esteem." [36] For the Jansenist, the Christian must discover this subtle venom in all his actions, believing himself to be sinning always, so long as he was not sustained by grace. "Concupiscence is the enemy which we have continually to combat; it is a malady which is only gradually cured and of which we are never perfectly rid save in heaven." [37] But now the Christian was experiencing a new burgeoning of hope. Man's nature, he told himself, was not as bad as one might have gathered by listening to the counsel of theologians of the old school; his nature, on the whole, had remained sound; let him keep clear of excesses, and all would be for the best.

Thus the sinner disappears—I refer to the classical sinner, the integral sinner—and we seem to become better and less repulsive in the eyes of the divinity as time moves on. In a synodal address delivered in 1783, man was described as "that being more weak than wicked, more fickle and inconstant than criminal, more unfortunate than culpable." Only the Jansenists were to take exception to such statements. Original sin, for them, remained "the key to all religion." [38] The worldly, for their part, were thinking and acting as though Adam had never existed. "What is the cause of crimes, and by what means can they be stamped out?" was the question set by a provincial academy around 1773 as the subject of a prize essay. The reply, for a Jansenist, could not be in doubt. "Does not religion indicate clearly enough that the cause of crimes has lain in the depravity of human nature since the sin of the first man? Is it not absurd to suggest that the matter be investigated, as in a case where the cause is unknown?" And how should a cause which makes sinners of all men be destroyed? "To suggest the destruction of a cause so intimately ingrained in sinful man, and of its resulting effects, is possible only in the system of those who take no account of Revelation." [39] Crime was thus but a manifestation of the malady inherent in the human race since Adam. How, then, could it be thought that any means discovered by humans would suffice to cure it?

We cannot, then, be healed of sin save by destroying the sinner within us, and that is not within our power. But is it not true, also, that once man ceased, in his own eyes, to be a sinner, sin could no longer exist for him; and that what he formerly described as sin had become for him a crime or a transgression, a moral and legal concept of an altogether secular character, and far removed from that religious perspective which related all human action to the next world and made of it an affair between God and creature? The doctrine of original sin puts the sinner, we might say, before the sin. But once it is ignored, there remains only sin without sinner, and in that condition sin cannot long survive. For in order to find the true features of sin in human actions, we have always to come back to the sinner, since "all the children of Adam are as streams contaminated at their source." [40] Hence, according to the Jansenists, if man was displeasing to God, it was not because the deity particularly reprehended this or that action but because God was angry with him for being what he was. But as the idea of sin became increasingly dissociated from that of the sinner, it ended, like so many other religious concepts, in becoming secularized, to be applied only to isolated actions which could be judged individually, according as they were more or less nefarious, without going back to the human heart and without the divine mysteries entering into it at all.

SINS WITHOUT A SINNER

The Dissociation of Sin

"Every day," says Bossuet, "our rule of conduct is beset by so many questions and so much caviling that the most complicated lawsuits cannot outdo them in number; and if God does not put a stop to the course of the pernicious subtleties which self-interest suggests to us, the laws of good faith and equity will soon be seen as only another problem." [41] To "these vainly subtle minds, who reduce the whole of the Gospel to problems";[42] to "these subtle and ingenious sinners who twist and turn the Gospel and find reasons for hesitating about the fulfillment of all the evangelical precepts, who weary the casuists by their endless consultations," Bossuet proposes "simplicity and good faith," both "excellent teachers." "By the grace of God, gentlemen, a pious and Christian life does not depend on subtleties or on the exquisite inventions of the human mind; to know how to live according to God in simplicity, the Christian needs neither much study nor any great literary apparatus." [43]

Having lost the simplicity of faith, the eighteenth-century believer wished to go into the matter of sin, to find out when an action was sinful and when it was not. And he was to seek answers to his questions in "those huge collections of cases and decisions which we find increasing and multiplying daily, and whose authors, at least for a great part, belong to the Jesuit order." In these compendiums, "all the most indisputable principles of the moral teachings of Jesus Christ have been reduced to little more than problems; there is no duty concerning which corruption has not raised difficulties and a false scholarship has not found mitigations; everything has been argued over, contested, put in doubt." [44]

The confusion engendered in people's minds was compounded by the circumstance that different schools had emerged on the subject of sins and sinners. "People no longer know whom to believe . . . ; some condemn you, while others announce your salvation; here certain points are conceded, there they are condemned; here you observe the law by mitigating it, there you mitigate it only by transgressing it; here reasons are adduced for prohibiting, there for permitting; in a word, here you are a saint, and there you have not so much as begun to be a Christian." [45]

What was gradually building up was what might be called a crisis of sin. The worldly-minded, overcurious to find out about their sins, came eventually to wonder whether any particular action of theirs had been sinful. They were to find, in pushing their analysis far enough, that in many cases what they had thought to be a sin had in fact been perfectly legitimate, and that in order to determine the issue, distinctions had to be made which would clearly show that they were not in fact as bad as they appeared in the eyes of those overrigorous or oversimple minds who saw sin everywhere.

The casuists, according to Père Lamy, "are dangerous for the most part, because they seem to wish to insure sinners against God and teach them to quibble with him by showing them how far they may offend him without his being entitled to punish them." [46] Their concern was "to discount sin, and to justify many actions which the ancients, less subtle but more sincere, judged evil." [47] To do this, it was often necessary to engage in "mental contortions." But "the singular thing about it," remarks Lefranc de Pompignan, was that those who worked out all these dubious stratagems "elaborated them coldly in their rooms" without having "any personal axe to grind." They rejected for themselves, he continues, "things far less reprehensible than those which they permitted to others; and walking in the narrow path, they imagined they were rendering a service to God by widening the road to heaven for the Christian people." [48]

The casuists, then, were felt to have made concessions to the worldly and in so doing simply to have followed in morals the policy they had applied to their doctrine. The basic assumption seemed to be, apparently, that since the Christian could no longer believe all that tradition taught, he should not be asked to believe what he found too difficult. Similarly, since he could no longer adhere to the principles in all their rigorousness, it might be necessary not to ask him to do the impossible. That did not imply, of course, that the Jesuits were prepared to take advantage for themselves of the concessions which they made to those who, in religion, were merely "the populace," those who were destined only to make up the mass of the faithful and who must be led to salvation at not too high a cost to themselves.

What was surprising, however, was that the Jesuits, who desired merely to adapt themselves to human frailty, often went much too far, as Pascal charged, making concessions to the worldly for which no one had asked and which sinners themselves were not prepared to accept. This seriously impaired their great achievement and fostered the development of the very disbelief which, by adapting themselves to the spirit of the times, they wished to prevent. If for a while, they paved the way to a secular morality, they also frequently offended bourgeois standards by excusing actions which the respectable were loath to admit. In evaluating sins, they were often unable to distinguish between those actions which must continue to be regarded as wholly sinful and those which might be discounted because they had become too widespread and too much in keeping with the spirit of the times. All of this implied that the tolerance which the casuists displayed in morals was the result not merely of pragmatic considerations, but also of other factors which took them farther than prudence demanded.

Bayle, deploring the errors of a lax morality, tells us that these were "the unfortunate fruits of disputation" and that "methods of study are at least as much responsible for them as corruption of heart. Before teaching moral theology, a teacher will have taught one or more courses of philosophy and will have got into the habit of hairsplitting about everything. . . . Argue as much as you like about questions of logic; but when it comes to morals, be content with common sense and the light which the reading of the Gospels sheds in your mind; for if you undertake to dispute in the manner of the Scholastics, you will soon be unable to find your way out of the labyrinth. The man who said that the manuals of the casuists were manuals on the art of quibbling with God was right. These advocates at the bar of conscience find more distinctions and fine points than the advocates at the bar of civil law. They make of the bar of conscience a laboratory of morality, in which the most solid truths go up in smoke." [49]

Lefranc de Pompignan wrote, "The Scholastic method, which is useful in speculative matters, but dangerous in practical ones, gave rise to lax decisions." [50] The casuists, indeed, might be described as theologians trained in the Scholastic tradition who applied the methods they had learned to the phenomenon of sin. In so doing, they hastened a process of destruction consisting in the point-by-point decomposition of traditional religious concepts. In their hands, sin fell apart, and after carefully picking up the pieces, they labeled them individually. Sins, now, were more numerous than ever before, of every shape and size and color, so to speak, with the result that, having become too adept at distinguishing between individual sins, the faithful came to lose the intuition of sin as such, whose infinite malice and unity of origin are never belied by the variety of forms under which it is concealed.

"We do not do all evil, but we incline toward it," says Bossuet; "only the opportunities are lacking. . . . Left to himself, man would avoid no evil." [51] It would, therefore, seem quite useless to enumerate exactly the thousand and one ways in which we sin; everything is of a piece and fits into man's fundamentally vitiated nature. Some distinctions, indeed, seemed not only useless, but even dangerous. If sins are treated merely as *entia rationis,* independent of the living and sentient sinner, what, ultimately, will remain of the sinner?

The human soul, then, would be regarded as neither good nor bad, but, rather, as a neutral substance, a substratum of actions susceptible of moral judgments but having in itself no specific moral character. A man would be evil only at the actual moment of sinning, or, rather, it was not so much he who, at that moment, would be evil, but a particular action of his, which must

be imputed to him as a fault because it was contrary to a particular precept. Man, in that case, would no longer be the total
sinner who drew down upon himself the wrath of God, the sinner who was corrupt of heart and full of malice, evil because
he was a child of Adam. He would continue to sin a great deal,
but his sins could be itemized and dealt with singly, without
involving the "substance" of his soul. Henceforward, the sinner
would be judged, not "by his heart, of which he is not the
sovereign master," [52] but by his actions, and, as he became more
proficient in distinguishing between good and evil, and in what
sense and in what degree his actions were deserving of divine
approval or disapproval, sin came to lose that terrifying character
which had previously made it a form of spiritual leprosy in
"the interior impurity of the soul . . . infinitely more to be
feared than that of the body." [53]

Sins and Offenses

A manual for the clergy written by a churchman of the old
school, Bishop Tronson, is highly instructive on the traditionalist
view of sin and the difficulty of avoiding it. In this work, entitled *Examens particuliers sur divers Sujets propres aux Ecclésiastiques,* the bishop proposes a detailed examination of conscience to his readers, reviewing with them all the things which
they have done and all the sentiments which they have displayed
in the different circumstances of their lives: "Do we have all
the hatred and all the aversion for the world which Our Lord
requires, and which his example must inspire in us? Have we
referred to it with indignation, distance and contempt; and have
we made it clear that it is filled only with corruption, vanity and
falsehood? . . . Have we loved what it hates and hated what
it loves? Finally, do we often lament with the saints to see ourselves constrained still to remain in the world?" [54]

Suppose, now, that the clerics whom he is addressing are ill.
"Let us examine the use we have made of our illnesses and the
way in which we have conducted ourselves. Have we regarded
them, in the light of faith, as a remedy capable of healing the
ills of our souls, as a portion of the cross of Jesus Christ, and

as a rich present from the hand of an infinitely loving Father? In that light, have we accepted them with joy, or at least with resignation?"[55] And now suppose that the cleric is in good health and is rising in the morning and about to dress. "Have we picked up our undergarments, which we wear in common with the rest of men, with sentiments of compunction, and have we remembered that, since these garments are the consequences and effects of sin, we should not touch them without lamenting the loss of our innocence?"[56]

Everything furnishes the Christian with opportunities for recognizing his imperfections, and in all his imperfections he finds the one which underlies them all, his condition as a man and a sinner. And, "as he has an ardent and continual desire to expiate his sin and knows that death will be both expiation and punishment, he envisages it with joy; sometimes, indeed, he cannot help but desire it as a blessing."[57]

Reading the pious Tronson's book, we might ask whether the author was not somewhat exaggerating the duties of the Christian and proposing a perfection difficult if not impossible of achievement this side of sanctity. But the objection, I feel, falls wide of the mark; our real grievance against the author is not so much that he imposes duties on the believer that are too onerous, but that he recommends sacrifices which, at best, might be regarded as absolutely useless. Thus, when the bishop describes the Christian as one who "does not pick flowers, or wear them, merely for the pleasure of smelling them" or as one who "never wastes time at a doorway or window, looking out at those who pass by,"[58] the ordinary Christian tended to say not simply that this was asking too much, but that what was proposed was of no consequence whatsoever, and he continued to smell flowers and look out of the window. Tronson might point out that "the concupiscence of the flesh," which "is spread through the whole body and all the senses," is "an evil which must be eradicated, a vice which must be conquered, a disease which must be cured."[59] The ordinary Christian of his day, however, had lost any inclination for mortification, and therefore found it hard to see why so many perfectly innocent pleasures should be forbidden to him and why he should be prevented from doing what could do no harm to anyone and therefore appeared morally justifiable.

"We note," says Nicole, referring to Jesus, "that he never laughed. Nothing has ever equaled the seriousness of his life; it is clear that pleasure, recreation, anything that could divert the mind, had no part in it. The life of Jesus Christ was utterly taut, wholly caught up in God and in the woes of men, and he gave to nature only what he could not have refused it without destroying it." [60]

But the man in the street wanted to know just why it was wrong to laugh and enjoy oneself and how far one might do so without falling into sin and risking one's eternal salvation. "People are constantly telling us that they don't understand why we object so much to parties and shows," says a preacher of the period.[61] These things were indeed hard to explain and define, and theologians often found themselves at a loss to know exactly what to say as to the degree of seriousness that should be observed in this valley of tears and how far one might give in to one's inclinations and indulge in small pleasures.

"The love of creatures, since it always diminishes that of God, deprives us of a part of our true life, which consists entirely in the love of God," says Nicole. "The soul which stops at creatures delays the course of the voyage by which it moves toward God; and by desiring to enjoy them, it proportionately deprives itself of the enjoyment of God." That is also why, "although all striving after unnecessary pleasures is not a mortal sin," such striving is not becoming to a Christian. For "it is difficult not to love an object in which one finds pleasure." [62]

The pleasures which we experience and which attach us to creatures are thus, in this view, so many infidelities which we commit toward God. "Since God has given me a heart with which to love him, he must be the sole object of our love," says Arnauld. Hence "it can be only a disorder and a sin when we take something of that love from God to attach it to creatures." [63]

But was it true, then, the worldly asked themselves, that our wills and our actions, to be justified, must all be reduced to a single and unique sentiment, and that there was only sin where there was no love of God? Yes, Quesnel answers, "there are only two loves, whence originate all our wishes and all our actions: the love of God which does all for God and which God rewards and the love of ourselves and of the world, which does not refer to God what should be referred to him and which for that very reason becomes evil." [64]

The Church itself felt that Quesnel had gone too far, and the proposition was condemned. For how could it be maintained without exaggeration that no action was good save one that could be referred to God and that all that was not dictated by a spirit of charity was sinful? What should be said, then, of all those multiple actions of our daily lives which are performed for many different motives and in which the spirit of charity and the love of God appear to have no part? "Spouses would sin in rendering to one another a duty attached to their state," says one of Quesnel's numerous opponents, "when they were not in charity, or had not taken care to propose to themselves the motive of charity. He who ate and drank soberly, without charity, or with the motive of temperance, or to preserve his life and health, would commit as many sins as the number of times he ate or drank. All those who worked, according to their condition, to support their families, would not cease to commit as many sins as the number of actions they performed." A Christian would thus always feel guilty; he would always have a guilty conscience. "A Jansenist penitent must accuse himself, in confession, of all his steps, of all his glances, of all his words . . . which were so many sins whenever he did not have charity as a motive, or had not proposed that motive to himself." [65]

Eighteenth-century life had become too complex for everything in it to be reduced to the two main principles of charity and concupiscence. That, at least, was the view of the worldly, and the Jesuits, always more accommodating than their opponents, took their feelings into account and let them organize their lives without always having to set themselves alternatives which, fundamentally, allowed them no other choice but to be saints or sinners.

"Scripture and the Fathers recognize only two principles of all human actions," says Bishop Colbert, "charity, the principle of all good actions; cupidity, the principle of all bad ones. The

Jesuits, on the contrary, introduce a host of principles of human actions." [66] There would thus be actions which were neither good nor evil, "an innumerable multitude of indifferent actions, of no consequence either for good or for ill. . . . God has abandoned them to men and will never ask for an accounting of them." [67] "These, according to the Molinists, are all the actions which neither benefit nor harm anyone, and concerning which God has prescribed nothing by any law known to man. To take a walk or not to take a walk, to enjoy objects of the senses, to eat and drink without need and merely for pleasure, provided that this is not injurious to health, are actions which they place in this latter category." [68] These actions "are numberless in the details of life, and it is not clear to what principle they should be referred." [69]

Thus man would have constituted for himself a sphere where there was no longer any question between himself and God either of sin or of virtue. He would be able to enjoy the pleasures that life afforded him, providing of course that he remained within the bounds of the law and of decency, and that he did no one any harm. God, at the last judgment, would not ask him to account for actions which were unrelated to his salvation and which did not concern the divinity. In that area, the Christian would enjoy a legitimate freedom, without fear of constantly sinning; he would be a sinner only when the occasion of sin arose, in specific cases. The rest of the time he would live between heaven and hell, between charity and concupiscence.

Nothing, then, would prevent him henceforth from living his life, a purely secular life, according to his nature and his habits, without having to ask himself at every moment whether what he had done was displeasing to God or not. And since he was no longer the sinner whose life, as soon as he acted by his own powers, was but sin, he would be able to enumerate separately the sins which he had committed on a particular occasion as well as his good works; knowing thus what good and what evil he had done in this world, he would be in a position to foresee what awaited him in the hereafter. At the same time, a great part of his life would be spent in actions which could not be exactly defined as either good or bad. God thus remained ignorant of his creature's conduct, and to judge man he would wait for him to infringe a particular commandment or to follow a particular counsel. It was only at such moments that he would be able to say to man, "you have sinned" or, "you have done this or that action which pleases me."

But this freedom which the worldly man thought to have acquired and of which he was to take advantage to make himself comfortable and at home in this world, though precious, did not suffice. Not only did he want God to give him free rein when, indulging in the little pleasures of life, he did no harm; he also wanted the deity to take part in his joys and to recognize that sometimes, when man follows his own promptings and acts from wholly secular motives, he is not only doing nothing harmful, but he may actually be doing something quite praiseworthy. In this sphere, which God had apparently abandoned to his creature, and in which man would spend the greater part of his life, there would be not only a multiplicity of actions too indifferent in themselves to be judged, but also a virtue having status and recognition, a virtue unrelated to God.

In the Jansenist view, as we have seen, God takes cognizance only of charity or concupiscence. But is charity alone good? Outside charity, is everything either sinful or at the least indifferent? "By allowing no intermediate position between what God rewards as an effect of charity, and what he punishes as arising out of love of the world, no place is left for the moral virtues," says an opponent of the Jansenists, "so that the love of a son who helps his father purely out of a sense of duty and gratitude is classified as a sin." [70] It must therefore be possible to practice virtues "for their own specific ends," [71] which was precisely the contrary of "the moral teaching of Père Quesnel, who, in honor of a chimerical charity, destroys and confuses all the virtues which God distinguishes and comments upon in particular." [72]

"They want to find an imaginary mean between cupidity and charity," says Arnauld, "as though our love could end and rest in any object other than God, this being charity, or in the creature, this being cupidity." [73] In this "imaginary mean" the new man had now established himself, and spent the greater part of his life; it was his spiritual homeland on earth. There he created habits for himself and made laws; he felt at ease and found ways of being virtuous and useful to his neighbors. God would not be angry with him for acting according to his own rules. Thus the worldly man was able to live perfectly well without thinking of a God who had formerly wanted everything done for his sake alone.

A point of doctrine would seem to have been abandoned: the obligation to "refer to God all the free movements of our hearts, loving him for himself and as the source of all righteousness." And there were many other maxims that were no longer held in honor: "the sovereign liberty of God in the distribution of the grace necessary to carry out the commandments," for instance, or "the insufficiency of fear to change the heart, when it operates alone," or again "the tests needed before absolution, to ensure the conversion of the sinner." [74]

Now, "an action performed purely out of honesty" might be "morally good, without having to be referred to God, or performed with love. . . . What a revolution this maxim effects in Christian morality," [75] and what "pitiable jargon" to maintain that "for an action to be morally good in every way it suffices that its object should be upright, and that it should be virtually and implicitly referred to God." [76] "By teaching men that their actions are good in the moral order once they perform them for an honest end, even though they do not propose God to themselves as their last end," [77] the very foundations of Christianity, it was maintained, were being undermined.

But while the Jansenists accused the Jesuits of conceding too much to man and not enough to God, the Jesuits accused the Jansenists of excessively belittling human nature. Thus, when "Abbé Esprit, and so many others whom it is not necessary to name" asserted "that all the human virtues are false both in their motive and in their end," the Jesuits felt that they were going too far. "It must be admitted," says the reviewer of the *Mémoires de Trévous,* "that these virtues are insufficient, nearly always mixed, often tainted by vicious motives; but to say that a man guided solely by the light of his reason can never perform actions of equity, obedience, moderation, humanity, gratitude, and so forth, save out of secret reasons of self-interest or vanity, is to think too slightingly of our nature. Our nature is disfigured, impaired, corrupted, no doubt, but it is not destroyed; on this, reason and religion agree." [78]

Some very curious discussions took place on this subject between Jansenists and Jesuits. The doctrine of the Jesuits, the Jansenists contended, would have us admit that "a Christian is not always obliged to act as a Christian." [79] In other words, the Christian might live as a mere man—an upright man, of course —and God would not hold it against him if, adhering to a moral code which Pascal, in his *Lettres Provinciales*, terms wholly pagan, he simply did his duty, without thinking of God. He could thus develop a morality without God or, if one prefers, without the Christian God, an independent morality which little by little would create its own deity or, if it still felt the need to preserve a supreme Being, would look upon him as a mere servant.

But what, then, of sin? There would be offenses and crimes; there would be no more sins. Sin must die without a God to whom all human actions are referred. God, it was believed, would still punish offenders in the hereafter. That function was still reserved for him, but he would no longer judge in his own cause. Whereas God and sinner had been linked by indissoluble ties, the offender (who replaced the former sinner) and God would be ignorant of one another. They would meet only at the last day, when God, in the interests of justice, would pronounce the verdict. God would thus avenge morality, the morality which the worldly had made an eternal law to which the deity himself must be subject.

Thus the moralist would kill sin. God might still exist, thanks to the moral code, but he would no longer have his sinners. His role would be reduced to imposing penalties and ruling on rewards, after properly distinguishing between right and wrong actions, a task which would at first be rendered quite arduous by the decisions of the casuists, but which the moralists would subsequently simplify. Basing their position on human considerations and taking account of human nature, the moralists had no difficulty in determining whether a particular action was good or bad, and God would have no choice but to approve their decisions.

Thus the reign of sin seemed to be over. A world had taken shape in which everything seemed to have been smoothed over and which no longer resembled the old world in which there were only elect and damned, a clear and terrible division which had filled the bravest hearts with fear. Now everything seemed to be more or less alike; both elect and damned held certain virtues and faults in common, and it was not possible really to contrast them and to establish any definite separation between them. Some, of course, might be said to have been more virtuous than others, and some would have faults on their conscience of such magnitude and in such multiplicity that they might well be expected to tremble before a just and severe judge. Yet basically they were all strangely alike, and on the last day it would not be easy to distinguish between just and unjust, for there would be so many intermediary degrees between the two and so many, too, who had avoided all extremes and been neither very good nor very bad. God, then, would not be able to hate his creature, who in a sense had been rehabilitated, since the issue was no longer the sin of Adam but the useful or harmful or merely indifferent actions which man performs during his sojourn in this world.

The New World

"The whole of faith lies in Jesus Christ and in Adam; and the whole of morality in concupiscence and in grace," writes Pascal.[80] Or to put it another way, Adam and Jesus Christ, sin and grace, corruption and redemption, wretchedness and beatitude . . . one cannot do without the other, and exists only in terms of its opposite. To diminish sin is to diminish grace; to diminish wretchedness is to diminish hope. The sinner needs Jesus Christ, and Jesus Christ needs the sinner; the power of the Son of God is made up of the wretchedness of men; what you give to man, you take away from God; what is of the earth no longer belongs to heaven. The less sick man is, the more ailing will God be. Happiness on earth proportionately diminishes the blessedness of the elect. God, in this view, needs sinners who are such with all their being and who are conscious of their wretchedness. So he is magnified by their prayers, and infinite through their infinite suffering.

But the time came when the child of Adam was transformed into the respectable citizen, and God found himself abandoned. The sinner was no longer regarded as such by origin and nature, but only by reason of actual and clear-cut sins. Sins, then, degenerated into offenses, and since everything in this area is connected, man, as he felt himself become more virtuous, found the world less filled with woe and more habitable.

"Nature," writes Pascal, "always makes us unhappy whatever our state of mind." [81] The honest citizen was now to say just the opposite. Gone were the days of the great Christian pessimists who claimed that "happiness is barely sensible to us in this life save as deliverance from evil" and that "we possess nothing real and positive." [82] The Jesuits, in any case, were already thinking and feeling quite otherwise. "The perfections of our God," contended an opponent of the Jansenists, "his goodness, his justice, his power, his mercy, his wisdom, make it clear enough to us that he had no other purpose in creating us, even after sin, than to make us happy." For confirmation, they pointed to nature. "God can do nothing in vain; all creatures are made for man, and man for God; all creatures have no other purpose than to make man happy." All things preach to us "the kindness of God." God "has made every man for felicity, . . . destined every man to beatitude." [83]

But if that was the case, what became of the claim that man was culpable before God and that this world was the place where he must expiate his crime? The Deity had clearly done everything to make his sojourn agreeable. Was that how one acted with criminals? God had embellished man's "prison"; he was full of delicate attentions for the child of Adam. It must therefore have been a mistake to have said so much ill of men, who could not be as basically bad as the Jansenists claimed, since it was God who had created them and since they were a part of the admirable order which so obviously reigned in all things.

There cannot be in man "a natural principle necessarily determined to evil; a principle which in itself can serve only for
evil; a principle which is thus in itself evil." Since "God is the
author of nature as well as of grace, nature must be good in itself, even after sin. And although it has been weakened, it has
not been totally corrupted." [84] That was the argument of
Quesnel's opponents, whom the Jansenists, in their turn, accused of not even telling man "that he was sick" and of having
made of concupiscence "a natural property of man, an attribute
of his nature, of which God might be the author." [85]

But people were no longer prepared to accept the views of
those who thought too ill of human nature and who saw in this
world only wretchedness and misfortune. "Theologians have told
me," writes Toussaint, "that optimism, in our present condition,
is mistaken, because, assuming that before sin the world was ordered in the best possible way, it is not equally true that it still
is so, since sin has disturbed its harmony. But," he replies, "it
is probably not mistaken to regard Providence as always wise
and just, since the fall of man as well as before." [86] Pascal's man
with his corrupt heart, full of concupiscence and full of malice,
who must necessarily hate himself, had had his day, and his God
could not long survive him. "Not only can one love God without
hating oneself," says Toussaint again, "but it is not true that one
loves him when one hates oneself. Should we have sentiments
contrary to his? He loves us; let us not, then, expect to please
him by hating ourselves." [87]

And why, after all, should man hate himself? Man, to quote
a writer of the period, "is the most noble, the most perfect of
beings, in form and qualities . . . his face is agreeable . . . his
manner noble, imposing, and gentle. . . ." [88] Here we no longer
have the miserable creature who, penetrated with his ugliness,
dares not lift his eyes to God without trembling; he knows who
he is, he knows what he owes himself. If anyone brings up the
doctrine of original sin, he will be able to answer that "original
perversity" should not be confused with "original sin." He
will be able to concede that he has the "faculty of sinning," but
he will not recognize in himself any "innate propensity to do
evil"; he is not born "perverse";[89] by nature, he is good. "Reli-

gion presumes man to be evil; morality presumes him to be good. . . . Religion says that man is born evil, in order to become necessary to him; it buttresses its contention by the history of an original sin. . . . Morality vouches for goodness; its foundation is the heart. . . ." [90] The respectable citizen opted for morality.

For the new man there must be a new God. The God of the sinner could not be the God of the respectable citizen. Hence the new man no longer believed in those "blasphemous portraits which somber and melancholic minds took pleasure in painting." He rather credited the "constant testimonies" which God "gives of his goodness." "God is a tender father," he would say, "good to all his children, prodigal with his favors to those who are submissive to him, indulgent and flexible with those who have offended him." [91] God was thus increasingly reduced to policing the world and making honest folk happy. And since the creature no longer believed in original sin, and had ceased to consider "man's state on earth" as a "composite of wretchedness and pain," [92] nothing need prevent humans from believing that the world was created for their happiness and persuading themselves that they could render no higher tribute to divinity than by working usefully for their own happiness and that of their offspring.

"Was man born to be unhappy?" we read in the *Avertissement du Clergé* of 1770. "Must his days be spent in sadness and bitterness, and is life but a deadly gift of Providence? Let us set far from us a thought so insulting to divine goodness." [93]

The respectable citizen was only too capable of setting aside this insulting idea. "I have seen that happiness walks in the footsteps of religion, religion in those of reason, reason in those of education, so that happiness depends entirely upon ourselves," [94] he would say, and, knowing how to enjoy a happiness within the reach of everyone, he taught his children to do likewise. No purpose was served in telling them that "happiness in this life is incompatible with happiness in the next. You will never persuade them that God created so many good things which they may not enjoy wisely. . . . Tell them that happiness presupposes health and a decent competency; that health is maintained by exercise and temperance, and a decent competency by wise economy." [95]

"What, indeed, does man need to be as happy as possible? Apart from the pleasure of existence, he has a thousand other pleasures, and experiences no pain, if he enjoys health, freedom, peace and the necessaries of life." [96] And is not everything in this world there to make men's sojourn pleasant and agreeable? "The waters run at their orders and bow to their will. . . . All the animals offer themselves for their pleasure and their palate. . . . Birds . . . fish . . . fruits of all kinds provide them with a variety of dishes constantly renewed and reproduced for them. The fertile earth offers its breast. . . . By easy tillage, which busies them agreeably, it renders a hundredfold the seeds which they entrust to it." Thus "everything in nature contributes to their happiness. What, then, do they lack? Will power." [97]

Before Jesus Christ, the miseries of the human race were "the disgrace of Providence. . . . It was left to the Gospels to teach us the great art of knowing how to be unhappy." [98] The respectable citizen, who felt he deserved happiness, had little inclination to learn an art for which he had no use; he replaced it with morality, which he equated with the art of attaining a decent happiness.

Montesquieu, referring to the "two worlds," tells us that "one spoils the other. . . . Two are too many. Only one was needed." [99] The new man no longer had the vision of two worlds dear to Christians. He had restored the world to unity. This world, now that there was no other, had ceased to appear to men as a place of exile. They settled down there and found it very comfortable. But who, then, had thus given humanity back its happiness? Who was this upright man who seemed to have finally triumphed over all the terrors which had formerly filled the hearts of the faithful? It was the bourgeois, master of a new world which God and demon both seemed to have deserted, and which, having neither sinners nor saints, experienced neither the agony nor the ecstasy of old.

PART THREE

*The Bourgeoisie and
the Social Teachings of
the Church*

9 · THE CHURCH
AND THE SOCIAL CLASSES

As men like Bossuet portrayed it, the world was divided into two distinct groups: the great and the poor. The great, to whom God had communicated "a spark of his power";[1] the poor, who were "the good friends of Jesus." Each had its own titles of nobility; the great were graced with the "splendors of power," the poor, with the "splendors of poverty, according to the teachings of the Gospels."[2] The great and the poor, two characters in a divine epic, which would lose something very essential were they to disappear from the scene. Warring and yet complementary, each must seek out the other, and exist, in a way, only for the other. And in order to play a part on the stage of the world, a man must be clearly seen belonging to one camp or the other. The important thing, then, was not whether he drew down upon himself anathemas or praise; he was in his place in the great Christian tragedy in which both God and the devil, sinner and saint, played their parts.

But what of those who, living in a condition of pleasant mediocrity, were neither one nor the other, neither saints nor sinners, neither poor Lazarus nor the wicked rich man, who experienced neither the splendors of power nor the wretchedness of poverty? Background figures, they did nothing to explain the significance of the drama performed here below. It seemed, then, that their lot was to live on the sidelines of the great

Christian tragedy, whose principal roles remained reserved for the powerful and the poor, each marked with the royal seal of divinity. Living in easy circumstances and outside the great conflicts dividing the universe, they represented nothing save ordinariness.

Reading Bossuet's sermons, one might almost be tempted to believe that the Church had forgotten the bourgeois, so small did his place appear in a world where the roles were distributed among those who lived in splendor and those who lived in want, both able to claim a special relationship to God. He appeared rather as a gatecrasher in a world formed without him, where he had no *raison d'être*. In vain does one search for his titles in the records of Christian tradition; legend seems silent on this score. Where had he originated, then, and who was he? The God of the Christians, in creating the world seemed not to have foreseen that one day the bourgeois would demand his place in it.

Yet, in the modern age, how could the Church still disregard this citizen? It could not abandon this upright man, conscious of his worth, to the secular world. As formerly it had been able to bestow a religious character upon those who, rich or beggars, had filled the stage of the world, so now it had to seek to interpret in its own manner the social phenomenon represented in modern times by the bourgeoisie. It had to be able to explain to the bourgeois why God had created him, and it had to assign functions to him on this earth. But how could the Church go about taking hold of this bourgeois with his altogether secular roots? How could it integrate into religious traditions the spirit and mode of the bourgeoisie, in order to be able to hallow it? What, in this order which linked heaven and earth and whose origins were traceable back to God himself, could be the spiritual significance of the bourgeois?

"Yes, my brothers," says Massillon, addressing kings and descendants of illustrious families, "it is not accident that has caused you to be born great and powerful. God, from the beginning of time, had destined this temporal glory for you, marked with the seal of his splendor, and separated from the crowd by the luster of titles and human honors." [3] There were thus transcendent reasons for titles of nobility, and, when a man was born great, he was of divine right. "I do not have to tell you," Bossuet says, "that it is God who grants the great births, the great marriages, children, posterity. . . . Let us be in no doubt, Christians; God in his eternal counsel has prepared the first families which are the source of nations, and in all nations the dominant qualities which were to make for their greatness." [4] But if Providence was concerned with illustrious families, the ordinary bourgeois could not expect it to attach any particular importance to his fate and that of his descendants. Hence it was hard for him to see how the divine wisdom had been thinking, since the beginning of time, especially of him.

While the bourgeois could not link their birth and particular destiny with an eternal counsel, the same might be said of the poor, who had even less reason than those who lived in decent circumstances to imagine that God took any great interest in their family affairs. Nevertheless, assuming that God, in creating a particular poor man, had no intention of establishing a genealogy for him, and was not concerned with his marriage or with the birth or number of his children or other details of his private life, it was nevertheless a fact—we are speaking the language of men like Bossuet—that in causing the poor to be born in their multitudes, he had prescribed their path for them, dooming them from the beginning of time to be in want and to remain so always.

A man was *born* poor; he was poor by birthright. One might almost say that poverty was a title of nobility which the deity granted to the poor, not to this poor man in particular, but to the mass of the disinherited. They, too, had their traditions to cite; they had their ancestry. If the power of the great was regarded as "deriving from the splendor of the first of Masters," the poor had the honor to "represent the God-Man . . . to be the living expression of the Word made flesh." [5] "On the foreheads of the great," says a contemporary preacher, "Jesus imprints some feature of his majesty and of his glory in order to invite us to respect them." But in the poor, "he imprints the seal of his cross and of his sufferings; he paints himself wholly, he breathes, he lives in his poor, to induce us to love them." [6] Thus the poor should be regarded as "portraits of Jesus Christ. The Divine Saviour lived on earth as they live today." [7] "The poor are the figure of Jesus Christ, poor and humiliated for us," says Nicole. "They are wholly clothed in the livery of Jesus Christ, and they represent him to us in the condition which should be most agreeable to us." [8] That, also, is why a poor man should inspire us with "something like religious reverence; he is the most worthy and most sacred object which the face of the earth can offer us. . . . Is not a poor man truly crucified in our midst? . . . Yes, a poor man is another Christ, Son of God." [9]

Thus the great and the small each had titles to display. But where, by contrast, were those of the bourgeois? God had not communicated to him a portion of his power, and the bourgeois life resembled not a whit the life led by the Son of God on earth. He was a commoner in the Christian world, a man of low birth. And that, too, was why it was less easy for him to recognize God's hand in what happened to him here below. Poverty was a destiny, and all the afflictions suffered by the poor were in the order of things; the poor man could see in them the hand of Divine Providence. He could "make a virtue of this necessity" and bless God "for refusing him that which is the loss and cause of damnation of many, and which might have been his." [10]

The great, of course, did not have the resignation of the poor and, trusting in their own strength, they appeared very sure of themselves, to the point that, while recognizing that it was to God that they owed their power, they often seemed to forget Divine Providence. At the same time, they were in a better position than others to realize "the fickleness of human affairs." "You live here at court," says Bossuet, "and without going much farther into the condition of your affairs, I should like to believe that your state was a peaceful one; but you have not so easily forgotten the tempests which so often agitate this sea as to trust yourselves altogether to this lull." [11] "The passion, the god of the great, is success," says Massillon. [12] "Success, deceitful in all else, is at least sincere in this, that it does not hide its deceits from us; on the contrary, it displays them openly and, in addition to its usual fickleness, it is pleased from time to time to astonish the world by terrible shocks, as though to recall all its force to the memory of men, and for fear that they might ever forget its inconstancy, its malignity, its eccentricity." It was at these moments that the Church awaited the great; it was then that, understanding that "success tricks us even when it is generous to us," they would realize that the power which it appeared to give was but "a great name by which it dazzles our ailing eyes," and, turning their gaze away from this pagan divinity, they ceased to be "captives subjected to the painful vicissitudes of its hard and malicious power"[13] and become Christians once more.

As for the bourgeois, his more regulated, more unified life seemed to provide fewer chinks through which the mysterious power either of blind fortune or of an infinitely wise God might penetrate. Acting by virtue of certain well-established maxims by which he abided, he was easily disposed to believe that it was he who had fashioned his life. He worked and he saved, he calculated and he measured, he reasoned and he looked ahead, and, establishing order everywhere and leaving nothing to accident, he was able, in his search for solid foundations for his life in the moral as in the economic sphere, to set aside the forces of mystery. He thus attained—and that was what he always had in view—to an honest happiness, unknown to either great or poor, a happiness which did not rule out the vicissitudes of fortune, but reduced and eliminated them as far as possible. Feeling himself master of his fate and conscious of deserving the decent ease which he enjoyed and which sufficed for him, he was less accessible than the mighty, however sinful they might be, to certain sentiments which are familiar to the Christian soul and which lead it back to God.

"The felicity of the worldly is made up of so many pieces that there will always be one lacking"; "its joys are soon transformed into utter bitterness."[14] The soul could then more easily divest itself of "exterior things" and begin to be "closer to itself."[15] "Vanity of vanities, all is vanity,"[16] said Bossuet to the great of his time, quoting Ecclesiastes, and the great sometimes understood him, and were converted.

The great were bored. "Yes, my brothers, tedium, which one

would have expected to be the lot of the populace, has taken refuge, it seems, only among the great; it is like their shadow that follows them everywhere. Pleasures which are nearly all exhausted for them offer them no more than a dull uniformity which benumbs or wearies; however much they diversify them, they merely diversify their tedium." Massillon shows us that the whole life of the great was "but an arduous defense against boredom. . . . Surround yourselves with every entertainment; there will always be spread over them, arising from the depths of your souls, a bitterness which will poison them; refine all pleasures, subtilize them, prove them in a crucible; the only result of all these transformations will be tedium." That, says Massillon again, is precisely what should bring the great closer to God. "The great are less excusable and more unfortunate in not attaching themselves to you, my God, because they realize better and more often the emptiness of everything that is not you." [17]

The bourgeois was not bored, or he was bored differently. He did not experience, or he experienced less, the great tedium which might lead to God, just as he knew nothing of the affliction which naturally caused the poor man to aspire to a brighter future. The great alone, says Massillon again, "experience the distress of a soul delivered over to itself, in which all the resources of the senses and pleasures leave only a frightful emptiness, and to which the whole world, with all the accumulation of glory and smoke which surrounds it, becomes vain if God is not with it." [18] The bourgeois, enjoying fewer pleasures, did not experience the great weariness which sometimes turned men away from the world and led their souls back to God. It would be an error, then, to sermonize to them too much on the vanity of human things or the emptiness of their existence, as it would be an error, too, to say too much to them about the afflictions of this world. Equally removed from the tedium of the rich and the bitterness of the poor, they had not sufficiently exhausted what life could offer them, nor had they suffered enough to embrace a life of piety.

At the same time, the bourgeois was not ambitious in the same way as the great, and it was therefore harder for him to see the nothingness of the things of this world. "Ambition, that insatiable desire to lift oneself on the very ruins of others, that worm that pricks the heart and never leaves it alone, that passion which is the mainspring of intrigues and all the agitations of the courts, which forms revolutions in states and daily displays fresh spectacles to the universe—this passion which dares everything and for which no price is too high, is a vice even more pernicious to empires than sloth itself." [19] But from "infinite pretensions" [20] might sometimes emerge pretensions to the infinite. The powerful and sublime God of Bossuet did not have to fear those who exalted themselves. He always had the last word so long as death was on his side. "Nothing can resist death. . . . It confounds and reduces to dust the proudest monarchs as well as the lowest of their subjects." [21] The great were better witnesses to the power of God than the humble, and their inordinate ambitions served divine glory. Sometimes they realized this and, turning aside from the "great drama of the world," took an interest in "the affair of eternity." [22]

"At court, far from regarding ambition as a sin, people regard it as a virtue," says Père Bourdaloue; "or if it passes for a vice, then it is regarded as the vice of great souls, and the vices of great souls are preferred to the virtues of the simple and the small." [23] Ambition, says Bourdaloue again, "is the great malady of our age." There is no condition "where ambition does not reign; it passes even for a virtue, for nobility of sentiment, for greatness of soul." [24] The bourgeois themselves may not have been exempt from ambition. But their ambitions lacked tragic grandeur, and the God of Bossuet would not deign to enter into competition with the *Bourgeois Gentilhomme* and would not overturn politics to show him his almighty power.

But if the respectable citizen did not have the ambitions of the nobleman, neither did he have the resignation or modesty distinctive of the poor. The latter, of course, had no particular awareness of the vanity of things which they had never known, and the reverberations of collapsing empires did not disturb them. On the other hand, they possessed by nature the Christian virtues which others might acquire only at great cost to themselves. A contemporary writer lists these characteristics of the poor: "Simple manners, hearts without conceit, minds without ambition, their cares confined to the necessaries of life; thus they are entirely prepared by their station to receive a Gospel which preaches only humility, detachment, contempt of human splendors; which gives great ideas only of the future life, and inspires respect and desire only for the possessions of eternity." [25] The bourgeois, for his part, possessed neither of the inordinate ambition of the great nor of the patience of the poor, would seem to have to remain ignorant both of the sins of those who exalted themselves and of the merits of those who humbled themselves.

Bossuet, speaking of his world, complains that the "license of great fortunes exceeds all bounds." This, he says, leads to "those prevailing sins which are not satisfied to be tolerated, or even excused, but which seek even to be applauded." The great liked to show greatness even in their sins. "How many have we not seen who like to play the great through their license in crime; who think they are exalting themselves far above all human things by contempt of the law, to whom modesty itself seems unworthy of them because it is a kind of fear!" The great are thus "bold and arrogant sinners," and Bossuet, following St. Augustine, contrasts them with the poor who commit only "servile and timid sins; when a poor man steals, he hides; when he is discovered, he trembles." [26]

The great, when they sinned, sinned wholeheartedly; they sinned in style, sinned well, so to speak. The same could not, I think, be said of the bourgeois. His sins were less definite, less tangible. Being an upright citizen, he was an amateur in sin, and the Church sometimes was very embarrassed in the presence of this man who, sinner though he was, seemed to elude its anathemas, adducing always his rectitude. In this respect, again, he was distinguished from the poor who, if they tended to hide, as Bossuet claimed, generally committed only well-defined sins, which everyone could agree to condemn roundly. Thus it was only the bourgeois who was bad at sinning and who, by assuming the attitude and manners of an upright citizen, seemed to diminish the idea of sin.

Thus the bourgeois, in more than one respect, appeared to elude the Church. The noble could cut a figure in a world where God, to demonstrate his almighty power, must find powerful men to cast down; he felt at home when he listened to the sermons of men like Bossuet and Massillon. But in one sense it might be said that the Church had done even more for the poor than for the great. For the Church, in a way, had created the poor man. The poor man was everywhere at home in the Christian legend, and could understand his lot only in the context of the ideology of the 'Church.

There remained the bourgeois, somehow out of place in the Christian universe. "Blood, education, the story of their ancestors sow the seeds of a natural tradition of virtue in the hearts of the great and of princes," says Massillon. "The populace, rough and untutored from birth, find within themselves, for the sublime duties of the faith, only the weight and the baseness of a nature given over to itself. . . . Born in the senses and in the slime of the earth, the poor man has difficulty in rising above himself." But did the bourgeois have seeds of virtue in his heart, or did he not? He was not of that "high birth" which might have prepared him, "so to speak, for the noble and heroic sentiments demanded by the faith." Massillon says again, "A pure blood rises more easily." The bourgeois, in this sense, was not pure-blooded. Was he then to be "rough and untutored" through "defective birth?" [27] It was a suggestion which he would have taken very much amiss.

So the Church had to find a new language in which to talk to him. It had to create a new ideology in which the idea of the bourgeois would have its due place; it had to trace of him a picture which could be set beside that of the great and of the poor, so that he might feel himself at home in this Christian world of symbols and allegories. Or to put it another way, the Church had to confer titles on this being of secular origins, so that he too might claim a relationship with God and find in religion the substantiation of his claims and the justification of the role which he regarded himself as destined to play in this world. But would it be able to hallow the bourgeois, to raise the bourgeoisie to the dignity of a religious symbol?

10 · ALMSGIVING

THE SALVATION OF THE RICH

"Nature, or to speak in more Christian fashion, God, the common Father of men," says Bossuet, "from the outset gave equal rights to all his children to all the things they needed to preserve their lives. None of us can boast of being more privileged than the rest by nature; but through the insatiable desire to amass wealth, it became impossible for this beautiful brotherhood to endure for long in the world. Men had to resort to division and possession, which resulted in constant quarrels and litigation; of this were born the words 'mine' and 'thine'—such cold terms, as the admirable St. John Chrysostom remarks—of this, too, was born the great diversity of conditions, some living in affluence in every respect, others languishing in penury." [1]

But in that case, how should we believe in the goodness and justice of God, and would not those who "languish in penury," seeing others "living in affluence in every respect," be entitled to complain? Not at all. God has provided for everything, concentrating "all these possessions in certain families only in order that they might be duly distributed to all the others." He has made "those who possess all in abundance" responsible for "those who lack everything." He has made the rich "the stewards of his Providence." [2]

Thus God made men rich not for their own sakes, but for

the sake of the poor. "For you should not deceive yourselves, Christians," says Père Bourdaloue, addressing the rich, "and not persuade yourselves, if you are rich, that you are so for yourselves. . . . You are rich, but for whom? For the poor. . . . What is God's wish? That you should be the deputies, the ministers, the co-workers of his Providence in regard to the poor."[3] Everyone with possessions owes a part of them to those who have none. "Not only do we have no real right to the things of the world," says Nicole, "because belonging always essentially to God they can never belong to creatures; but we are also limited by the laws of God in the use of those possessions; for it must not be imagined that God gives them to us so that we may dispose of them as we wish. He is too just to have made such an unequal distribution. These goods being the means destined by his Providence for the subsistence of men, he gives to some more than they need only so that they may distribute it to others. A rich man, in so far as he is rich, is thus no more than a steward of God's good things."[4]

How, indeed, should it be otherwise? "What," cries a contemporary preacher, "should Providence, in pouring an abundance of gold and silver into your houses, have had no other object but to furnish eternal and inexhaustible fuel to luxury and sensuality? No, Christians, God is not so eager to make people happy in this world, and to give our passions the wherewithal to kindle and satisfy them!"[5] What, then, is "his intention in showering the good things of the earth upon you in such profusion?" asks Massillon, speaking to the great. If God has made men great, it is so that they may be the fathers of the poor. "You take the place, here below, of God himself; you are the visible Providence [of the poor]; they have the right to appeal to you and make known their needs; your possessions are their possessions, and your bounty the sole heritage that God has assigned to them on earth."[6]

That, then, is why God has given wealth and titles to some. "You have communicated to the great of the earth a spark of your power; you have made them great in order to serve as fathers to your poor; your Providence has averted evils from them so that they might think of those of their neighbor; you have placed them at their ease and in freedom, so that they might perform their task of comforting your children." [7] What is true of the great is true also of the wealthy, whatever their social condition. God "has charged" the subsistence of the poor "to the wealth which you possess, in so far as you are rich." [8]

In this respect, then, no distinction could be made between those whose fortune derived from their ancestors and the self-made man. All owed alms; all, for the same reason, must regard themselves as fathers of the poor, as representatives of Divine Providence here below. The only difference that could be established among them related to the size of their fortune or, more exactly, to the extent of each one's superfluity. "As rich men," says Père Bourdaloue, "you have not only what you need, but more than you need, and the poor man does not have even the bare necessities. In order to provide him with these necessities of life which he lacks, you will use the superfluity which you have; so that one will supplement the other." [9]

This being settled, the only question that remained was how much each should concede to the poor, a very important question for the salvation of the faithful. "It is a law, a general and absolute law," says Père Bourdaloue again, "that alms and possessions must be proportionate; and when God comes to judge you, it is a matter of faith that he will take this proportion as the basis for his judgment. Your wealth compared with your alms, or your alms compared with your wealth, is what will determine your justification or your condemnation at God's judgment seat." [10]

Alms were thus regarded as constituting a form of graduated tax levied in favor of the poor from all those who, whether of noble birth or bourgeois, had any superfluity. Here the Church was basing its policy on a principle which the "respectable citizens" were later to introduce in the secular sphere. In this area, then, everything was methodical and extremely well organized; nothing was left to whim, and each could see just what was required of him. The bourgeois, who liked the position between himself and God to be quite clear, had no grounds for complaint. The Church was defining the divine will, setting figures, organizing charity. Preachers, it is true, sometimes complained of the way in which men of substance tended to carry out their duty toward the poor, and even protested against such "systematized charity." [11] But this was no longer the age of the "poor Francis, the most ardent, the most enraptured and, if I may so express myself, the most desperate lover of poverty whom the Church, perhaps, has ever known." [12]

Thus, taking account of eighteenth-century conditions, no longer suited to "triumphant folly" or an "immense and limitless charity," the preachers pictured God as saying, "You will share your possessions with your brothers. . . . Not that I oblige you to give them everything or the best part of what you have received from me. I do not mean that you should go so far as to impoverish yourselves to enrich them, or that through your bounty they should be in abundance and you in hardship." God's will was that men should measure "things in such a manner that there would be some sort of equality between them and you." [13] There would be cases, of course, where the proportion must be exceeded. "And if the need of the poor should become dire, then you would use not only your superfluity but even what was necessary to your station." [14] In ordinary circumstances, however, men should observe the rules dictated by a spirit of wisdom and moderation, which they must be sure to know well if they were not to deceive themselves to their own disadvantage and endanger their own salvation.

The wealthy must "buy their place in heaven by alms," says a Jesuit Father, Le Chapelain. But what should be the price? We know that the amount of the alms must be proportionate to a person's wealth. But are we really sure of always determining the right proportion? An awkward question. "For after all, this proportion between your alms and your wealth must be maintained, and if you do not maintain it, then your eternity will be at issue, for it is a matter of faith that God will judge you on this proportion." Père le Chapelain calls this a "terrible obscurity." But, he continues, "does not religion have resources to offer you? There is one, Christians, which this religion offers you, and which it is infinitely important for you to know. . . . Instead of relying exclusively on your own lights, which are always uncertain in so delicate a matter, address yourselves to those men who are the depositaries of the secrets of your consciences, and whom you have selected to act as your guides on the road to salvation." With their confessors, the rich would thus be able to enter into the minutiae. They would outline the position of their "affairs" to them "in good faith," "without concealing from them what might render their decision more sure," and they would make "of that decision the rule for their alms." [15]

Thus everything would be solved, and the bourgeois, well counseled during his lifetime by his notary and his confessor, would by his death have put his affairs into perfect order, both for this world and for heaven. There therefore seemed to be no reason why he should not accept an arrangement which insured him to the greatest possible extent both against risks here below and against the infinitely more serious ones of the hereafter. Of "all the obstacles which the devil places in the way of our salvation, none is greater or more deadly than riches," [16] states Bossuet, and the sentiment was often repeated. But there was nevertheless a way whereby the rich could save themselves, namely, almsgiving. "If the rich man can have some assurance of his eternal predestination, and some safeguard against this unhappy reprobation which envelops him, it is through alms. Oh, how many rich persons have safely reached the haven of salvation after treading the corrupt paths of the world for so many years!" God would speak thus to the rich: "It is true that you deserve the severest punishment, and my justice should descend upon you in a thousand cases; but you have set up a barrier which stops it—your alms." [17]

So it was not bad business for the rich to give to the poor. "You will live in slavery to sin, and you will die in it," says a preacher to the rich. "It is no small matter to be treated between God and you, that of your reconciliation; but important though it is, you can settle it at small cost; present to God the sacrifice of your alms, and he will cause the treasures of his grace to descend upon you." [18] Another preacher, after comparing the kingdom of heaven with "that precious pearl referred to in the Gospels," tells us that it is "offered to the generosity" of the rich. It is "bought" by alms. "Hurry," he says, "the right moment for this profitable transaction is short!" [19]

The bourgeois was being offered a very profitable and very secure investment. For, as a writer of the period puts it, "alms bear a considerable resemblance to remittances made for eternity; on your arrival, you will find them payable at sight." [20] And "not only is Jesus Christ himself your surety, but it is also in his divine hands, and on his adorable head, that you invest your capital. Could you invest it more soundly or more profitably? This kind of funds will never perish . . . the interests will be in perpetuity." [21] Thus without even touching the funds which provided him with the necessaries of life, the bourgeois could create a perpetual income for himself.

All this would seem to be very congenial to the bourgeois temperament. The bourgeois liked to save, and he was sometimes taken to task for this from the pulpit. But why, as a prudent and sensible man, should he not save for heaven, which would be by far the most profitable investment he could make? The bourgeois liked to make an income for himself. Then let him make one for eternity, and this love of earthly goods, although wholly worldly in itself and dangerous for the rich man's soul, would become the most powerful instrument of his salvation. "We see men working three-quarters of their lives to make a happy life for themselves for the rest of their days, although they can hope to enjoy it for only a few years; how much more reasonable it is for them to work for a happy eternity, if the thought of that eternity sometimes comes to their minds, if they but reflect that they have a soul and that this soul is immortal!" [22]

THE MYSTERY OF THE POOR

While the man who was ignorant of the precept of almsgiving might be able to see "neither justice nor wisdom nor reason in the distribution which God has made of the things of the earth," it would be quite otherwise of the Christian who, understanding the true designs of Divine Providence, might easily be persuaded that "the inequality of this distribution, which produces inequality of conditions, is what is most admirable in the government of the universe, where we see rich and poor meet and joined by the worthiest of bonds. The rich man regards the poor man as one whom Providence has entrusted to his care, and whom he is responsible for feeding, while the poor man regards the rich man as the agent of Providence, as the steward of the good things which the earth produces for the subsistence of all men." [23] And it seemed that whatever the changes introduced in the social order, the admirable system to which the Pastor of Gap referred must last forever. To anyone with an understanding of the designs of Providence here below, a society without rich and poor was inconceivable. Either, or both, might change in aspect— the rich bourgeois, for example, might replace the nobleman. But as for the roles assigned by Divine Providence to rich and poor respectively, these, it seemed, could never change. Rich and poor were figures established by the Christian legend for all time, transcending the mutations which the mind of man might introduce in the secular sphere.

"The whole human race, as you know, is divided into two conditions: that of the poor, which is the broadest, and that of the rich, which is the most restricted." In both, a man might attain salvation, but by different means. "By what road can the poor man attain salvation? By that which his condition itself offers him, namely, humility and patience. And by what road can the rich man arrive at the same goal? It is not quite the same, Christians, but it will lead him there none the less surely; it is that of charity and almsgiving. . . . For thus says the Saviour: give alms . . . and all your sins will speedily be blotted out; your riches have most often been the cause and the instrument of your irregularities; may they be their remedy and expiation." [24] In this way Providence had provided for everything. By creating rich and poor, God wished to sanctify the rich "through wealth, the poor through poverty. He has ordained that the poor man should honor the supreme authority by his submission; he has ordained that the rich man should imitate the infinite mercy by his good deeds; to one he wished to give the reward of his patience, to the other the reward of his charity." [25] That, too, was why the rich man had "no reason to look down upon the poor man. Each is equally God's handiwork, and created for the other." [26]

Thus it had always been God's will that there should be poor and rich; the poor, whose "condition" should be to ask because they were in need, the rich, whose "condition" should be to give, because they lived in affluence. [27] "He created the rich man that he might redeem his sins by helping the poor; he created the poor man that he might humble himself through the aid he received from the rich." [28]

We were looking for a function for the bourgeois in the sacred sphere; here we have it ready made. The bourgeois, in his turn, was to be the providence of the poor. The poor were to see, in the rich, "visible Gods." [29] What more could the bourgeois desire? Everything had worked out; the newly rich who could not appeal to a divine right by reason of their birth might be admitted as a matter of course to the traditional world of the Church once they bestowed alms on the poor and served as stewards of Providence. It might even be anticipated that, with the increasing affluence of the bourgeoisie, there would soon be only the rich, nobility and bourgeoisie, on the one hand, and the poor, on the other, the former giving, the latter receiving. To be "stewards of Providence" and to serve as "visible Gods" in relation to the poor, all that was required was to be rich. And the fact that, in the designs of Providence, the bourgeois might exercise the same functions and be vested with the same dignity as the great seemed to bring closer together all those, whether titled or not, who enjoyed a certain affluence, leaving finally only two categories, the rich and the poor.

In this perspective, the bourgeois might be regarded as a kind of nobleman, minus the title. Vested with a sacred function, he could enjoy a certain prestige conferred on him by the Church, which, making wealth the common measure of a whole class, seemed to place the newly rich commoner on a footing of equality with the traditionally wealthy. At the same time, by satisfactorily performing the honorable functions which he exercised in common with the nobility, the bourgeois might believe himself assured of salvation, no small thing for a self-made man, who often had much on his conscience and everything to fear, for all kinds of reasons, from eternity.

The rich, we read in a seventeenth-century sermon, had very special reasons to be grateful to God. They could save themselves by giving alms. They "are very unfeeling if they damn themselves eternally, having in their hands the wherewithal to open heaven for themselves, to open it as easily as it is easy for them to extend and to open a charitable hand." The rich must therefore thank God more than all the rest. They had the means of redeeming themselves from hell, of purchasing eternal glory. They would be given "for their gold what costs others blood and tears; what the poor can acquire only at the cost of their sweat and suffering." [30] Thus the rich were in a very privileged position, and, if the Jesuit whom we have just cited was exaggerating somewhat, perhaps, and oversimplifying, it was nevertheless a fact that almsgiving was regarded as a powerful means of attaining salvation. Innumerable sermons testify that the worldly-minded long continued to feel uneasy at the approach of death, when they thought of hell and of what might await them in the next world should the Church, perchance, be right. Here, then, was a way to allay their remaining anxieties. Taking advantage of the means of salvation which his riches offered, the bourgeois could live confidently, knowing that he was prepared for any eventuality.

Thus everything seemed to be for the best, and the bourgeois, in the legendary world created by the Church, which it traced back to God, had a perfectly respectable place, with functions that ensured his salvation, provided he carried them out well. But that being so, why did this new officeholder make so little of a dignity which, for this world and the next, seemed to offer him so many advantages?

"The law of God is as it were destroyed as soon as it attempts to touch our wealth," says a preacher of the period.[31] "People do not believe as they should in the truths contained in Holy Scripture, and that is the source of all the evils in the world. You leave property to your children because you believe that it will be useful to them; you would be even readier to leave some to the poor if you believed that this would be to your advantage. Had you the least suspicion that the alms which you give would serve you in the next world, you would give them the more willingly, since you must have more affection for yourselves than for your heirs."[32] And yet men distrusted the word of God. "People believe a liar, on a piece of parchment signed by a notary and two or three liars, since Scripture says that all men are liars; and I speak on behalf of the Creator of heaven and earth; I promise on behalf of him who is the arbiter of life and death, preservation of health, assistance in sickness, increase in possessions and, better than all that, life eternal, if they will give alms . . . and they are unwilling to believe me!"[33]

Clearly, the bourgeois was not as believing as he might have been. He was not altogether sure that everything he was told was true. So he was cautious. But over and above these more general reasons, related to modern unbelief, are there not others, more particularly connected with the very essence of the bourgeois mentality, which might explain why the newly rich felt less disposed to serve as stewards of Providence than those who had inherited their fortunes from their ancestors?

"Without the precept of almsgiving," cries a contemporary preacher, "I see only frightful disorder in the universe; men no longer appear to be the children of the same father."[34] When the great lavished alms upon the poor, they were justifying Providence at the same time as they were working usefully toward their own salvation. The position they occupied in the universal order placed this responsibility upon them; they had obligations toward God who had caused them to be born wealthy. But did the bourgeois feel the same? And even though he felt that he owed to God the riches which he possessed, was he prepared to act as the voluntary agent of the designs of Divine Providence?

Between the noble and the poor on the one hand and the bourgeois on the other, there were certain quite essential differences, connected with their very origins. The bourgeois was born in circumstances altogether different not only from those attendant upon the illustrious birth of the noble, but also from those surrounding the very ordinary birth of the poor.

The little marquis was born in a castle, the little beggar in a shack. This might appear a somewhat strange dispensation of Divine Providence. Add to this the fact that all the little marquis had for centuries been born in the same castles, and that all the little beggars had successively seen the light of day in the same shacks. Clearly there was something here that eluded understanding unless it was seen as harboring a secret intention of Divine Providence. But did the birth of the little bourgeois in his father's house represent an equally strange phenomenon? First of all, his father's house, having the externals neither of great wealth nor of extreme want, had nothing of the symbolism inviting us to reflect upon the destinies of men. And then, again, most people usually knew when and how this house had been built, as well as the wholly secular origins of the fortune of the owner. Since the fortune had been acquired and the house built in the same generation, it could arouse little curiosity in a mystical vein or stimulate speculation on the origin of things.

The bourgeois was the being born without providence, or at least, without a class providence. A God was needed to explain the nobleman and the poor, but none to explain the bourgeois as such. There was no reason to ask God why he had created the bourgeois. The bourgeoisie was without mystery. It was an essentially secular social phenomenon, governed solely by the laws of this world, with no need, in explaining it, to go any higher and appeal to the counsels of Divine Providence. Why, then, should the bourgeois feel any particular obligation to justify Divine Providence by lavishing alms in reparation for sin?

The nobleman was aware that everyone could not be great and powerful and live in mansions. But why should there not be modest and well-appointed little bourgeois houses all over the land? The nobleman knew that his greatness needed the poor; their existence enhanced his dignity, greatness being always a wholly relative attribute, requiring contrast. But the bourgeois did not to the same degree require a negative complement to assert himself, the bourgeoisie being the normal condition of humanity, the condition which everyone should achieve, in the view of the philanthropists. No one could hold it against you that you were not a duke or a marquis, but it was always a little your own fault if you were not of the middle class. The poor man was the bourgeois who had failed, and poverty could easily become a reproach.

"I shall not affect for riches a contempt which I do not feel, and which in every writer is no more than dubious ostentation," says a contemporary author. "It is doubtless a noble heritage," he goes on, "to leave to one's children the example of an upright life; but if by honest means one can leave them some money, I think he would spare himself cruel anxieties at the hour of death." Alas, it was not given to everyone to be spared such "cruel anxieties," and our author regrets it. "I have examined man in the midst of riches, I have examined him in modest circumstances; would that I might abolish only the third class of men, who languish in poverty!" [35]

The rich often accused the poor of not working hard enough, and the preachers sometimes protested against accusations which might be cited as excuses for failing to give alms. "Do not say, my brothers, that the poor should work, and do not be such severe censors of their laziness," [36] says a preacher of the period. But would the bourgeois still listen to the Church's exhortations? The poor man had lost his mystical quality; he had lost that transcendent dignity which had conferred a divine right upon him. The poor man, says the Church, should not be blamed for being poor. "The condition of the poor is in itself and of itself a condition of salvation; to be saved, it is sufficient for the poor man to maintain himself in his condition." The same did not apply to the rich and the nobility, who "will be saved only to the extent that they succeed . . . in guarding themselves against the perils of their conditions . . . in detaching themselves from their conditions." [37] The rich must not forget that "The poor man, after all, is on the road to heaven; he has only to stay there to save his soul. The greatest temptation to which he is exposed, if not the only one, is to lack patience and resignation to the will of God; while the rich are subject to temptations of every kind." [38]

The poor must thus be regarded as treading the path of salvation, destined to lead to that path those who had not yet reached it. "How your benefactions would increase were you to delve into the mystery of the poor!" cries Abbé Poulle. "Not only is Jesus Christ hidden in them; but he entrusts to them the treasures of his graces and heaven itself, and he commands the great of the earth to turn to them if they want to receive those treasures." [39] For it was they who, "standing in your path," were the "distributors of spiritual graces"; it was they who, "creeping at your feet," were the "arbiters of your eternity. However destitute they may be, however contemptible their appearance, how great they are, how fearsome in the eyes of faith! They have in their power maledictions and benedictions, war and peace, famine and abundance, storms and calm, death and life!" [40]

But the poor, as well as the nobility, seemed now to have lost their power, that mysterious power which they were believed to possess from God. A whole universe was disappearing, the universe of the great, those openhanded sinners, and of the poor, children of God who stretched out their hands humbly and submissively. The bourgeois had emerged, and all seemed to have changed. It mattered little, then, that the bourgeois, too, now and then, continued to give alms. His gesture no longer had the mystical significance attached to it by the nobleman when he found himself face to face with the poor.

For the nobleman, almsgiving was not only a function incumbent upon him; by showing charity he was classifying himself in a higher order. Nobility itself, as was constantly reiterated, had absolutely nothing Christian about it; charity alone could justify it and relate it to the values of the hereafter. In the nobleman, there was a secular side and a religious one. To his secular duties he must add that of relieving poverty; in other words, from a Christian point of view, charity must enter into the very concept of the great.

Was this true of the bourgeois? Almsgiving certainly did

not characterize him. He was no nobleman who sought entertainment (a not very Christian attitude) but who at the same time was generous with his alms (an altogether Christian attitude). The bourgeois was prepared to please God by asserting his workaday virtues, which, for him, formed an integral part of the ordered life of people of his class. Whether he added charity to his duties or not, the general plan on which he ordered his life would be little affected. Had he or had he not fulfilled his domestic duties? Had he or had he not been upright in his dealings? These were the questions which he would authorize God to put to him. The great had their wealth and a pleasure-loving life for which to obtain forgiveness; to do so, they must make an act of renunciation and abandon their way of life. The bourgeois wanted to be judged on his own life, on his everyday life; he did not have to obtain pardon for belonging to the middle class.

"I do not condemn the ordinary concerns of the world," says Père Bourdaloue, "a family which must be cared for, a property which must be administered, an inheritance which must be improved, even a lawsuit in which one is involved and which requires attention. . . . I shall go farther, and admit that there are certain commitments, certain circumstances, certain affairs, which it would be more sinful to neglect than to attend to." Nevertheless, "you cannot better sanctify all these concerns in which you are involved by your condition than by combining them with care for the poor." [41]

But did all these concerns in which the bourgeois was engaged really need external hallowing? They contained their own built-in standards, and the bourgeois was unwilling to recognize any other. If religion was to signify anything in his life, it would have to connect with that life itself, exalt the motives which determined it, not only tolerate them or approve them from a distance, but penetrate them and model itself on the very special morality which governed it. The duality of life, which existed necessarily in the great, was not to be found in the middle class. The bourgeois must be accepted as he was, and virtues and sins which were not of his condition should not be attributed to him.

Would the Church be capable of meeting the challenge? To do so, it would have to shift its ground and change its methods and, instead of having in mind a life characterized by excessive pleasure and expiatory almsgiving, envisage an existence of decent comfort and reasonable foresight and find a way to sanctify it.

11 · CHRISTIAN LIFE
AND MIDDLE-CLASS LIFE

THE EDUCATORS OF THE BOURGEOISIE

The bourgeois who sought to give a shape to his life could elicit from Jesuits and Jansenists alike any number of good counsels which he could use to advantage. In the case of the Jesuits, this is not surprising. Although they sometimes erred by discussing certain points of morality which respectable citizens, however tolerant they might have been in other respects, did not want to have discussed, the Fathers were too alert not to know how to talk with the bourgeois. The Jansenists, for their part, might have been expected to find it harder to hit the right note. If the Jesuits were sometimes overtolerant, the Jansenists seemed disinclined to make the slightest compromise. It is, therefore, surprising to find that the layman often came to their defense.

"For in order to understand easily the obligation incumbent upon us all to imitate the life of our Lord as the Gospel describes it to us," says Arnauld, "we have to consider that we are all religious according to the general religion established by Jesus Christ, and obliged to observe its rule."[1] Yet it was not by looking upon himself as a "religious" that the bourgeois would be able to grow rich and get ahead. The important thing, says Nicole, "is to die well." "Sufferings," he continues, "whether

[155]

long or short, great or small, vanish and are lost in eternity. There these little differences which terrify us so much are unknown. Let us seek to have eternity in our hearts, and all will appear the same to us—riches, poverty, health, sickness, honors, lowliness, glory, ignominy." [2] The bourgeois had to be able to forget eternity and attach importance to the things of this world. He was among those whom the mind of a Pascal could not bring itself to fathom, who were prepared to build "magnificent dwellings" without thinking of death.

The objection might be raised, of course, that whatever his vision of the next life, man would always try to accommodate himself to this one and satisfy his earthly necessities. The Jansenist, however great the passion which moved him toward God and eternity, also had to "rest in the company" of his fellow men and live the common life. What did he retain, then, of that faith which caused him to sense the great universal tragedy and to seek infinite treasures? Something very important, which could not be effaced: a mode of being, an attitude which he was to preserve toward everything, certain ways of acting and feeling which were to give his life its peculiar texture, a style of life, if you like. And that was precisely what the bourgeois found among the Jansenists.

"The righteous man acts according to the precepts of religion in the smallest things," says Pascal.[3] And Nicole explains, "Not even the most ordinary actions are to be excluded from the rule of faith. We have to get up, for example, out of obedience to God who grants us sleep only for the needs of the body and who orders us, once these needs have been satisfied, to busy ourselves with the work which he prescribes according to our condition. We have to eat out of obedience to God, who orders us to support our life; and in eating we must observe the rule of temperance which obliges us not to seek pleasure for pleasure's sake, and to have as our purpose, in eating, only to satisfy bare necessity." [4]

The disciple of the Jansenists would go even farther and deprive himself of licit things. "It is no small sin," says Nicole again, "to grant oneself all the comforts which can pass as necessary or useful; for it is a great sin not to do any penance." The

Jansenist sought a spiritual circumcision, which consisted "in depriving oneself by mortification and penance of the legitimate use of many things which are permitted." [5]

Did a disciple of the Jansenists desire to get married? He must look for qualities of seriousness and a high moral character in the person with whom he was going to link his life. "These qualities are to have an ordered, reasonable mind, . . . to be established in the practice of Christian living, . . . to love retirement, work and ordered living, . . . to be capable . . . of managing the family's property without dissipating it through luxury, unnecessary expenditure or neglect." [6] The life which the spouse should lead was a "Christian life, which is in itself a sober life, a life of work and not of recreation, games and pleasure," and they would never forget that it should be "filled with some useful, serious occupation, corresponding to one's station." [7]

The Jansenist, as we know, bore with him a terrible secret, the mystery of predestination. The mystery would remain in the depths of his soul; it would be buried there, and life would not allow him to think of it constantly. But watching his actions, we perceive in his attitudes, his daily conduct, a something which shows that he was not unaware of the terrible God whom the damned implore in vain. And this man would tell himself, in his anguish, "Let us bear in our lives the marks of the divine election which are the Christian virtues," [8] and he would order his life "in such a fashion that there might be reason to believe that he was moving toward heaven, and not toward hell." [9]

The Jansenist was a man of "rigorous probity" [10] because, realizing the seriousness of life and the tragedy of the human lot, he owed it to himself to be so. Living a uniform and ordered life, a "serious life," he did not seek to exalt himself, knowing that "each degree of wealth, honor and grandeur increases our dangers, and renders salvation more difficult." [11] Therefore, too, he did not envy the great of the earth, for he could not fail to know that "the condition of the great is a condition of violence for Christians." [12]

In order to grow to self-awareness and develop an ethic which reflected its spirit, the middle class might well have gone to the Jansenists for sound principles and forms of life. In adopting them, it would have acquired a certain moral prestige, which would have been useful in its struggles with the aristocracy. The bourgeois who had passed through the school of men like Arnauld or Nicole did not seek pleasure; he abhorred anything that offended the proprieties. This might have conferred upon him a sort of moral superiority over the nobility, or, rather, he would have represented morality, as the nobility personified power and glory. Integrity would have constituted his specific character, his specific differentiation from the nobility; he would have been the unswerving man of principle and, for that very reason, would have been clothed with a dignity which kings and nobility did not possess by virtue of their station and to which the poor were unable to aspire.

But if the bourgeois had many things to learn from the Jansenists, the teaching of the Jesuits could be no less useful to him in very many ways. For who were better able to preach the blessings of order than the disciples of St. Ignatius of Loyola? "Order and virtue are two names which signify practically the same thing," says Père Crasset. "Order creates paradise; disorder creates hell." [13] Order is divine. "Order, we might say, is the creator of the world; it preserves and restores the world. We proceed from order; we subsist through order, we live in order. All that God does, he does in order, and nothing that is done without order is from God. Order leads us to God." [14] This divine and universal principle must be rigorously applied by everyone in their everyday lives. "Set yourselves a rule for the day, which you will keep unswervingly unless you are prevented from so doing by a superior order which obliges you to set it aside. Rule the time of your rest, of your meals, of your study and of your recreation. The life of heaven is a life of order; begin a life which you will continue in eternity; it will be all the more agreeable to God, more convenient to your family, if you have one, and more profitable to your salvation." [15]

Thus the man of regular habits, who loves order, prepares himself for heaven, where he will continue his habits without having to relax his discipline. And in order that everything in his life might be ordered and organized beforehand, the Jesuits did not refuse to discuss with him the most minute details of his life. "Arrange a fixed time for getting up and going to bed; and as far as you are able, try to retire early in order to be able to rise early. Nothing is more contrary to a regular and Christian life than to get up late." [16] "Undress with decency and modesty, take some holy water and sprinkle a few drops on your bed." [17] And above all, shun "idleness," [18] and never forget that "all your devotions must be subordinated to the necessary duties of your state or of your employment." [19]

All this appears to apply perfectly to the bourgeois life, and the members of the middle classes, we might think, must have been delighted to find educators who spoke so sane and reasonable a language to them, one which would benefit them both in this life and in the next. We might go even farther and say that the words of the Jesuit Fathers seemed to be addressed to the bourgeois in particular, for they applied much more to well-to-do persons of regular lives than to the nobility or to the poor, both of whom, either because they were too exalted to emphasize "little duties" or because they felt the exigencies of life too keenly to make rules of them, were less able to appreciate the benefits of order. It was thus his own ethic that the bourgeois could find among the Jesuits, and in that respect he could find no better educator than Père Bourdaloue.

"In truth," says Père Bourdaloue, "if there is any innocence in the world, where is it to be found if not in the conditions and states of life where the law of work is unswervingly observed? Among the great, the nobility, the rich—that is, among those whose life is nothing but recreation and indolence—do not look for true piety, and do not expect to find purity of manners. . . . Where, then, can we find it?" he asks. "In the huts of slothful poverty, where there is no occupation but mendicity? No, Christians! Idleness is the undoing of these as much as of the rich; and this type of poor, whom Jesus Christ does not recognize at all, also tends to indulge in libertinage. Where, then, is innocence confined? I have told you—in those undistinguished states of life which subsist through work, in those less brilliant conditions, but conditions which are safer as far as salvation is concerned, of merchants engaged in the pursuit of lawful trade; of craftsmen who measure their days by the work of their hands; of servants who fulfill to the letter the divine precept, 'you shall eat according as you work!' " [20]

Through the mouth of Père Bourdaloue, the Church seemed to be giving its blessing to an entire world, the world of work. The pleasure-loving nobleman was excluded from it for the same reason as the beggar who suffered patiently. The great, for whom, despite their faults, Providence had paid particular attention, would feel humbled in the presence of these undistinguished stations of life in which men lived industriously and in innocence. As soon as he did not work, the poor man, whose poverty had sufficed to create his title in the world of pious legend, who had been regarded as bearing a sacred character because he symbolized the great affliction of mankind, was no longer the good friend of Jesus Christ. There was thus a type of poor whom Jesus Christ did not recognize, any more than the police did.

The Church had talked too much about the great and the poor. In the modern age, it had to insist more on the characteristics of the intermediary states. Why talk to the bourgeois of the vanity of splendors which they did not know, or cite the example of poor people whom fundamentally they despised? They must be spoken to about themselves; they must be shown that God was not less interested in them than he was in the great or in the poor; that he was satisfied to have such honest and hard-working people in his world. The Church must preach to the bourgeois on his duties, must reveal to him values that were more especially his own, must set the seal of divine approval on his efforts, on his work; and, satisfied with himself, he would be no less so with God and with his Church.

"All your piety is contained in your station and your duties. I say in your duties faithfully carried out; do not neglect anything that is required by your work, by your responsibility, by the various relationships which you have more directly either with God, as ministers of the altar, or with society, as judges, or with servants, as masters, or with children, as fathers and mothers; with whosoever it may be and in whatever situation it may be, embrace it all, fulfill it all, do not neglect an iota of it all."

That was reasonable talk! That was what would touch the heart of the bourgeois and what he would be pleased to repeat to his children. The bourgeoisie would have a professional morality, a well-defined morality of duty. It would merit heaven by a well-regulated and properly occupied everyday life.

"I say, in your duties assiduously carried out; in your rule of life, you should have certain principles whereby you distribute your time, divide your attentions, arrange your practices according to the nature and extent of your obligations; set these principles for yourselves, and, in order to act more surely and in a more Christian manner, ask a wise director to prescribe them for you, and make it your steadfast law to abide by them." [21]

Great man and poor man had been legendary figures with symbolical gestures; the reality was no longer gesture but order, the well-regulated life of every day. And let it not be said this moral code was undemanding. "A long and wearisome continuity" could produce "tedium," and this tedium must be overcome and one's duties must be carried out "with holy zeal; not always with a sensible zeal but with zeal of spirit, independent of sentiment and transcending all obstacles." That was the morality described by Père Bourdaloue in his sermon on the feast of St. Francis de Sales, a morality which required that everything be done "according to the ordinary obligations of one's state, and without the ceremony or brilliance which eccentricity lends to other works." [22] It was a morality governed by a spirit of prudence and a sense of reality, a morality of good sense in which the bourgeois could feel at home and recognize precepts that he could turn to good account.

Neither nobleman nor poor man had had a profession as such. What they were was more important than what they did. The nobleman had his rank, he had his dignity, and whether he performed a function or not made no difference to his character, which was acquired by birth and hallowed by God. The poor man, too, whether he worked or not, played a specific role on earth. In this respect, great and poor were alike. The bourgeois, on the other hand, existed primarily in relation to his activity. The Church must talk to him about his work, about what preoccupied him in his everyday life; only thus could he recognize his own moral code in the Church's teachings. The Church must not present him with far-ranging concepts or try to raise him out of his own sphere but, rather, talk to him of the daily round, of the minute concerns of life, and tell him that God required no more of him. That was what the Jesuits realized very clearly.

"True virtue contracts our thoughts and opinions, our movements and our undertakings, within the confines of our state. It excludes from the economy of our action whatever does not pertain to order, and in all our occupations keeps us under the hand of God. It causes us to walk toward a blessed eternity in the path which Providence has traced for us, turning neither to right nor left." [23] Thus the bourgeois could be sure that God approved of him when he faithfully fulfilled the duties of his state. "We serve God in serving our prince with fidelity; we serve God by developing our property in accordance with the rules of probity and justice. There are duties to be fulfilled in every condition, and it is by fulfilling these duties that a man sanctifies himself." Nothing need prevent the bourgeois from attending to his business, making a decent competency for himself and enjoying the esteem of his neighbors. "May God deign to take account of what we do even for ourselves, when it is for the love of him that we do it, and then there will be no incompatibility between duty and business. A man is a soldier, a lawyer, a business man; but he is a Christian. In all these different states one can serve the same master, and work usefully for God, for men and for oneself." [24]

If the bourgeois, then, found good educators among the Jansenists, he could find no less satisfactory ones among the Jesuits. Middle-class life could be governed by the principles of Père Bourdaloue as well as by those of Nicole. Yet there were differences. "We do not judge people by the austerity of their lives, but by their docility of mind," says Père Bourdaloue again.[25] A Jansenist would not have said this, or at least not in that way. The bourgeois who had passed through the school of men like Arnauld and Nicole was likely to have a captious attitude. For Père Bourdaloue, perfection should be not in "extraordinary and singular things" but in "what is most habitual to us, . . . in that

which fills the days and years of our lives." [26] The Jansenist was
not equally concerned to avoid singularity, and his common
sense was less solidly developed. He sometimes liked to distinguish himself from the rest. "It is necessary," he might say, that
the Christian "should distinguish himself from the crowd by
a singular conduct; that he should walk almost alone along
a by-lane, where he will have to suffer the scorn and sneers
of false Christians." [27] For while "there are worldly singularities,
there are Christian and salutary ones, too; and this singularity by
which one is differentiated from the crowd who tread the broad
path is what constitutes the straight and narrow path of the
Gospels. . . . Holy things will never be established or reestab-
lished so long as we have this fear of appearing singular." [28]
The Jansenist, then, would not be like "everybody else"; he
might sometimes have a nostalgia detaching him from his social sphere; the idea which he conceived of his perfection would
be less circumscribed by social duties, more individualistic in
character.

We might easily pursue these contrasts between bourgeois of
the Jansenist school and those of the Jesuit school. One, of upright and rigid character, was himself in the various occupations
of daily life; the other had the personality of his state, which
would make of him less a moral personality than a socially
determined being, subject to rules which it would be improper
and unChristian not to observe, the "first duty of probity" always being, as Père Bourdaloue puts it, to "submit to authority." [29] So that while the disciple of the Jesuit Fathers might be a
reliable man, who most probably would always remain prudently within the confines of mediocrity, the disciple of the
Jansenists might sometimes indulge in eccentricities. He was less
reliable; he might take the counsels of perfection literally, and
not be so docile. Under a middle-class exterior, he might often
conceal a romantic spirit, preserving a predilection for the heroic
feats of olden times.

"We should not imagine that, for our salvation, God demands
great austerities of us, or very extraordinary things. Each of
you, within the sphere of his own station, can easily achieve
salvation. The duties which must be performed, the obligations

which must be fulfilled, suffice to make you walk in the way of the saints." So a preacher tells his congregation (his sermon is preserved in Houdry's *Bibliothèque des prédicateurs*). The disciple of the Jesuits took care of his family; he saw to the education of his children.[30] He carefully carried out all his domestic duties, and was tempted to believe himself released from any other. "When everything is planned, and we do each thing at the proper time, we act like Christians, and it is in this way that many believers become holy and perfect, although they do not do any more than others. . . . Often they cannot be distinguished from others of the same walk of life save by their industry and their punctiliousness in carrying out their duties; they do what everyone else does, but they do it with a scrupulousness which takes the place, for them, of the greatest and finest actions."[31]

Such a man, abiding by what his masters had taught him, did not, of course, have any of the divine folly of Christianity. He might, perhaps, be lacking in grandeur, but, as a Jesuit Father put it, "To omit nothing small is a greater thing than the most difficult enterprises. It is in this sense that we are entitled to say that a number of *nothings* make up great virtue. Let us carry out all our duties . . . then we are dispensed both from great austerities and from the most heroic deeds."

The Jansenists did not share this view. "Here are saints of a singular kind," we read in the *Nouvelles Ecclésiastiques*; "they canonize themselves; they make saints of themselves *with many nothings;* and thanks to those *nothings,* they are dispensed from great austerities and heroic deeds, which cannot be of obligation for them. What an idea of sanctity! Nevertheless, if you do not adopt it, then according to Père Martel you are a harsh prophet, a teacher bristling with hard precepts, who has on his lips only the ancient discipline, only the severity of penance, only the maxims of an excessive rigorism."[32]

But whatever the differences between Jansenist and Jesuit approaches, what was most important for the bourgeois was to be able to find in the teaching of the ministers of the Church certain maxims which he might turn to his advantage. And it is a fact that the representatives of both camps were agreed in exhorting their flocks to carry out the duties of their state and in emphasizing the importance of a commonplace life, well planned and well regulated. Thus the Church seemed well qualified to educate the middle class. But would the bourgeois be willing to follow the path it indicated; would he be able to recognize himself in the image which the Church had formed of him and identify himself with the ideal which it proposed to him?

THE BOURGEOIS, DISCIPLE OF THE CHURCH

"How many obscure duties there are in every state of life," observes Père Griffet, "and how many others appear small and insignificant!" But for religion "there are no small or indifferent duties, because the overriding consideration, here, is duty." [33] In order to capture the hearts and minds of respectable citizens, the Church had to be able first and foremost to recognize and hallow commonplace values. This the eighteenth-century preachers realized very clearly. Thus, when Abbé Cambacérès exposes the all too common error of identifying virtue with "noble deeds," recognizing it only in "illustrious actions," [34] he appears to be championing the cause of the bourgeois paterfamilias who conscientiously carried out duties without glamour or distinction. "We have heroes of the stage," says Abbé Cambacérès again, "but few in private and domestic life." [35]

In speaking to the aristocracy, preachers had succeeded in striking the right dramatic note to enhance the luster of power; in speaking to the bourgeois, they lowered the pitch, estimating the values of ordinariness at its true worth and speaking a sensible and, if need be, sentimental language when they wanted to give added emphasis. If high tragedy was the Church's business, so was bourgeois comedy. At the same time, if worthy bourgeois living in contented mediocrity must not be approached in the tones used for the great, the proud, or the ambitious, neither must they be treated on a par with the poor, for the latter, while displaying a humility beyond all praise, were often far from respectable. Hence preachers, while continuing to laud poverty, were well prepared to concede the advantages represented by a decent competency and to agree that it facilitated the salvation of those who enjoyed it.

"It is very hard to preserve great virtue in great poverty," says a Jesuit Father; "it is a privilege granted to only a few chosen souls. The poor, usually, are so busy thinking about keeping alive that they have no time left to think about living virtuously." Therefore, he continues, "the wise man asked of the Lord, if not great riches, then at least enough to secure him against poverty." [36] That was what might be called the language of a reasonable man, without any of that excessive love of poverty which was little to the taste of a hard-working and orderly class of men. These words were written at the beginning of the eighteenth century; as time passed and the world became more "reasonable," the bourgeois were more easily to find priests who avoided all extremes and told them useful and sensible things, who knew that it was permissible to acquire wealth and useful to save in order to avoid poverty.

"I have told you before: poverty is the principal cause of the sorrows of households such as ours. But poverty is always a consequence of laziness and disorder in the affairs of the home." [37] Thus spoke a priest who lived in the latter half of the century, in the French provinces and who was in the habit of saying very reasonable things to people who wanted to hear nothing else. To avoid poverty, he recommended that they work and duly order their affairs. "Waste of time, negligence in the internal order of the household, unnecessary little expenditures, failure to harvest in due season and to sell the various products of one's land—these are so many causes of poverty and unhappiness." [38] In so doing, of course, there must be no departure from the rules of strict probity, "for to emerge from indigence and to get rich through fraud, ruse and injustice is the way to perdition and misery. Can there be any happy condition in this world without the witness of a good conscience? The answer can hardly be in dispute. But to provide for one's necessities and even to grow wealthy through work, through saving and through sober conduct is something God permits, and is highly esteemed by men." [39]

The bourgeois who enjoyed a modest fortune could not have put it any better; he was grateful to his pastor for showing him that God was of the same opinion. But the pastor was to go much farther; he knew that the life of the bourgeois was not always easy and that he often had trouble with his servants and workers. He told the latter that they were at fault in making life hard for their masters and complaining of their lot. "It is for men's welfare that God wished them all to be subject to one another; it is his Providence that has established inequality of conditions, so that some are born to command, others to obey. Some need servants, others are obliged to serve in that capacity." [40] Hence servants and workers had no reason to be dissatisfied with their lot. In any case, "there is a strong bias against the worker or servant who is always complaining; the best workers and servants are usually the least demanding." [41] It was always their own fault if they were not as happy as they could and should be. "The happiness of servants is nearly always in their own hands; and if they are not as happy as they would like to be, they should blame the fact on themselves alone."

The Pastor of Mayet opens up a whole little world for us, a world composed of worthy bourgeois and peasants living in contented mediocrity. They possessed both integrity and religion, the two being inseparable. "The designation, 'an irreligious man,' is enough to make it impossible to expect such a man to have been a good son, or to become a good husband, a good father, a good neighbor, a good citizen." And since the parishioners of Mayet wanted to be all these things, they were not lacking in religion.

As Christians, they were not too unkind to each other, but they were cautious and disinclined to trust the first comer. "We have to believe in the probity of all; nevertheless, without detriment to probity, we may be inwardly suspicious of those we do not know." Concerned with their good reputation, they wished to enjoy the esteem of their neighbors. "Conduct yourselves with such uprightness and good faith that no one may even suspect you of the least lack of probity. Always, and down to the least detail, be what is known as an upright man, that is, punctilious and just to the point of scruple." Though unassuming, and making no attempt to compare themselves with the great, they could not fail to lay claim to the dignity conferred upon them, in their eyes, by a life of probity and toil. "Birth and honors are of course respected; but a man is to be esteemed only by reason of his probity and the qualities that flow from it, and he is contemptible to the extent that he possesses the contrary defects." [42]

Abbé Froger, Pastor of Mayet, we should remember, was writing in the second half of the century; here was an enlightened priest, a "modern" man, laying down the moral law for his flock, giving counsel to farmers. But the ideas and maxims he developed are traceable to certain more venerable traditions to be found in Bourdaloue, Abbé Fleury, and also Nicole.

In the Church's legend, the bourgeois played a less brilliant part than the nobleman on the one hand and the poor man on the other; but he, too, wanted to find his place in the sanctuary, and be included among the characters hallowed by the Church, kings and beggars, monks and bishops, and so on. But this meant that the bourgeois had to fulfill certain conditions. He had to take his place between the great whom Providence had destined to be rich and the poor whom it had appointed to penury; that is, "between wealth and poverty, beyond the reach of the temptations of one or the other." [43]

He had to have qualities possessed neither by the great nor by the poor. The "nobility think that saving should be left to the vulgar conditions," [44] and the poor did not have the wherewithal to save. The bourgeois continued to save even if he was ennobled and displayed a spirit of order unfamiliar to the representatives of the old nobility. Referring to one of these nobles of undistinguished birth, Toussaint says, "he spends only his income, never touching the capital, which he intends one day to leave to his children. So true it is that the spirit of the commoner always pierces through some chink! Would a true nobleman descend into these details of bourgeois economy?" [45]

The aristocracy was concerned only with pleasure, the poor only with lamenting; the bourgeois was industrious and did useful work. And he was upright. These were not qualities which could gain him much glory, either in this world or even in the next; but such as he was, he might claim membership in the Christian world, provided that, in fulfilling his professional duties and his duties as a paterfamilias, he remembered that whatever he did, he was doing in obedience to God.

Thus the Church appeared prepared to receive the bourgeois and to confer titles of nobility on this commoner of secular origin. It showed him the path he should follow, proposed to him an ideal to which he should conform, made him conscious of his dignity, and recommended him to God. But if the Church thus endeavored to give much to the bourgeois, it seemed that what it said and did in his honor did not always correspond to all the aspirations of the bourgeoisie. And while the bourgeois could easily find in the sermons preached to him precepts in keeping with his mentality and related to values asserted by his class, he often found others directly contrary to what he wanted, and must want, according to the exigencies of social and economic development. When the Church urged him to be upright and honest, it seemed to want him to be content with that and have no other ambitions. Let him confine himself to his role between the great and the poor, without seeking to climb higher. Let him be content with modest comfort and not seek to get rich. Let him never seek to rise from his station, and let his children remain in the station of their father. In this bourgeois, the Church was hallowing the daily round, duties faithfully fulfilled and daily repeated, a monotony which ended only with death, the divine principle of order applied to the smallest things, social stability resting on solid foundations.

The type of middle class to which the Church was speaking consisted of sober persons, satisfied with their humdrum existence. They had no wish to climb higher, and were to continue in their professions and daily routine to the end of their days. Their children were to do likewise. These were steady people, leading a well-regulated existence which confined them within their particular spheres, from which they must on no account attempt to emerge. They were industrious folk, despising a life of mere idleness such as that of the aristocracy and carrying out their duties conscientiously, with particular emphasis on the principle of duty, duty being always translated in a series of small duties precisely defined according to concepts of class and profession. But in so doing, they expected no great success in life. They remained what they were and died respected by their neighbors; they were men of sober temperament, who never carried their ambitions very far.

Thus the Church translated the bourgeois mentality into a language in which mystery and common sense often formed a strange alloy. The bourgeois could not fail to recognize in it something that was familiar to him. Nevertheless, as the middle class evolved in the course of the eighteenth century, he did not find in it everything he wanted. The Church was far from underwriting all the values of the bourgeoisie; there were certain aspirations of the bourgeois class which it was unable to mold to a form that might be integrated in the framework of its traditional concepts, on which it could not set its seal, could not declare them approved and blessed by a divinity which had displayed greater liberality toward princes and nobles.

WORK

"Life is too small a thing that we should trouble to change our condition unless God's command requires it," says Quesnel.[46] "Nature loves . . . to expand; the spirit of Jesus Christ moves us to contract and to remain in our littleness. . . . Blessed is he who loves lowliness." [47] The Church, in this view, condemns those who exalt themselves. But the bourgeois by definition seeks to advance; it is in the nature of the middle class, as a social phenomenon, to spread, to be dilated, as it were. "I do not ask whether you are perfect, but I ask: are you Christian?" says the Pastor of Gap. "Are you content with the low or indifferent estate in which Providence caused you to be born? Had you been able to have your choice, would you not have preferred a condition which raised you up and placed you far above your present station? Do you not think that it is infinitely preferable to be rich rather than poor?" [48] The bourgeois was indeed unable to deny it. He had no difficulty in admitting that he infinitely preferred riches to poverty, and not only did he see nothing in the least wrong about such a preference, but ultimately he was even unable to understand why there should be such insistence on wanting it to be otherwise. He was proud of having made an income for himself; he regarded it as a virtue to succeed in business through intelligence and industry.

The middle class had its own built-in standards. It recognized some values and rejected others, and the bourgeois found nothing arbitrary in the judgments dictated to him by his class spirit. So long as the Church condemned what he considered sinful, as being contrary to the work he must do here below, he could take the Church's part, and was pleased to obtain divine confirmation of what his social sense prescribed. But when the clergy interpreted their God's commands in a manner too obviously contrary to the aspirations of the bourgeoisie, conflict was inevitable. The bourgeois wanted to work his way up, and the Church exhorted him to be humble. He feared nothing so much as to be poor, and the Church glorified poverty. He seemed to be challenging Divine Providence and, unconcerned with God, to be administering his affairs himself, an attitude of which the Church could not approve. How, then, were the aspirations of the bourgeoisie to be reconciled with the commandments of the Christian God?

On one point, nevertheless, the two powers might be expected to agree, namely, the importance they both attached to work. And since the God of the Christians blessed and rewarded toil, there was nothing, surely, to prevent him from approving the effort of the bourgeois. True, the bourgeois' wealth was often far from being the product of his own labor, but he always liked to be told that it was, and if he was to be made a Christian it was necessary to insist on this point and to repeat constantly that God wanted men to work and that he had a very particular predilection for those who toiled well and usefully here below. And in a certain sense, the Church appeared to take the bourgeois' part. It presented work as of divine institution and made of it a duty binding upon all its children, without any distinction whatsoever. Since its doctrine appeared to promote economic development, it must meet with the approval of the bourgeois. "Religion, by making of work a sacred duty, and of idleness a crime, is the soul and sustenance of useful industry," says an eighteenth-century preacher.[49] Why, then, should not the bourgeois support a religion which, by bestowing its blessing upon work, seemed to set the seal of its approval upon all who led a respectable life here below?

Jesus Christ lived on earth as a worker "in order to show that the general duty of men is to work in silence,"[50] says Abbé Fleury. The Church, so the faithful were told, censured those who did nothing; it condemned "a life of idleness, of pleasure, of visiting, of worldly ceremonies."[51] And why must the Christian work? "A laborious life always diminishes love of the world," says Nicole; "it diminishes love of life, attachment to temporal things, self-satisfaction."[52] A life of work, on this theory, prepares men for Christian virtues. But there were other, more fundamental reasons why it would be contrary to God's commandments to wish to shirk the duty of work. "We have to consider work as a penance which God has imposed on man, and from which no one is dispensed."[53] The obligation of work, the faithful were told, went back to Adam and Eve. Work, "to which God has condemned all men, is a consequence of and a punishment for sin."[54] And since all men were equally sinners, no one was entitled to think himself dispensed from work. "Since we are all born sinners, we are all without exception included in the sentence which condemned the first man to work, to infirmities, to death. Since, then, neither birth nor riches dispense anyone from the necessity of dying, no one, either, should believe himself dispensed from the obligation of working, under the pretext that he is of a distinguished condition, or that he does not need to work in order to live."[55] The rich, therefore, had no justification for thinking that they were dispensed from working. "But I am rich, you say, and why should I be obliged to work since I have enough to live on? Why, my dear hearer? Because all of this world's possessions cannot preserve you from the curse of sin, . . . because God, in giving you these good things, never intended to abdicate his rights."[56]

Work was a penalty; the Church never wearied of repeating it. But did the bourgeois see it thus? As far as the aristocracy and the poor were concerned, the Church seemed to be right, but not in regard to the bourgeois. The noble did not work, and it would have been a penance for him to do so. The poor, for their part, either worked or begged. And because it was hard, unprofitable labor, they would be perfectly willing to regard it as penance. But the bourgeois at work had nothing penitential about him. He worked and he succeeded, and the joys of his successes made him love his work. He was making money . . . that was the all-important point. Why, then, should he be pitied and looked upon as some sort of galley slave? He would be bored in a paradise with nothing to accomplish, and he was content where he was. It was, therefore, a waste of time to try to prove to him that God had cursed him. All he needed to refute the assertion was to point to his well-appointed home, his securities, and his income—tangible proofs that work was profitable—and he might argue, "The obligation to work is not a condemnation; it is the decision of a father who makes all creation tributary to our needs." [57]

Judging by the sermons of the period, the Church's terminology, nourished by venerable traditions, never quite succeeded in interpreting the modern concept of work as represented by the bourgeois. The Church, it seemed, had more understanding for the poor man who worked in the sweat of his brow; it consoled him, explained his fate to him. But if the sin of Adam could explain the fate of the poor, it did not explain the life led by the bourgeois, peacefully enjoying the fruits of his labor. What resemblance had this bourgeois, capably running his business, managing his property, increasing his revenues, to a child of sin? Would a criminal build such a clean and spacious dwelling for himself? Would he be surrounded by a happy and respectable family? Would he enjoy general esteem or have heirs who would bless him after his death? To listen to some ministers of the Church, there was no other kind of work but that of the galley slave, which led absolutely nowhere; they were apparently prepared to ignore the work of the bourgeois, which led to prosperity.

The Church seemed to have preserved a view of life to which the bourgeoisie was giving the lie. Preachers insisted on the vanity of human effort and pointed to what might be called the negative aspect of work. "This work which, in the state of innocence, would have been but an agreeable pastime, becomes in the state of sin a penalty which afflicts and wearies to the point of sweat." [58] This was why "an occupation which is merely pleasurable and which one undertakes by choice is the work of innocent man, but not that of the sinner, whose whole life must be one of continual penance." [59] What was particularly meritorious in work, according to this view, was the constraint which man imposed on himself by his work and which made of work a form of penance. Man is "exiled like a criminal in an accursed land," says the Pastor of Gap. As proof, he cites the example of the merchant. "How much bustle, discomfort, journeying, night and day, in all weathers and all seasons of the year"; he shows us the lawyer, "with so many things to learn, so many volumes to read, difficulties to clarify, sleepless nights." [60] He was forgetting that this "exile" had deliberately chosen to become a merchant or a lawyer, that he was making money, that his work was profitable. He failed to see that all the trouble was compensated by the completely unified middle-class life which was its fruit and that the bourgeois' work could never be considered in isolation from its objective, which was to create a position for himself, and achieve a life of ease.

The Church always seemed to be looking at the form rather than at the content of work, at the effort rather than at the result. To work, we read, meant to order one's life, submit to its rules, subject oneself to discipline. Preachers liked in this connection to bring up the example of religious orders, where carefully planned days followed one another in monotonous succession. This example they would cite to members of the bourgeoisie, living in some affluence. "Those who have to work constantly to earn their living," says the Pastor of Gap again, "know their obligations and want to fulfill them." The Church, therefore, did not need to prescribe a regular life for them. But to others, whose "living was already made, as they say," the pastor addressed accusations and exhortations. "It is a great disorder," he says, "to live at haphazard, and at the whim of chance, never knowing in the morning what one must do, nor in the evening what one has done. Apart from the fact that such a life must necessarily lead to much tedium, it is absolutely incompatible with the spirit of Christianity, which is a spirit of order and activity, a spirit of wisdom and caution, a spirit of fear and trembling, by reason of the temptations of every kind to which we are exposed, and against which it is not possible to defend ourselves if we live an idle and useless life." The wealthy bourgeois should create obligations for himself, and to incite him to do so our pastor tells him how life is organized in the cloister. "One of the greatest advantages enjoyed in religious houses and in all those where men live in community is that they abide by a certain rule which embraces all the hours of the day, prescribing the use of every minute. . . . And how comes it, my dear parishioner, that you do not draw up for yourself a rule indicating in detail what you should do from morning to night?" [61]

The bourgeois was only too inclined to regulate his life; he was a man of order. But he was more than that; he was an enterprising individual who wanted to get ahead in order to succeed. Imagine the bourgeois trained according to the rules of the Church. He would retire and rise at regular hours. He would have his hours of work and of rest. He would never make excessive efforts; he would not exceed the limits he had set himself. His life would breathe regularity. His days would follow each other in perfect uniformity, and nothing must be disturbed in the established order. Work, for him, would be a part of the general rhythm of his life; he would work not out of an urge to succeed, but in order to give substance to his life, which otherwise would have none. The Church would bless him because of his steadiness and because he was content with the *status quo*. That bourgeois undoubtedly existed in flesh and blood; he was the model employee.

The Church helped to form a type of average bourgeoisie and to populate offices. A respectable man, this unassuming and well-ordered bourgeois would go to Mass every Sunday, as he went to his office on weekdays. Everything about him exuded regularity; he worked out of a spirit of order, not out of ambition; his advancement was regulated beforehand, leaving no room for those extravagant hopes so dangerous to the Christian soul. The Church, he knew, loved order, as being of divine institution. He, too, loved order. And coming to church, he found in his pastor's sermons, as well as in his books of devotion, useful confirmation of his convictions. For he was told, to his entire approval, that a man's life must be regulated, that he must form habits and stick to them. That, he learned, was useful not only in order to make a position for oneself here below, but also for salvation. "The great advantage we draw from this practice is that we can achieve holiness with less difficulty." The road to heaven would always appear arduous. "To facilitate that road, and cut short this path which is represented to us as so difficult and requiring such long toil, all that is needed is to order the ordinary actions of our lives and walk in that path; for then nothing can stop us, habit will smooth out all the difficulties and will make easy for us what previously had appeared impracticable; one day will regulate the next; we shall know what we have to do at a certain hour, at a certain time; and thus, treading an even path, and taking the same road every day, we shall find nothing to disturb us." [62]

The Christian, therefore, would not fear the monotony of a life in which the days succeeded one another uniformly, hour repeating hour; on the contrary, he would wish it to be so and would not desire to move out of the circle he had traced for himself. Indeed, he should wherever possible choose one occupation rather than another if it was the one he had set himself in his rule of life, "because it has this advantage over another, that in preferring it we avoid frivolity, disorder and change, and therefore have reason to believe that we are acting in a manner more consonant with the will of God, all of whose works are ordered." [63]

That should be the manner of life of all who submitted themselves in all things to the will of God, never swerving from the path they had traced for themselves. "They have established a program for themselves which they follow, and nothing disturbs them, neither family difficulties, nor duties arising out of convention or propriety, nor visits of relatives or friends. As they have started, so they continue always; the same spirit leads them, the same guide shows them the way. They are subject to it in all things, and observe everything exactly according to rule; and since that rule is marked for them from above, and they seek not their own will but the will of the heavenly Father which is immutable, they persevere in the pattern laid down for them." That was the part of the righteous man. For "the truly righteous man is one whose life is unified," a man "settled and ordered in his habits, . . . who does nothing astonishing, . . . nothing disturbing or bizarre," [64] and who, living "a uniform life outside which all would be confusion," always respects order "which he knows to be of divine origin." [65]

In its glorification of the spirit of order, the Church seemed to be giving its sanction to the type of bourgeois who was concerned to fulfill his duties scrupulously and content to remain within his own sphere. But this bourgeois, whom modern eighteenth-century society certainly could not dispense with, was far from summing up in himself the whole spirit of his class. There was another type of bourgeois who had nothing about him of a monk transplanted into an office. He was energetic, pushing, by no means content to confine himself to a life rhythmically punctuated by work; rather, he was concerned to grow, to achieve power and wealth through his own effort. But what would the Church say of this bourgeois who was to become the monarch of the modern age? It did not like him; it could not like him; the impulse that moved him was too contrary to its own. He seemed intent on flouting God; trusting in his own strength, he seemed to want to organize his life independently of the plans of Divine Providence.

PLANNING AND PROVIDENCE

"If the thought of Divine Providence is to produce in us that constant attention to God of which we are now speaking," says Nicole, "we must not be satisfied to recognize and adore it in great events; but as it extends to everything, and there is no situation, however insignificant, which is not ordered by God, we must accustom ourselves to honor him in everything, and to refer to him the smallest things that happen to us." [66] But the worldly persistently reduced the area in which Divine

Providence was permitted to hold sway. "We do not doubt that a general Providence exists, but are we really convinced that this universal Providence becomes a special Providence for each one of us?" The reply could not be in doubt; even if people did not deny Providence, "they act as though there was none," and the example of those who sought to make money was sufficient evidence that they did not place their trust in God.

"God has told us a thousand times that all our confidence must be in him. . . . But what of this man who means to get rich no matter by what means, or who possesses great wealth? Even if he does not say that he does not need God to make his fortune, and that he will make it regardless of God, he acts as though he had no need of God's help or favor." [67] How otherwise explain the urge for riches that had seized all hearts? "Whence comes this acquisitiveness? From the small confidence that we have in Providence, from our excessive fear of failure, from the fact that we take no account of the help of God, who is able, if he so chooses, to assist us in our necessity." The faithful, apparently, were disinclined to believe such teachings. "People worry, they are restless, because they suppose that by human exertions we can achieve what we lack; we do not want to believe that God has undertaken to provide for us." Or again, "You place all your trust in your own strength, whereas religion requires that you place it in the blessing which God gives to your labors." [68]

Planning, for the bourgeois, had become "the universal panacea; combined with moderation, it prevents all ills, of whatever kind they may be." [69] The bourgeois did not rely on divine intervention; he preferred to trust in himself; he acted and looked ahead. "Do I have to expect God to work miracles in my behalf?" he asked. "I have children; don't I have to work to establish them? I have possessions; must I not look to their conservation? I have a considerable rank; should I not maintain it?" Those were the questions which he put to his pastor when the latter preached confidence in God to him. Those were the arguments which justified him in his own eyes, the "most common pretext in which self-interest and ambition are clothed in the world." [70]

But what gave the bourgeois such self-confidence? How was it that he appeared sure of the success of his undertakings and that the unknown did not frighten him? "The successful or unsuccessful outcome of our affairs usually results from a thousand particular circumstances," his preachers told him, "and from a thousand incidents independent of ourselves; a meeting, an incident, a trifle, it seems, has often halted the greatest enterprises or brought them to a happy conclusion." How should a man ever control circumstances, take account of all eventualities? "Use every ounce of human prudence; you will never be able to foresee those circumstances, those occasions, those adverse or favorable seasons; you will never be able either to bring them nearer or to sweep them away. Thus it is only God whose wisdom and power are sufficiently far-reaching to know the future from afar, to dispose it little by little, and by means absolutely hidden from us; to arrange, to proportion, to combine so many means which sometimes seem directly contrary to one another and to pull all the multiple strings at the appropriate time." [71] The bourgeois, nevertheless, looked ahead, calculated, ensured himself against the unknown; he deliberated with his notary in order to have contracts in good and due form in his hands; he established himself solidly; and, confirmed in his judgment by ever recurring experience, he felt himself master of his destiny and forgot Divine Providence.

"Were you born poor? God wanted it so. This destiny emanated no less from the counsels of his wisdom than the fall or the establishment of kingdoms and empires. Again, if you were born to be rich, and are fallen into poverty; if normally you should have been able to count on a fortune which has eluded you, then God wanted it so; it is he, you need not doubt it, who stripped you of all the things which you have lost; he could as easily have left you in abundance." [72]

But that was precisely where the bourgeois disagreed; had he become poor, he must be in some way to blame; had he become rich, he took the credit himself. He was establishing his own responsibilities as against the deity. There were laws governing the economic order which must be respected if the process of business was not to be disrupted, as, for instance, "that communication in transactions of the superfluous for the necessary which is so consonant with the order of Divine Providence." [73] But after instituting this admirable order in the world, the deity should have to leave men to their own devices, so that they could get rich. What would then become of God? When "God is nothing in relation to ourselves, of what consequence is it that he exists in himself?" asks Abbé de Boulogne. And he continues, "Of all the errors concerning the divinity, the most dangerous and the most incurable is not to deny his existence, but to forget him; not revolt, but indifference." [74] The worldly, for the most part, did not deny the existence of God, but they set him aside; they closed the doors of their houses to him, while complimenting him profusely on the admirable order which he had established in the universe.

"Will he who commanded the waves, and set limits to its mutinous tides, be vanquished by the false prudence of men?" asks Touron.[75] Foresight had triumphed over Providence, reasoned calculation over confidence in God; the prudent and alert bourgeois no longer expected prosperity in his business or happiness for his children save from his own effort. Thus God was gradually eliminated from everyday life, and men were to take over the responsibility of ordering the small details of life themselves.

"Since a philosophy . . . can believe only what it understands, it reduces all happenings to general laws. And the mass of the faithful, through the inclination of their hearts, develop somewhat the same attitude." [76] It is a fact that the philosophers contributed quite substantially to limiting the attributes of the God of the Christians. But it remains a moot point whether the wary and farsighted bourgeois did not do more to dethrone the ancient divinity than did the philosopher or scientist. He, too, experimented, and his experiment was successful; he could prove by his own example that an existence might be built up from which unknown factors, illness or death excepted, might be ruled out. He, too, applied calculation to the data of experience. He, too, recognizing the laws governing the order of things and connecting effects with causes, was able to plan and thus to extend effective human action in an area which previously had been most elusive, namely, his destiny. Was not everything in his life falling into place, connecting up? Had not the investment which he had made a few years earlier in fact produced what it was supposed to produce; had he not been right in refusing a particular contract; was there not a perfect logic in all this? Capricious fortune and the Christian God alike were out of place in this system of logic, too closely woven to leave room for any mystical influences from beyond. Divine Providence had no place in this expertly regulated and ordered life; the end-of-year balance sheets were in the nature of manuals of experimental science, driving out mystery.

"If there is a Providence . . . on which all things depend," we read in a sermon of the period, "why, then, children of men, do you rely on the frail support of creatures? Why, seeing yourselves deluged with possessions and riches, according as Providence has ordained, do you attribute them to your own industry, as though they were its fruit?" [77] But the bourgeois knew that he owed his fortune to himself; books in hand, he could show how everything had been accomplished. God had made man, but the bourgeois had made himself. How should he still see in the fruit of his farsighted action, of his intelligence and probity, some miraculous intervention of Divine Providence?

The prudent and farsighted investor was entering into competition with the God of the Christians. For the most part, as yet, he did not set his aims too high. He confined himself to desiring the necessary; he had in view only a modest competency. To achieve it, he preferred to rely on well-planned dividends and contracts in good and due form rather than on Divine Providence, whose effects, he felt, were always incalculable and sometimes gave the lie to the best established prognostics. But, as time passed, he was to acquire a taste for riches, and he would be accused from the pulpit of avarice and ambition.

"I concede," says the Pastor of Gap, "that a man who has only the salary from his job to live on, and who cannot be sure of keeping that job as long as he wants, may, without offense to Providence, save up a certain amount in order not to be reduced to beggary should he lose his job." Similarly, he did not condemn those "whose only livelihood is from their work, and who save against the day when they will no longer be able to work." But, he says, "the man who amasses money in order to spend the rest of his days doing nothing is not upright of heart," and, he adds, "his conscience is far from easy."

But Réguis' astonishment and indignation exceed all bounds when he comes to speak of the bourgeois whose income "is assured for always." "There are some among them who hoard," he says, "and it is laughable, or rather, pitiful, to see them accumulate money, coin by coin, contract by contract, rent upon rent; each year turning interest into new capital, which produces more interest, from which more capital is formed, and so on, as long as their hands and feet remain to them!" So the Pastor of Gap could not help but look upon the fundamental principles of nascent capitalism as altogether ridiculous. And what was his argument to show that people were wrong in planning and building up incomes? "Is Providence nothing, then? You don't believe in it, then? Or you do not trust it? Is it your money, then, which secures you against any accident which might befall you? Is money, then, your god?"

For Abbé Réguis, all this was mere folly; it was a sickness which gradually attacked the whole human organism and rendered the soul unsusceptible of salvation. "At first, you will look with complacency at the small sum which you have put by in case of need, and for very good reason. If you come to feel like increasing it, rounding it out, forming a little capital, and if you succumb to that temptation, you are lost; a canker forms which will devour you to the bone; a gangrene will have infected your heart and will slay your soul; and you might just as well—God forgive me!—have apostatized."[78]

According to this view, then, the urge to build up an income was proof of a corrupt heart and a disordered mind, and capitalism was a malady. But let us listen farther. "Your frenzied hoarding deprives your fellow citizens of a currency needful to them. What would become of workers? or of trade? What would the poor live on, if all those who had money piled it up and locked it up, as you do?" How could reasonable men, concerned with their salvation, act in such a manner? "It is thus a twofold folly," says the Pastor of Gap, "to lie sunk in forgetfulness of one's salvation in order to acquire wealth or get ahead in this world. For apart from the folly of sacrificing one's soul for money, for a little smoke, it is also folly to bustle, to worry, to be concerned, as are the ambitious and the miserly, to acquire the things which Providence has promised to give gratis to those who first and foremost seek the kingdom of God and his righteousness." [79] Clearly, the pastor and the new bourgeois did not agree; a profound misunderstanding separated the Church and the newly rich.

"What a terrible opposition!" says a theologian of the period. "A faith which teaches men only scorn for terrestrial and perishable things, and a life entirely oriented to acquiring, conserving and accumulating them by whatever means, whether just or unjust, and dictated by insatiable avarice." [80] Persons "of a certain sort" were not prepared to agree on this point. "After all," they said, "what harm is there in being or becoming wealthy, when one acquires or possesses only lawful riches?" [81] What harm, once they had become wealthy, in wanting to move up in the world? "I have acquired nothing save by legitimate means; what should I do with my income and my savings if I did not advance above the condition of my fathers?" [82] The ministers of the Church answered that such doubts could come "only from the bewitchment of riches themselves, or from failure to reflect on the sentiments which they usually inspire, sentiments contrary to all the duties which we should fulfill, either toward ourselves or toward our neighbor, or toward God." [83] But this did not prevent the worldly from wanting to be rich and getting ahead. "The only concern, now, is to become wealthy," says a preacher of the period, "and self-interest becomes the sole principle of emulation." [84] "In vain do the Scriptures tell us that to amass goods on earth is to amass a great heap of sand, which at the first push will collapse over our heads," says another preacher.[85] The worldly were increasingly self-confident and defiant of Divine Providence; they were becoming masters of a world to which the Church would continue to refuse its recognition.

THE NEWLY RICH

"Woe to the man who constantly desires to multiply his income, because in multiplying his own, he inevitably despoils his neighbor," says Père Bourdaloue. "To become rich through long savings or assiduous industry was the path followed in the simplicity of the early centuries; but in our day people have discovered much more convenient short cuts. By discharging an office, or giving advice, or joining some group, . . . a man finds himself in a few years, or a few months, as though transfigured, and from the dust in which he was crawling, he is lifted to the pinnacle." Père Bourdaloue was amazed and outraged at the great fortunes piled up in dubious ways. "It is inconceivable, for instance, that with settled profits and emoluments one should suddenly make fortunes such as those to which we refer." Consequently, Père Bourdaloue concludes, "Bad faith, not to say double-dealing, must have been involved, and it must have lent wings to cupidity to make it take so prompt and rapid a flight." [86]

Hence suspicion inevitably attached to those who made their money too fast. "Men very rarely acquire great possessions in a short space of time without committing many injustices," observes Mésenguy. "Wealth thus acquired will soon be dissipated, or will become a cause of eternal unhappiness to him who has acquired it." [87] For what were the means employed by those who sought wealth at any cost? "People think that money should be put to work, and at the highest available rate," says a Jesuit Father in a violent diatribe against those who were laying the foundations of the new economic order. And he continues, "People manage in a short time to obtain interest equal to the principal; and in so doing to take advantage of the misfortune of their neighbor, who is lucky, they say, to have any money left at all." [88] The Church could not but deplore a situation where, "in order to get rich quickly, a man jettisons innocence, relinquishes probity, divests himself even of humanity, devouring the substance of the poor, ruining the widow and the orphan." [89] But although the objection seemed often to be only to certain excesses, what the Church was really proscribing were the new economic and financial methods leading to the capitalist era. It adhered to the principle of ordered profits and emoluments at a time when large-scale speculation was emerging on the scene.

God, we read, "only tolerates" the successes of the rich. "In many cases, they have arrived at such great possessions against his designs." [90] The clergy were reluctant to place responsibility for great fortunes on God; the role of Providence was obscured. For the God of the Christians could not approve of such men, "poor by birth, rich by industry, formed out of nothingness by nature and glorified by fortune," [91] and they, in turn, did not like the clergy. The Pastor of Gap notes among men who had grown rich "a marked aversion for the ministers of the Church." A whole class was coming into being composed of men who sought to advance in life and who, avid of success, were casting aside old traditions. They gave priority to economic values, and the character which they assigned to private life, as to political life, did not square with the positions represented by the Church. "Today we are told only about the force, the splendor, the security of empires, and we are told nothing about the obligation of fidelity to the Gospel"; instead of emphasizing the evangelical principles, "we are constantly told that the important thing is to get rich, to get ahead, to live in luxury, to criticize the clergy and abolish celibacy." [92]

The Church seemed to hold aloof from the new middle class. There were constant references to the confusion created by those who sought at all costs to "better themselves—cutting right through the crowd, turning aside, jostling one another, . . . taking one another's place." Such men were everywhere, "among the military, at the bar, among merchants, in the Church, in our poor villages, among the lowest of the common people. . . ." "I want to get rich, they say; to buy offices and lands; to change my name and station; to shake off the dust in which my fathers lived." They would stick at nothing. "You have to suck the blood of the widow, despoil the heritage of the orphan, oppress, stifle, devour the poor who have not the strength to resist you; you have to raise your houses on the ruins of twenty families, and batten on the purest substance of the region in which you have settled—to the misfortune of those who live there." [93]

The Pastor of Gap accused these new men of falling into the sin of ambition, a sin having "this property, that it directly attacks the principles of all the Christian virtues, that is, humility and self-abnegation." [94] He held it against the newly rich that they were disturbing the established order by creating a regrettable confusion in the estates of which that order was composed. "But what is the use of speaking of estates? They are all mixed up today; we no longer know each other, and our ears are constantly ringing with the words, 'he isn't better than I'; 'I'm as rich as he is.' The son of a wretched artisan, whose father had amassed some property, sells his tools and boards up his store, and then suddenly changes his clothes, his tone, his language, I almost said his face. In public records he has himself credited with the title of 'Sir,' and he would take it amiss were we not to describe him thus in our registers—in our registers, where he is named son of a mason, or of a furrier, or of a shoemaker or something of that kind. . . . Your father tilled his field himself, and you want to have tenant-farmers; your mother was dressed in wool, and you want silk for your wife and daughters, and everything else in proportion," he continues, speaking in particular to peasants who had grown prosperous. "The frenzy to lift yourselves above your condition almost completely extinguishes the spirit of Christianity in you," he tells the ambitious bourgeois and those who aspired to become bourgeois. "I see only pride, envy, jealousy; you are damning yourselves. Oh, in the name of God, be what you are, each of you! Be as your fathers were, live as they lived, and don't try to depart from the station in which Providence caused you to be born."

As we see, Réguis' sermons provide very keen insights into the origins of the bourgeois mentality. We are witnessing the emergence of a new world, and at the same time we hear a pastor defying those who, after grasping social power, were soon to grasp political power. There is sometimes a tragic grandeur in his blunt and often forthright language. "How I love to see among you, my dear parishioners, those truly Christian homes where the children preserve, from generation to generation, simplicity, modesty, sobriety in everything which they have inherited from their forefathers, having no other ambition but to enrich their fields, increase their flocks, establish their families, not by brilliant but by solid marriages, and with persons of their own station." [95] The Pastor of Gap was fighting a lost battle, opposing an irresistible movement, whose extent and importance he did not realize. And like the humble pastor, the Church seemed ill at ease with these new men who ignored the counsels of Divine Providence, yet succeeded in life and were to gain the ascendancy.

"If there is a station in life in which the possession of wealth seems legitimate, it is probably that of the nobility; they are born rich, and Providence, which caused them to be great, seems to have made them rich at the same time in order to sustain their grandeur. Removed from trade, they are ignorant of its deceits and sordid gains, and owe their possessions to their birth alone." [96] The ministers of the Church seemed to look askance at the bourgeois for getting rich without asking God's permission and to have a preference for the old nobility.

"Our blindness is extreme," says a defender of religion. "Beguiled by the luster of opulence, we have unfortunately given riches too high a rating. Our more religious fathers, who were also, unwittingly, more astute, preserved a respect for blood. The power of States based on nobility holds up best. Accustomed to looking to the antiquity of his race and the virtues of his ancestors as sources of pride, the noble sees his greatness less in what he is than in what he has been and what he will be to the most distant generation. The more he contemplates the centuries before and after him, the more a secret and just pride fills his soul. His personal existence is barely more than a moment in his greatness. What he loses for himself, time will pay to his descendants. The rich man, on the contrary, sees all his glory gathered up before his eyes. Only the present moment belongs to him. Nothing suggests to him ideas of perpetuity. He feels that the luster of gold can reflect nothing durable on his name; everything prompts him to enjoy himself, and to do so as quickly as possible." [97]

Thus the newly rich were intruders, men without a past, children of the present. Whence had they come, and what was their function in a world where Divine Providence had foreordained all things, tracing for each station and for each individual the lines along which each must evolve? "No longer do we see a single order of citizens where the ancient customs are preserved. No longer are we able, in the most exalted estates, to . . . distinguish between refined and common society. There are as many moral codes as there are individuals. Oh, strange manners!" [98] The Church could not discern the emerging pattern in this society in process of transformation, in which all values seemed to be displaced. It was unable to meet the new rulers halfway; it refused them its sanction and seemed to wish to halt the movement leading to the development of industrial and financial capitalism.

"In the interests of the public weal, the prince should not permit manufactures which damage the interests of the poor and of small artisans by taking away the substance of their work and employing machines, driven by wind or water, to do the work formerly done by the common people. He should also oppose all inventions whereby one man takes the place of several, and which therefore deprive them of their work and livelihood." [99] Such was the view of Abbé Duguet, a convinced Jansenist. Fontenay, in his *Lettres sur l'Education des Princes,* criticizes such principles. "He who would act in accordance with these principles would destroy not only the arts, which constitute the glory of a nation, but even the manufactures most useful to a State. On the pretext of correcting a few abuses, he would run the risk of destroying everything. He would have all theatrical performances closed, all paintings burned and all statues smashed. Were the Goths any worse when they sacked Rome? Will such men always preach barbarism to us, on the specious pretext of devotion? Is it the way to inspire devotion to paint it so barbarous? What bizarre fanaticism to wish to turn towns into cloisters, and princely palaces into retreats for solitaries! Let us blush for eternity for all these excesses, and impute not to religion but to a spirit of authoritarianism, which possesses most of these extravagant doctors, teachings which lead only to the destruction of society." [100]

It was not necessary, then, for the Church, "on the pretext of devotion," to oppose all economic development. Had it chided kings for building splendid palaces and fostering the arts? It was the newly rich that the Church objected to, those who had acquired riches without asking permission of Divine Providence. What it combated above all was the spirit underlying nascent capitalism itself, which was destroying the established order. "Hands which amass wealth on every side, and accumulate with such haste, are not very clean," says Père Croiset. "More or less instantaneous fortunes have something miraculous about them; was it God who performed the miracle?" The riches of those who had thus deliberately piled up wealth were not "legitimate"; their owners were upstarts who had no right to them. They were usurpers, as proved by the fact that "one finds few of these new mansions which are not built on the ruins of the old, and these newly rich rarely appear on the scene without several ancient and universally respected families disappearing, and virtually reduced to beggary." [101]

Riches should be regarded as but the external sign of rank; they should exist only in relation to the place one occupied in the social hierarchy. To be rich was not an isolated attribute; it was the privilege of persons of quality. If kings combined magnificence with magnanimity, a "magnificence which appears in the great works devoted to the public good, in constructions which bring glory upon a nation, which command the respect of subjects and strangers and render immortal the names of princes," that was in the order of things. But what business was it of this bourgeois, who, grown rich, often made himself equal to the powerful of the earth, without being able to justify himself before God, without being able to show titles authorizing him to combine "great expenditures with great designs"? [102] By what right was he rich? From whom did he hold his power? By what sign could it be recognized that God approved of him?

Kings, noble lords, men of quality of lesser rank, were rich, each according to what he represented. To seek to separate titles and riches seemed contrary to the order of Divine Providence. For those who had thus *become* rich must have wanted to be rich. And that was what could not be squared with the spirit of the Gospels. A man might remain rich once he was rich at least if the proper distinction was made between counsels and precepts, but he could not want to become rich without ceasing to be a Christian.

But what, then, of all those business men, merchants, bankers, and the like, who sought riches and were proud of it, who considered that riches were the due of those, more intelligent and enterprising than others, who were able to look ahead and take advantage of circumstances? Were they not intruders in a world where it was God's business to distribute riches, and not the business of individuals to acquire them according to their own will?

12 · THE CHURCH AND CAPITALISM

COMMERCE

"Those who accumulate possessions without end and without measure," says Père Thomassin; "those who are constantly adding new fields and new houses to their heritage; those who hoard huge quantities of wheat in order to sell at what to them is the opportune moment; those who lend at interest to poor and rich alike, think they are doing nothing against reason, against equity, and finally against divine law, because, as they imagine, they do no harm to anyone and indeed benefit those who would otherwise fall into great necessity." And yet, continues Père Thomassin, "it is an injustice, and one which includes many others, for a single individual to possess so much land and so many houses, and to think daily of acquiring more, which cannot be done without dispossessing a large number of former owners; that a single individual should gather the fruits of all the lands of a fairly large region, and should thus deprive a large multitude of men who are thereby reduced to beggary; that a single individual should concentrate all the fertility of the countryside in his own hands, and force so many people to live on his largesse; that a single individual should seek to be the arbiter of the life or death of an entire population. It is the greatest of all injustices, . . . since it means declaring war on the human race, and driving more people from their homes than can a war."[1]

The dealings of these grabbers, we read, created the great number of poor. "If no one acquired or possessed more than he needed for his maintenance and that of his family, there would be no destitute in the world at all. It is thus this urge to acquire more and more which brings so many poor people to penury. Can this immense greed for acquisition be innocent, or only slightly criminal?"

In directing his attacks on the monopolists of his time, Père Thomassin might seem to have had in mind only the excesses of a criminal cupidity. But in fact he was attacking a whole class, "that small number of rich people who grab for themselves the common heritage of the human race,"[2] all those possessed by the desire for wealth. Whatever their efforts in other fields, they always endangered their own salvation; this applied to all "merchants, bankers, tax farmers and business men," who exercised a "very dangerous" profession, as an eighteenth-century writer put it, citing Père Thomassin, "because self-interest and the urge to accumulate wealth being the soul of these professions, he who exercises them is constantly exposed to the temptation of acquiring wealth by illegitimate means, when he cannot do so by just and lawful ones."[3]

It was thus very hard for the Christian to be a merchant without endangering his salvation. To quote Bayle, "of all the occupations of life, there is hardly any more blameworthy, judged by the criteria of religion, than that which is the most common, namely, that of those who work to acquire possessions, either by trade or by other honest means. The means of gaining wealth which, humanly speaking, are the most legitimate, are contrary not only to the spirit of the Gospels, but also to the specific prohibitions of Jesus Christ and of his apostles."[4] Theologians did indeed attempt to determine more just procedures of conducting trade so as not to condemn it out of hand. But the point remained, how could a man be a merchant according to the spirit of the Gospel? Obviously a man engaged in trade only with a view to acquiring wealth; how, then, was he to acquire wealth without contravening the law of God?

"For although commerce is in itself innocent, it is not so in the manner in which most people conduct it. Fraud, deceit, perjury, excessive love of gain are very often involved. A man is in an habitual disposition to prefer his own interests to those of his neighbor, to take advantage of his losses, of his ignorance, of his needs; to deprive him of what he needs in order to achieve abundance for himself. Those who buy and sell rarely have a spirit of justice, good faith and sincerity. When they buy, they pay less than the price; when they sell, they overprice." [5] So speaks a Jansenist. Let us listen, now, to a Jesuit, Père Croiset, on the subject. "When a man conducts trade in a Christian manner, he is very careful, industrious and prudent in his affairs, but not oversolicitous; however hard-working he may be, he never transgresses the limits of the law which God has prescribed. Industry, here, is always governed by the spirit of the Gospel maxims. He seeks to profit by everything, but never takes advantage of anything." [6]

But this was hardly typical of most of those engaged in commerce. The same Jesuit observes, "They take advantage of everything—loans, services, acts of kindness, even of the scourges with which God afflicts his people. The crop failure which should open the granaries closes them." Thus each sought to enrich himself at the expense of others; no holds were barred, not even speculation on the public distress. "Yet this, today, is called being lucky, being farsighted, having a knack for money-making; it is little short of being regarded as a dispensation of Providence, in favor of the most detestable cupidity." [7]

The Christian merchant would have little solicitude about his business, says Père Croiset. He would always, it seemed, be afraid of getting rich too fast. And since his conscience would not be altogether at ease when his business was too profitable, he would be eager to lavish alms in order to ensure his soul's salvation. Even if he abided by the most exacting standards of honesty, he would always have scruples, never being really sure that he was on the road leading to heaven. For once he was wealthy, he would find it hard to prove that he had not tried to reach that condition and that he had not preferred to be a rich man, according to the world, rather than a poor man, according to the Gospel.

But how many in fact conducted business in the spirit of the Gospels? The reply was not in doubt. "Is a man in business? He wants to make his pile." [8] "People think only of discovering new ways of getting rich." [9] The great ambition was to emerge from "Christian ordinariness," [10] no matter by what means. "They want to get rich, and they hope to be as lucky as many others who did not start with any greater funds. They are ambitious, and they think they are smart enough. Success seems hardly in doubt for the bold man. The sea on which he travels is very stormy, filled with reefs, and famed for shipwrecks; but people continue to travel on it. They figure that, when the winds are contrary, they will use oars; and despite pirates and a hundred other dangers, each hopes to arrive safely in port."

The ministers of the Church fought the new mentality. While the Church was prepared to bless the reasonable efforts of the small tradesman whose undertakings did not overstep the boundaries set by human and Christian prudence, it was nonplused by the bold and enterprising merchant who sought to get rich quick. This figure was a stranger in the Church's world, not merely a sinner who flouted God, but a strange and bizarre personage whom the preachers could not understand and whom they even regarded as a little ridiculous. "A business man can be recognized wherever he goes," says Père Croiset. "A thoughtful and troubled mien, eyes always inflamed, the face of a solitary man, awkward manners, tacitly dismissing whatever is not concerned with loans, exchange or interest; all this entitles us to ask whether there is any state of life in the world more painful and more austere; might we not add, more laborious and unrewarding? . . . The day does not suffice for their crushing occupations, and they deny themselves the rest which one does not refuse even to slaves. The night seems to dispute their industry with the day; meals, rest, all is interrupted by business —payments, commissions, accounting; in all things there is a constraint, a servitude, which barely leaves them time to remember that they are Christians." [11]

The Church would, of course, condemn the pleasure-loving

worldling, but it could understand him, love of pleasure being a vice too natural to require long inquiry into its motives. It was quite another matter with these new men who were always busy, who "spend their days and wear out their health in an application of the mind, in a multiplicity of occupations which oppress it."[12] How explain the workings of their minds? For "what more cramping assiduity at a desk? What more stubborn and more tedious work, what more intense concentration than that of businessmen. . . . Glued night and day to their account books and piles of letters and papers; inaccessible to any but agents and clerks; invisible to their best friends, and often even to their own families; their minds always taut, always preoccupied; their heads always filled with projects, incidents, companies, new methods of trade and banking."[13]

That was Père Croiset's picture of the businessman who had made his appearance in a world of idlers athirst for pleasure, forming a strange contrast with his contemporaries, the men of quality, whom Père Croiset upbraids for their indolence. But if idleness was the "mother of all vices," might not those who denied themselves even sleep and who wore out their strength by work be entitled to regard themselves as virtuous? For "what more laborious condition, what less idle life," than theirs? "Desiccating study, devouring cares, unremitting attention accompany even meals, even rest. No leisure to relax, no day without trouble, no success without alarums, . . . engulfed in a welter of business. What solitary is so busy? And in what cloister is so wearying a retreat to be found? No, the vice of this kind of people is not indolence or idleness; no one can live a harder life, or spend less peaceful days; and if heaven were to be won only on such conditions, the price might well be regarded as exorbitant. . . .

"Would one dare call these men idlers? Will they be accused of laziness? Will their lives have been useless?" asks Père Croiset. "Alas," he replies, "perhaps at least as useless as the lives of those who do nothing. . . . They are not idle, but will God be pleased with their works? And should eternally unfruitful works be accounted as having some value?"[14]

The God of the Christians could not, then, be pleased with

those who worked too hard, with the sacrifices which they imposed on themselves. Their lives were as useless as those of men who wasted their time. The idle worldling and the zealous businessman were on a par, and it seemed that, if the Church had to choose between them, its preferences would lie with the former, for it was better able to speak to him and to persuade him to be converted and he would be more disposed to listen.

The worldling might say, to justify himself before God and men, that "some are born subject, and others masters," that "Providence" had "determined all the different conditions," and that it "therefore authorized their privileges. . . . When a man lives on his income, he has a right to do nothing; and it is even, by worldly standards, proof that a man is of high birth and well-to-do if he does nothing." To this Père Croiset might reply, for the Church, that while idleness might be a proof of noble birth and affluence, it was hardly proof of being a Christian. And since the worldling would be at a loss for an answer, he might eventually be converted. "Idleness benumbs," says Père Croiset again, "but it does not at first render insensible those whom it lulls to sleep. There are intervals of religion and reason which cause a man to perceive with terror the chaos of sin in which a useless life nurtures worldly persons. However much he may pretend, he feels the sting of remorse and the bitterness of the fatal fruits of idleness." [15]

But what was the Church to say to the man whose fault was that he worked too hard? "What, to work, to deny himself even sleep, to wear out his strength," exclaims Père Croiset, "and even to hasten his death by working too hard, knowing that during all eternity that work must be useless to him! *Quid nobis profuit?* At most, he will have worked for others; and what sorrow, what despair, to have done nothing for himself!" [16] But was it not precisely the strength of the man who was to be the master of tomorrow not to put the question to himself, not to ask to what purpose all his efforts had been made? And that was why it was so hard to make a Christian of him again. "As soon as a man becomes religious, he is useless," [17] he would feel, and what more was there to say?

Yet, from another point of view, might there not be some analogies, however strange they might appear, between this "businessman" who worked without surcease and the man who renounced the joys of life to consecrate himself to the service of God? Père Croiset, speaking of the tortured existence of most businessmen, says that their life "is harder, more painful and also more mortified than that led by the greatest servants of God in the cloister or in the desert." [18] They were ascetics, then, and whatever the motives which had caused them to abandon the pleasures of the world, it really seemed that their self-imposed "constraining assiduity" and the stubbornness which they displayed in their work should assure them of certain advantages, in the eyes of faith, over worldlings who did not work, if only because, by working as they did, they seemed, in their own way, to be obeying God's command and expiating the original sin which the idle, pleasure-seeking worldling always appeared to wish to forget.

But people who felt that they were entitled to do whatever they pleased were thoroughly dishonest, said the preachers. "Insatiable greed for gain," says Père Croiset, "causes men to grab whatever they can lay their hands on. Provided they can put their money to work at high interest, they endanger even the sacred trust of orphans and widows." [19] The man intent on getting rich at any cost knew no scruple. "The prospect of fat profits soon does away with that delicacy of conscience which is nurtured only in a modest Christian existence. As soon as we want everything to serve our profit, we want everything to be permitted." [20]

But it did not have to be so. The businessman might be a very "upright man" and might even aspire to be so; he would certainly like to hear himself so described. The fact remained, nevertheless, that the businessman thought only of getting ahead and making money, and this was what the Church could not forgive. "God who in sacred Scripture ceaselessly inspires in us contempt for riches; God who by terrifying analogies shows us the fatal consequences of riches; God who declares that cupidity, the first motive of great commercial enterprises, is the source of all evils, did not make man to raise piles of money and then have them circulate to the glory of trade and the State; he created individuals, like societies, for his own glory." [21]

So a writer of the period put it a few years before the Revolution. But was he really sure that it was so, and did not the enterprising merchant believe that by getting rich himself he had increased the prosperity of his country and labored to the glory of God, which for him was identified with a profitable trade and a prosperous country? Trade, he insisted, made countries prosperous. "To be persuaded of it, we have only to compare the condition of certain regions where there is no trade or industry with that of regions where the spirit of trade causes agriculture to flourish and animates all the arts. We shall see, on the one hand, a half-savage way of life, general inertia, unrecognized talent, a general indigence with the vices attendant upon it, and very low taxes, which are very hard to collect. On the other hand, we shall see prodigious activity, a constantly increasing population, a civilized way of life among all classes of citizens, an industry which multiplies capital in every direction, immense and constantly renascent aid furnished for the needs of the State, easily collected, and even sometimes in excess of the demand." [22]

And what could the Christian reply, once the discussion was shifted to this new ground? "An honest and happy average existence may be found among an agricultural population, but it would be vain to seek it in our commercial cities. For what do we see there? We see, side by side with a rich man overwhelmed with abundance, a host of workers collected, almost herded, in a work room, hustled, covered with sweat and rags, reduced to perish of poverty and hunger through a thousand accidents as frequent as they are inevitable—the death of the merchant who makes of their hands the instrument of his affluence, bankruptcies, war. . . ." [23]

These were not the right things to say at a time when capitalism was developing, and the problem which faced the Church was a different one. That problem was to have the big businessman sanctioned by the God of the Christians, to show that, by fulfilling his mission, he was following his vocation, a vocation foreseen by Divine Providence from the beginning of time, and thus to sanctify the duties of his state.

God, we are told, "has from all eternity disposed" the vocation of each individual, "having destined some for the cloister, others for the world, these for the Church, those for the bar, these for the army, those for honorable offices and functions, these for trade and skilled occupations." [24] It might seem, however, that the big merchant of modern times had not received a vocation; that the profession which he exercised placed him somewhere outside the order established by Divine Providence. Yet he, too, was aware that he had certain duties to carry out. He established values for himself, he distinguished between those who had succeeded in business and those who had not, he imposed on himself a certain way of life, he created a new order, he made his own moral code, he formed an ideal for himself and his mission here below, an ideal which was his own. But what else could he be but a worldly man?

"God delights in confounding the designs of those bold, ambitious persons who want to raise their fortunes to the skies," says Père Croiset. "A gust of wind overturns the enterprise within sight of port; a small pebble upsets, destroys the valuable colossus." [25] Clearly the God of the Christians was not fond of big businessmen. "I should frighten you perhaps," writes Abbé Liger in 1774, "if I told you what the Fathers of the Church, and particularly St. Gregory, said about the dangers of commerce . . . a condition which they regarded as the lowest in the order of salvation." [26]

But the big businessman was not going to let such a notion worry him. He was sure of himself; he knew his own worth; he knew what was owed him. He had emerged from that "modest Christian existence" so much praised by the ministers of the Lord; he was proud of it, and looked down upon those who remained in it. As for him, he took the large view and despised those who confined themselves to those "little duties" which, conscientiously fulfilled, would assure the salvation of Christians. "Incapable of extending their views, of perceiving other causes than luck or fate, having only the example of others to justify their conduct, they crawl, work, obey and all their lives constitute a necessary and undistinguished cohort." These were the eternally ordinary persons, who would always remain in the estate to which God had assigned them, whereas the big businessman would rise and reach the summit of magnificence. That was why he despised them profoundly and was very careful to prevent anyone from identifying him with the mass of mediocrities, of small shopkeepers, who seemed to him to dishonor the splendid profession of commerce. He would not be of those who simply helped to make a crowd. He was a somebody, born to command others, to extend his dominion over the whole world.

"The merchant of whom I speak," we read in an address made before the Académie des Belles-Lettres of Marseilles in 1755, "is one who, towering over all the rest by reason of his vision, his talent and his enterprise, by his fortune increases the prosperity of the State. He is a citizen, traveler, politician, man of letters and man of the world, and he can aspire to all the functions that talent should fulfill. While his ships loaded with foodstuffs and the products of our manufactures sail off to seek the products of the most distant climes, his agents everywhere serve him, inform him, act for him. His couriers carry his orders to all parts of Europe, and his name on a commercial bill ensures that the funds which he wishes to transfer or to circulate will move and multiply. He orders, he recommends, he protects." [27]

There we have the master of the modern age. The Church did not give him recognition; at most, in any case, it granted him tolerance. It was to accept the fact that he was rich, without concerning itself overmuch about the means whereby he had acquired his wealth. To assure his salvation, it insisted on telling him exactly how much of his wealth he might keep for himself and what he must give to the poor, it being understood that almsgiving alone was meritorious. But did this satisfy the merchant conscious of his own importance? Did he have any use for a God who, far from rejoicing in his prosperity, was always warning him against the dangers he had incurred by making his fortune? He was only too ready to say that not only had the divinity nothing to pardon him for, but indeed that it could only approve of him, since in acquiring wealth he had contributed to the development of industry and commerce and consequently to the public weal.

On this point, then, as on so many others, there was disagreement between the bourgeois and the Church which, whatever he might say in his defense, could only repeat to him that "zeal for temporal things whose purpose is to raise a man's status and establish him in the world" [28] did not befit a Christian and which continued to hurl anathemas at those who made money.

How were the two points of view to be reconciled? The merchant conscious of his own worth and of what society owed him, could never appeal to any other right than a secular one, and the order which he instituted here below could have no breath of the divine. What did he have that he did not owe to himself, to his work, which Père Croiset regarded as excessive, to his ambition, which the Church condemned?

BANKING

"Go up, my brothers," exclaims a preacher, "go up to the heights overlooking your cities, and from there take a look at all who dwell in them! Alas, what will you not see! You will see men moving, bustling, revolving great projects in their minds, talking, visiting, concerning themselves with every business but that of salvation." [29] But if men had thought of salvation, would they have conceived or constructed "great projects" at all? It was a question which the worldly seem often to have prompted, and which the philosophers answered as follows: Commerce "is contrary to the aims of a religion whose founder pronounced anathema against the rich and excluded them from the kingdom of heaven. All industry is also forbidden to perfect Christians, who live a transitory life on earth and should never be concerned about the morrow." [30] What, indeed, could be the industry "of a people who are daily told that their God wants them to pray, suffer, live in fear and groan unceasingly?" [31]

Yet it would be a mistake to believe that the Church overtly warred against modern industrialism and commercialism. The

Christian religion is directed to the individual, and must look upon any economic system only in the context of the human soul. Hence, when the Church said that the merchant was possessed by an inordinate desire for riches and was therefore losing his soul, it was not attacking trade as such or claiming to lay down any laws in that area. The big businessman, therefore, continued to act as before, seeking to profit by his trading and to make his fortune. If he were still a Christian, he might, of course, have scruples, and, not finding in the Church's teaching the endorsement of the values which were his, he might have to seek the moral support which he needed from others better able than "theologians" to appreciate the benefits of trade. Nevertheless, if there was opposition between priest and businessman, it was a latent conflict rather than open warfare.

It would have been otherwise had the Church, instead of attacking the merchant's "cupidity" or showing him in general the "dangers" inherent in the exercise of his profession, objected to a particular economic practice. If, for example, it attempted to forbid the industrialist to use machines or the capitalist to invest his funds in a particular way, the conflict would have become acute. It would, then, no longer have sufficed for the rich man to moderate his cupidity, to give alms, to work less, and to give more time to the thought of his salvation; he would have had to make a clear and definite decision either to continue practices which he felt legitimate or even necessary or to obey God in order to avoid the danger of hell.

Our supposition might appear at first sight to be absurd. What the Church opposed was "the rich," their attachment to earthly goods, their avarice, their ambition. It really mattered little what form the sins of the rich took; it was the desire for riches itself that must be combatted, that was the sin and its various disguises. The rich merchant, the industrialist, the banker, the capitalist who lived off his investments, all were sinners, first because they were men and next because they exercised a profession which was "very dangerous" to salvation. But there it had to end, and it is difficult to see what might have prompted a priest to enter into greater detail with the businessman concerning the methods which the latter used in the exercise of his profession; for, necessarily, that would lead to envisaging a whole series of thorny questions in the area of commerce and banking concerning which theologians—or so at least the businessmen claimed—knew nothing.

However, on one question of a "practical" nature the Church took a definite stand; it forbade loans at interest. That prohibition led to a lengthy debate, which set the Church and the new middle class at odds and in the course of which were raised all the questions which flowed from the fundamental and irremediable antagonism between two forces, two irreconcilable attitudes.

"Usury is never divorced from robbery," says a missionary priest in a book entitled *La Guerre aux Vices,* "because it is a species of robbery and derives from it, as a stream from its source. Thus all usurers are attenuated robbers who steal more cleverly and more slowly than the others, but who are not therefore less harmful or blameworthy. This is evident in that the usurer . . . lends his money and his goods only in order to extract from them an unjust interest rate in excess of the value of the goods or the sum which he has loaned." [32]

Thus anyone who loaned money at interest, whatever the rate, was a usurer, and consequently an "attenuated robber." And that, indeed, was what the learned theologians of the Sorbonne decided. "At the Sorbonne, everything is regarded as usurious which is required over and above the capital loaned," and "it is held as a constant doctrine that the vice of usury consists in the exaction of that additional sum." [33] The borrower was required to pay "more than the thing is worth—*plus exigit quam res valet.*" That was why lending at interest must be forbidden. For "a loan of 100 crowns" the usurers "demand 105, although 100 crowns are worth only 100 crowns; . . . these five additional crowns are thus the price of injustice." [34]

This, then, was usury, that "vice detested by God" and "condemned by the Church." [35] "Everything additional to the capital, whatever its quantity or quality, from whomsoever it is received, whatever the condition of the borrower and the consequence of the loan, . . . is usury." [36] And, adds a theologian, those who plead the cause of "this monstrous hydra, which the Church has so often anathematized, and whose ever reviving heads present horribly gaping jaws, always prepared to devour the substance of others and to batten on the blood of the poor, are surely declaring themselves champions of cupidity, destroyers of charity, enemies of justice." [37]

While a merchant, then, need not despair of salvation, the usurer was condemned beforehand. "For although there are many dangers in commerce," says a theologian, "and although the conscience is often gripped by an inordinate desire for gain, as St. Augustine says, . . . nevertheless, as the same Father recognizes, a man may trade in an innocent manner and without violating God's law. For avarice, fraud, falsehood and excessive desire for gain may be the vices of individuals who engage in trade, but they are not vices attached to trade itself. . . . The position with regard to loans at interest is not the same as that in regard to trade," continues the same author. "Moneylending at interest is vicious in itself, whereas trade, which is harmless in itself, becomes evil only through the injustice of those who do not conduct it in a manner corresponding to the law of God." [38] Thus, whereas the profession of commerce, while "dangerous," was not "criminal," [39] those who loaned money at interest were actually criminals.

The anathemas of the theologians perplexed the worldly. So many people, after all, were lending money at interest, and among them were very honorable persons. "We may say with sorrow," says Père Hyacinthe de Gasquet, "that this fault has today become as it were the dominant note in all countries, all peoples, all conditions, with this single difference, that some disguise it, while others teach or practice it openly." [40] The laity asked in their turn, "But how is it, then, that so blameworthy a profession should have been able to take root in Christendom without anyone thinking of halting the course of injustice? How is it that, without anxiety and without remorse, a host of Christians should have engaged in commercial operations involving credit and money at call, and have made this the basis of their trading? How is it that, among the countless Christians who have entered the field of commerce, not one should have been found to resist the torrent of example, to perceive the iniquity and cause others to recognize it?" [41]

It was strange, indeed, and enough to make one doubt that moneylending at interest was so detestable a crime as the theologians made out. "For to whom would it ever occur that God treats as a detestable crime a modest profit which I derive from my own money, which greatly benefits my neighbor?" said the moneylender appealing to "all men of good sense." [42]

In their debate with men of "good sense," the theologians sought to demonstrate that moneylending was in fact unjust and contrary to right reason. Money, they said, "is unproductive by nature, being merely of human institution—a conventional sign representing the things of life." But capitalists could not concede that money was unproductive. "A capital of 50,000 pounds is generally regarded as equal at least to a house, or a piece of land estimated at the same value, and it usually produces more in industrious hands. Money is actually less sterile than a field which, if it is not cultivated, ruins its owner through the charges or taxes with which it is encumbered." [43]

So there was the answer. Indeed, "to know whether we may deduct the cost of the rental of our money . . . the crucial factor is whether the money can be useful to the one who rents it, that is, who borrows." And that was hardly subject to doubt. "When money provides the physical necessities, or amenities, or superfluities, or consideration, or distinctions, or favor, or nobility, or dignities, or titles, or whatever else; when with money one can have people's opinions, or suffrages, or generals, or armies, or provinces or populations; when its stability becomes that of the land, and maintains the equilibrium of the whole of Europe, is there any need to show that its possession is useful?" [44] In a word, "we have to decide either that money is an unproductive and lifeless substance which . . . can in no case produce interest, or that it is a useful thing which represents all others and may be rented as well as sold. There is no intermediate position." [45]

A distinction should nevertheless be made according to whether the borrower was rich or poor; so at least the "champions of usury" maintained. "We have to distinguish," they pointed out, "between two kinds of loans: the simple loan and the compound loan, or the subsidiary loan and the lucrative loan, also known as the loan of consumption or loan of increase. The simple, auxiliary or consumption loan is the one by which one provides for the actual necessities of the poor, who will physically consume the substance of the loan; as when one lends them wheat, or bread or vegetables to eat, or wine to drink, or money to buy these foodstuffs which they need to live. The compound, lucrative and increase loan is the one whereby one gives the means to the rich or well-to-do to increase their possessions, either by the purchase of some building, or by trade, or by some other means. The first loan," they add, "is a loan of charity, which should be free . . . but the second is a commercial loan, from which it is lawful and even just to derive a profit, because it produces a profit for the borrower." [46]

That, as the author of a paper published in 1730 put it, was the crux of the problem. The question was whether what would be unjust toward a poor man would be equally so in regard to a rich merchant, "whether it is contrary to natural law to derive some profit from a rich merchant, from a man in easy circumstances," when one lends him money at interest "to negotiate or buy lands, houses, etc., and thus to augment his property." [47]

The argument from reason was as follows: "Why should God prevent a man from deriving a profit from what he lends? It is something so just and so useful to the community. Is it not a matter of natural equity that he who uses our goods should repay us for such use? . . . There is no evidence that God forbids a contract which does no harm, and which produces so much good." [48] Provided that the interest rate was reasonable, there should be no harm in the practice.

On the other hand, "in the state of fallen nature, reason alone is almost incapable" of distinguishing between the just and the unjust; "its vision is too weak and too short; it easily detects the injustice of the great usuries which oppress and destroy one's neighbor, but not easily that of the small and medium ones which accommodate, or do not notably inconvenience those who borrow, and which are covered by an appearance and a false tincture of justice." [49]

Hence, if the mind alone was our guide, we might well lose our way in the labyrinth of usury. Faith must therefore come to the aid of reason. "Let the philosophers not object if, in regard to moderate usurers, I defer little to the judgment of reason," says the author of the *Traité de l'Usure*. The "quickest and surest solution is first to become a disciple of the faith." [50] "It is not for us to interpret the decrees of God; it is for him to impose upon us his laws, and for us merely to glory in obeying them." [51] We should, therefore, beware of the "deceitful discourses of reason." For if we allowed ourselves to be persuaded by those who defended usury and "stretched out our hands to take this illegitimate gain, it would be as fatal to us as was the forbidden fruit to Eve; it would cause us to lose life and paradise." [52]

Thus all that was left to the Christian was to submit, as must human reason itself, in the presence of a mystery. But in the matter of usury was there really a mystery, such as "original sin, or the Incarnation?" [53] The problem of moneylending at interest, as posed by the Church, is a moral one, writes the author of the *Traité des Prêts de Commerce*. And "there is this essential difference between dogmas and morality, that in dogmas reason should not be consulted save to make sure of the reality of Revelation and, once it is convinced that God has spoken, it must make a halt, sacrifice its own light and believe blindly whatever he says, whatever the difficulty that has to be surmounted. But since the moral precepts are merely the principles of the natural light which God has allotted to all men, there are none whose justice reason is not capable of recognizing." [54] This was the opinion of a theologian writing in 1731 and citing Abbé Fleury. And the ordinary citizen agreed, since he could see nothing mysterious about trade.

Right reason, then, had to decide whether it was lawful to lend at interest or not. But that was precisely what those who opposed all compromise refused to concede. "To appeal to all men of good sense to judge whether a thing which God forbids is detestable and deserving of eternal punishment," writes an orthodox author, "is to misunderstand God's holiness, his authority over us; to affect not to know his will, as Holy Scripture teaches it, and to seek to make of those who today are called men of good sense judges of his judgments; which cannot be done without blasphemy. For if we except certain sins which are criminal in themselves, because they directly outrage God, such as blasphemy, what makes the ordinary malice of sin, and draws eternal damnation upon all mortals? Is it the action in itself or its prohibition?" And to prove that it sufficed that God should have forbidden a certain action for the man who performed it to commit a sin, the author cites the story of the fall. "Suppose the men of good sense were asked to decide what great harm there was in eating one fruit rather than another in a garden, and whether that was a reason for drawing down a curse upon so numerous a posterity and hollowing out so hideous a hell under their feet for all eternity! God wants to be obeyed," and that sufficed. "If, therefore, there was nothing against usury, or moneylending at interest, save the Lord's prohibition, that would be enough to qualify it as a detestable thing. . . . To seek to cast doubt on the justice of God for that reason is an impiety and a horrible blasphemy. And that is where philosophical egotism leads, referring everything back to itself." [55]

God wants to be obeyed. The whole question, then, was to know his will. "Is it true that he commanded, that he forbade? That is the sole legitimate object of our study; once there exists a firm precept, our only business is blind submission." [56] "We must do what the law of God commands, refrain from what it prohibits, because he is master and Lord. *Ego Dominus!* If we do not see the reason for a command, we must still obey. *Ego Dominus!* . . . God has spoken, God commands us, what more is to be said for a man who is not without religion? . . . God speaks. We have to be silent or declare ourselves atheists." [57]

But would God be obeyed? Those who spoke in his name did not seem very sure. "In their greed for gain, merchants refuse to walk in the narrow paths of justice which would lead them to eternal life; they give way to the onslaughts of cupidity." [58] Wherefore, "moved solely by objects of the senses, blinded by the inordinate love of frail and perishable goods, these spiritual goods, these eternal interests touch them little. They will go on just the same with their usurious loans, motivated by the same sentiments as the avaricious Pharisees. . . . The prodigious multitude of the reprobate will follow them along this beaten track; and all our efforts will result only in rendering them inexcusable, only in preserving a small number from the contagion of their bad example, only in justifying the teachings of sound morals, as well as the decrees of divine justice, concerning the eternal damnation of so many prevaricators who have refused to follow its precepts." [59]

The long struggle initiated between the Church and the new mentality seems to have focused on a single point. There had been discussion of the mysteries, but whether, in the end, some had decided to believe what the human mind was unable to understand or had declared themselves content with the data of reason, their temporal interests were not affected, and the discussion could have continued indefinitely. Similarly, there had been disagreement on moral questions; but there, too, temporal interests and a particular conviction relating to life as a whole did not, for the most part, clash directly. "Does the Gospel forbid you to look to the preservation of your goods, and even to work to increase them, by lawful means? Does the Gospel condemn the desire to provide for your family, to get jobs for your children, to harvest the fruits of your lands, even to defend your dignity with honor, and according to the rules of justice? . . . By no means," replies Père Croiset; "it condemns only excess, cupidity and too great solicitude." [60] That, after all, left plenty of margin, especially if one really knew how to distinguish between counsels and precepts. The Christian could temper his zeal without having to give up his business, which continued as before. He thought more of death. He was less likely to forget the important business of his salvation; but if he himself changed in certain respects, nothing was changed in the conduct of his affairs, which continued to be regulated by a series of "practical" considerations which, being of an altogether secular order, should not interest the Christian deity, who could not be expected to go into all these details.

So long as this remained the position, everything seemed satisfactory, and both the man and the Christian should benefit equally, the former for this life, the latter for the next. But the whole question was reopened once the Church, abandoning a policy of prudent reserve, ceased to concern itself only with the soul of the merchant, and concerned itself also with the secular being who conducted his affairs, bought cheaply and sold at a higher price, and made out annual balance sheets. God then had to change his language; instead of speaking of mysteries, he had to use the commercial idiom. And that was precisely what the businessman found it hard to accept, taking the view that, in order to talk business, one must have very specialized knowledge, which could be acquired only through experience.

If that was the case, was it for God to adapt himself to the needs of men, or was it not rather for men to fall in with God's will? Could businessmen claim privileges which would exempt them from the obedience which every Christian owed to divine authority? They sought to explain to the "theologians" that "moneylending at interest is good for trade." The theologians, for their part, replied, "Before all else, we must examine what God permits and what God forbids; our neighbor is not the sole or the primary object to be considered. Interest, therefore, should not be permitted merely because it fosters trade and feeds the desire of merchants for riches. We must realize that it is not for the law of God to comply with the needs and conveniences of trade, but for the conduct of Christians in trade to be governed by the law of God." [61] Or were merchants laying claim to acquired rights? "Since when," ask the theologians, "have they acquired such rights against the express decisions of the Church, the spouse of Jesus Christ, to whom sovereign power has been given under heaven, whose reign is eternal, and whom all peoples and all the kings of the earth must obey with submission?" [62]

A theologian whom we have already quoted compares moneylending to the forbidden fruit. Adam disobeyed a first time, and the capitalists seemed quite prepared to do likewise. God was putting them to the test. "Rationalizations are useless; we have to obey or cease to be Christians." [63] The question was clearly stated. The point, then, was not how, precisely, the world of God was to be interpreted or whether certain theologians had attempted to narrow its relevance. For was it not clear that the gravity of the problem consisted in the fact that it raised the question whether God was ever able to make a stand against a particular business practice which merchants found profitable and even necessary. The theologians seemed to be putting God's power to a final test. "Am I still God," they made him ask, "and does my will suffice to have the merchant abandon a particular advantage?" Those who favored moneylending at interest "would be damned." [64] But what if that threat did not suffice?

"Let us assume that one-third of mankind lives only on trade, that interest lending is the soul of trade, and that merchants have no other means of subsistence than their condition; is the conclusion true that in order to secure their livelihood they must be allowed to do that without which they cannot subsist?" "Obviously," the theologians reply, "it is not and cannot be." For whatever arguments might be advanced in favor of interest, they were of no account in the face of the supreme argument of salvation. "What, is it possible to forget that it is not permissible to transgress the law of God for the sake of a flourishing trade and State? It is obvious that it would be a crime to buy all the treasures of the world at that price, and the world itself. . . ." God must be obeyed before all things. "As soon as he speaks, as soon as he forbids, men and whole nations must respectfully listen and obey. The legitimacy of interest loans does not consequently depend on their usefulness to the public weal. . . . It were better for the world to perish a thousand times over than to use a means which the law of God condemns." [65]

But to put the question thus seemed, as we have said before, to reduce the long debate between Church and bourgeoisie to a single point. The two adversaries are thus seen confronting one another in a final debate where the question is one of determining, in a specific case, how far the power of God still extends and what can be the influence of the Church once some vital in-

terest is at stake. Here they come to realize how wide is the gulf
between their sentiments.

THE BUSINESS WORLD

"The legitimacy of interest-paying loans in business has been
the burning question for the past ten years. It is discussed in all
publications," [66] writes an observer in 1783. What would happen to trade, to the State, to each individual, if ever the Church's
will in the matter were to prevail, the worldly-minded asked
themselves, feeling affected in their most vital interests. We are
lost if we obey God! "There is no longer a trading center on
earth," says Turgot, "where most undertakings do not operate
on credit; there is probably not a single merchant who does not
often have to resort to another's purse; not even the man with
the most abundant capital could be sure of never needing to
borrow save by keeping a part of his funds idle, and consequently reducing the scope of his operations." [67] And there
would be no funds for all these merchants to borrow if they
were forbidden to pay interest to the lender. "Without interest,
there will be no money at call," says the author of a letter to the
Archbishop of Lyons on the question of interest; "without
money at call, there will be no funds; without funds, there will
be no trade, no business; everything will come to a standstill,
everything will be lost." [68]

The same author points to the situation in the city of Lyons.
"Independently of the mass of money which is the basis of the
city's trade, that is, of each company, of each commercial house,
some 16 to 17 million usually circulate in the form of credits
to meet the requirements of trade." This "conjunction of funds
and industry" made it possible for Lyons commerce to "operate
independently, without encouragement and without protection;
the ravages of war are repaired; the gold which had been ex-
ported is flowing back from all sides; the national debt has
been reduced; foreign countries have become our tributaries;
our provinces are made fertile; 200,000 subsist, work and bless
heaven; the State has more citizens, the Church more children,

and all is for the best." But "of those two mainsprings, money and industry, take one away, and the machine will break down." [69]

And that would spell ruin not only for those who needed loans to run their business, but also for all who provided them with funds. "What would happen to so many modest bourgeois families run deep into debt, younger sons, retired soldiers, widows and virgins, incapable of turning to account the money of their patrimony, of their portion, of their legacy, of their dowry, of their small capital, in any other way?" [70] And what would become of the artisan, accustomed as he was to invest his savings in the form of interest-paying loans? "I have worked all my life, says this artisan, and I have put something aside to form a nest egg for myself to help me in my old age, and you don't want me to get a profit from it by lending it to my neighbor, who urges me to lend it to him, whom I would help, and who would do good business with it; but if I have to do it gratis, I shall have worked only for the benefit of another; on the other hand, if I leave my money idle, I shall have to pray God that I may not live longer than my money lasts. What a hard and unreasonable religion, if such was the case! Oh no, God is better and more just than that; he does not want me to risk starving to death!" [71]

And what would become of the working man, if ever the position of the foes of interest were to prevail? "One hundred thousand workers without bread, because they would be without work; children abandoned on all sides; fathers lamenting of being born in a murderous faith; mothers detesting the life they have given even more than that which they have received; everywhere destitution, hunger, despair, groans, cries, sickness and death—and it is in the name of my God that they would thus be slaughtered! . . . Arrogant rigorists, cruel fanatics who, for all answer, would probably call me an impious and rebellious man, permit me to say that I despise, abhor and combat a doctrine which would lead to so much evil!" [72]

But was it really possible that God should prohibit "a thing that is absolutely necessary to the prosperity of societies," [73] the laity asked themselves, and the theologians sought to show that it was quite possible to dispense with loans at interest without the disastrous consequences envisaged by those who constituted themselves the champions of usury. "It is, in a way, to conspire against the welfare of the State," declares Père de Gasquet, "and to blaspheme against religion, or at least to speak of it without reflection, or out of self-interest, to claim and to teach that such moneylending is useful, beneficial and even necessary to trade, which could not subsist without it; since it is to assert that trade and religion are irreconcilable, whereas each is respectively necessary." [74]

But what if the conflict were in fact irreconcilable? The reply for a Christian must not be in doubt. "The champions of interest," writes a pious author in 1710, "make a great stir about the need for the circulation of money among merchants, bankers and businessmen. You hear them saying all the time that the State cannot subsist without it, because, if you take the interest or profit away from money, you destroy trade, which is conducted only for profit; and that, by destroying trade, you ruin the State in which the money that moves and passes from hand to hand is like the blood which circulates in the veins of the human body. They claim that this is the decisive justification for the interest ordinarily charged in the trading of notes, bills of exchange and money; as though man had no other business in this world but to get rich at whatever cost, and as though the first of all these necessities, or rather the only one, were not concern for his eternal salvation." [75] The arguments of the defenders of usury in favor of moneylending at interest might hold "if trade were the great affair of man and if all divine and human laws were subordinated to that end. But Jesus Christ brought another doctrine to the world when he taught us detachment from riches and said that he who does not renounce everything, at least as regards his interior disposition, cannot be his disciple." [76] Hence, "if these maxims appear harsh to most worldly persons, and as though impossible to carry out in practice, it is because most of them are concerned only with the cares of the present life, and very little with the life to come." [77]

That, at least, was clear. "If you cannot conduct trade save by means of usurious loans," says Abbé Liger in 1774, "you are obliged to give it up." [78] But perhaps there was no need to go so far and to place the merchant in the cruel dilemma of having to give up his business or risk going to hell. For what were the undertakings that needed credit? They were not the "ordinary commercial enterprises, conducted everywhere and every day"; they were the "great commercial enterprises" which, requiring immense sums, "cannot do without credit. . . . I conclude that it is necessary to abandon these great . . . enterprises which cannot be conducted save by means contrary to the laws." [79]

Thus all the attacks of the opponents of usury were directed against the large-scale enterprises, which, they said, had corrupted manners. "If manners become as pure as they used to be," exclaims a theologian, "and as they ought to be, trade based on moneylending at interest will cease to be necessary; and I conclude from this that it is not truly necessary." [80] For proof, another theologian invites us to make a comparison between "two societies, in one of which services are sold, save to the most needy; and in the other, the precepts of the Lord are observed, especially not to hoard, and to do to others, when you can, as you would have them do to you, and not to take interest on loans; we should then see which was the happier, and in which the necessaries of life were cheaper." [81]

Thus the great debate was on between those who condemned modern developments and those who favored "progress." "Only the most obstinate fanaticism can fail to realize the need for trade," [82] say the latter. And they pointed proudly to "this host of operations and the advances they require which necessarily present so many lucrative uses for money; commercial enterprises multiplied to infinity employ immense capital." [83] "Are we happier than our forebears whose capital was less than ours?" ask the others. [84] "It is through trade that civilization spreads," say the former. "In the provinces which have no trade," answer the theologians, "manners are less civilized, but they are purer; minds are less cultivated and talents less developed, but hearts are more religious, and with less science there is also less ambition and less demand." [85] Only nations which had developed trade and "cultivated the navy" had played a great part in history, asserted those who defended modern trade and its practices. "But in order to play that very great part, how many people have been ren-

dered unfortunate! How many citizens have been lost! How
many nations have been humiliated, ravaged, depopulated!" And
"can these reflections be weighed without agreeing that it is
at least uncertain that commerce, as it is practiced in our day, is
less fatal than useful to society?" [86]

And so the debate continued. The theologians became increasingly aroused and, abandoning the prudent reserve which
sacred language appeared to demand, proceeded to deal with
realities and call a spade a spade.

Why should loans at interest be forbidden, the ordinary citizen
asked, since they benefited precisely the one who borrowed
money? "Your arguments about moneylending at interest are
wrapped in a thick cloud, as far as I am concerned," remarks a
"good paterfamilias" in a "natural and sensible comment" on
the "theory of money." "All that is clear to me," he continues, "is
that the crime of a usurer consists in impoverishing those who
borrow from him, whereas the man who borrows from me is
growing rich on the product of my money. He admits it to me
at each payment; he is always protesting his immense obligation
to me for the preference which I have shown him in entrusting
my capital to him." [87]

All the same, the adversaries of usury replied, borrowers must
find some way of indemnifying themselves for the interest which
they had to pay. That indemnity, "the wholesalers will seek, and
always find with advantage, from the retailers, and the latter from
the people, who thus defray the cost of the interest on commercial call money, of fixed-term or promissory notes, of bills of exchange, etc., as well as the amount in excess of the price of the
merchandise sold on credit or bought for the account. Is it surprising, after this, that businessmen should run after call money,
and say they have no disadvantage, no prejudice from the interest which they pay? All the prejudice, all the damage falls upon
the public, and hence on the poor, who are in a majority." [88]

If "eighteen million in loans cause the Lyons trade to flourish,
notwithstanding the interest paid on it by the traders," says
Gasquet, "it is only because the latter are careful to indemnify
themselves at the expense of the people, by raising the prices of

the merchandise and foodstuffs which they sell to them, and defrauding them in a hundred other ways." [89]

Thus the issue was being narrowed down. The people, led by the servants of God, were seen as rising against the capitalists and cursing their new masters.

"Industry's capital is multiplied, but for whose benefit? . . . For that of the artisans who give of their labor? Most of them have only work, poverty and abasement as their lot. The funds which are accumulated are poured into the coffers of a small number of businessmen, fattened on the sweat of a host of workers who wear themselves out in dismal manufacture. In commercial countries, industry supplies immense and ever recurring assistance to the needs of the State. But by whom is this assistance provided? By the hard-working citizens whose industry multiplies capital funds? A fatal source, which ruins the people to succor the State. By the tax-farmers to whom the money belongs? But are the tax-farmers who provide the State with the assistance it needs generous enough to lend freely the funds which they make available? . . . If they lend, it is for their profit and for the ruin of the State, which in order to refund the money which the capitalists have supplied to it is forced to increase its taxes." [90]

Thus a whole class of society was the target. It was not the newly rich or the rich in general—who, although sinners, or just because they were sinners, had a place in the Christian legend—that the ministers of God attacked; it was the big industrialists, the big bankers, the merchant contractors, to whom they pointed by name. The Church appeared not only to refuse them the benediction which it granted those of the other professions, kings or beggars, feudal lords or bourgeois living off petty trade, but to condemn them out of hand and refuse them recognition. They were all classed as "capitalists" and "usurers," as men who deliberately ignored the commandments of God. And what did they not do in the service of their idol, which they insolently set up against the God of the Christians? "What do you immolate to it?" asks Père Hyacinthe de Gasquet, addressing the money-lender; "is it not the blood and the substance of the people that you suck, on which you fatten through your usuries?" [91]

And it was just because the Church directed its anathemas against a whole class of society, a whole profession, that the "usurers" paid so little attention to the anathemas hurled against them by the servants of God. They were merely carrying out their duties; they were secure in their consciences, they had their moral code, the moral code of their class. How could it be held against them that they were what they were? "Criminals? We?" they seemed to ask. "But we are perfectly respectable men!"

"If the subtleties and the rantings of our casuists against the value of money and interest are well founded," say the authors of the *Théorie de l'Intérêt de l'Argent,* it will have to be said of trade that it is the sole source of the public welfare and yet that all those engaged in it, and those who supply it with funds, are thereby excluded from the path of salvation; that both violate the first rule of conduct, which is justice; that the number of usurers is simply being multiplied indefinitely through the continuous extension of the branches of trade; that the famous fairs of Europe, our maritime cities, and other commercial centers, in Catholic countries as in others, are but meeting places and breeding grounds for thieves, who have agreed to deceive one another, since the basis of all their operations is the injustice of lending at interest; and that finally all capitalists, contractors, bankers, merchants, and traders must, in conscience, give up their professions, restore all the interest and rebates they have received, and themselves get back all those they have paid. Such consequences, the author concludes, would "strike horror into the heart of every civic-minded person," [92] and they must not come to pass. It was only because "vague notions" had been attached to the word "usury" that it was applied "now to the man who exercises his full rights rigorously against all and sundry, now to the businessman who by his talents and skill has managed to make a solid fortune for himself, and now to the smart trader whom we see every day borrowing on the one hand and lending on the other. Can these citizens be charged with committing injustice? It is agreed that their probity rules out any such suggestion." [93]

All these people whom the ministers of the Church were consigning to perdition were thus men of known probity and great utility to the State. "I am merely exercising my profession, a profession that is useful and necessary above all others," the business-man said. "The true reason which justifies bankers' profits is thus that they fulfill the duties of their state, and that this state is use-ful and legitimate. . . . Any establishment recognized as useful by society is also a legitimate establishment; because the supreme Wisdom could not have placed the order of things in opposition to the rules of conduct." [94]

But in that case was it conceivable that all these respectable citizens should be damned? Yet that was what the die-hard the-ologians claimed. The consequences of God's commandments, they pointed out, were terrifying. "They make me tremble my-self," says the author of the *Observations sur le Prêt à Intérêt,* "but does that make them less true? What more terrifying than the doctrine of the small number of the elect, what more horrible than hell, what more susceptible of freezing the rich capitalist's blood than those words of the Gospel, 'Woe to the rich!'? Instead of en-couraging the culpable cupidity of capitalists by sophistries, in-stead of bemusing them at the brink of the abyss, should they not rather be woken up and frightened by the terrible reali-ties?" [95] "It is a misfortune to be reduced to this extremity," says another theologian, but "this is a case where it is better to tear out one's eyes or cut off one's hands and feet to avoid doing any-thing displeasing to God rather than run the risk of being thrown into hell with all one's members." [96]

That such arguments made some impression on contemporaries is borne out by the authors of *La Théorie de l'Intérêt de l'Argent.* "Among the capitalists of the kingdom, probably one-third dare not trade their money and introduce it into the channels of com-merce, some through fear of being regarded as usurers, others in order to avoid hurting or embarrassing their consciences." [97] The Church should, therefore, declare that God never forbade money-lending at interest as it was currently practiced in commerce. "Traders and bankers" would thus be able to "serve the public and maintain their state, without by so doing committing as many mortal sins as they contracted loans; the door to salvation would be open to them." [98]

But many others among the laity, less timorous and with a more firmly rooted class consciousness, put it quite clearly to the theologians that they were meddling in things that did not concern them. "There is not a businessman, banker or trader who does not think he knows more about usury than all the Church Fathers and theologians put together. According to them, the churchmen understand nothing; they know only what they have found in their books, and all those books are uninformed about trade. In a word, they are blind men who want to argue about differences of color." [99] "Oh no," exclaims Turgot, "men don't have to be metaphysicians to be virtuous." [100] They knew what they had to do without going to the scholastics for advice. Did not merchants "know best what is most profitable to them? Will a casuist, who looks upon trade only from his study, understand it better than those who practice it?" [101]

But was this not tantamount to forbidding the Church any interference in human affairs? "It is not within the competence of theologians to make judgments concerning usury, to teach the faithful what is in conformity with or against the law, to determine the morality of actions and human conventions? Let us return to the principles of order," replies Abbé Liger. "The law of God extends to all actions, foresees all circumstances, applies to all states. It is an invariable rule, according to which the works of prince and subject, magistrate and trader, priest and people will be examined, discussed, judged." [102] How could the Church's "right to judge of usurious loans" be disputed? "Has not the Church received from Jesus Christ the power to bind and loose? . . . And how should it exercise that power if it is not to declare what is just or unjust, what is sin or not? And who then should judge what is for or against the law of God, if not those whom God has established to judge of that law, and whom he commands to explain it to the peoples?" [103]

Thus the debate was broadening. The issue was now the moral influence which the Church might exert in human affairs. Were its judgments still to count for anything in secular life? So long as it confined itself to condemning what the respectable disapproved, whatever the differences in motive and spirit behind the decisions of the two adversaries, the conflict might not be too apparent; but in the question of interest-paying loans, it suddenly erupted. A decision had, therefore, to be made, and it was in connection with a specific point, but one affecting the very foundations of bourgeois existence, that the division between the two forces appeared most clearly. The merchant, the banker who felt himself directly challenged in his vital interests did not merely say that he did not need to consult the theologians to know where his duty lay, but, turning the tables, he attacked those who appealed to evangelical morality and defended his own rights, his own moral code, the idea he had formed of himself and of his duties.

"The scholastics say," we read in *La Théorie de l'Intérêt de l'Argent*, "that those who lend at interest should be tolerated in the State only to the same extent as female prostitutes, both trades being equally proscribed by natural law." [104] Such an analogy was to appear altogether inappropriate to merchants or bankers who prided themselves on their utter respectability. They took the view that, by causing money to circulate, they were performing a thoroughly virtuous action, and, far from being content to know that God was not too displeased with them for acting as businessmen, they wanted him to approve and encourage their practices. The theologians, it is true, told them that it would be much more generous on the part of capitalists to lend their money gratis. "To maintain that, without interest, there can be no more call money," says Souchet, author of a *Traité de l'Usure*, "is to assume that there is no longer in society any principle of generosity; that cupidity has corrupted all hearts. . . . To judge thus of all men is to give a very poor idea of oneself." [105] Indeed, "should not the bonds of fraternity banish usury from cities and from human society," asks Père Gasquet, "and should they not finally impel citizens to contribute to the general welfare, and to prefer that good to any particular interest? But not at all. The individual interest prevails," [106] he notes regretfully.

According to the champions of interest-paying loans, the theologians felt that "traders should suspend all operations which depend on loans until capitalists are pious enough to lend them for the love of God the sums which they possess." [107] That, they maintained, was patently absurd. "As it is impossible to preserve order in society solely through disinterested contracts, so our social structures simply cannot subsist save through the free operation of mutually advantageous contracts. . . . To ban the free and uninterrupted movement of trade, in which each finds his advantage, would be to ruin all classes of society at once; for it is clear that the natural law does not confine itself to approving of charitable compacts, but that it also approves of contracts entered into for reasons of self-interest." [108] "I serve both my family and my country by putting my money into trade," [109] the capitalist said, and he did not understand why the Church should hold it against him.

But the capitalists were to go still farther. Taking the offensive, they excoriated the "angelic morality" which would lead to "disorder, idleness, depopulation, ruin, . . . [whereas] in all the religions of the world, happiness, population increase, rest and order are the supreme law." [110]

And who were those who preached this moral code? People who lived at the expense of others and contributed nothing to the good functioning of business. They were the ones who wished to forbid those who worked hard to use methods as legitimate as that of interest-paying loans. "It is easy for you to talk," they said, apostrophizing the clergy, who, they maintained, knew nothing of the details of commercial undertakings; "you, having to concern yourselves only with the next world, who should be strangers to the affairs of this world, yet in every society manage to form a state within a state; you, again, for whom family and posterity are of no account, for whom idleness is a right and trade a crime; you, finally, whom the general poverty never affects, who owe everything to society and never give it back anything but words; you who earn as you sleep, and have only to receive and to enjoy here below—it's easy for you to orate!" [111]

The ministers of God did not leave such attacks unanswered and in their turn challenged the capitalists. "You, wholly concerned with this world," says Père Gasquet, following his opponent's phrase, "who are wholly estranged from the affairs of the next life and claim to form a state within a state in the bosom of Christianity; you for whom the good things to come and an eternity of misery are of no account; you for whom trade is a title for misdeeds and who prefer its criminal operations to

the salutary work of your salvation, . . . who secure yourselves
against the general poverty by impoverishing so many; you
who owe everything to the people and who oppress them by
your monopolies and a thousand other deceits. . . . You who
till without a plow, who harvest where you have sowed nothing, who earn both sleeping and waking, and who spend nights
and days doing nothing, but feeding on the work, the sweat and
the substance of others!" [112]

But were not the Church's objections to capitalism really a
form of nostalgia for the past? That was what its opponents
maintained. Thus we read, for instance, that "nowadays," people
were better informed about the changes that had taken place in
the business world [113] and that this was what the "theologians"
refused to see when they inveighed against interest lending. And
the author of the letter to the Archbishop of Lyons on loans at
interest says that "it is no more reasonable to say that such loans
should not be contracted than it would be to maintain that the
use of carriages must be condemned today because, under King
Henry II, the women of the court rode pillion behind their
husbands, seated on a little fresh straw. . . . In morals, as in the
physical sphere, there are revolutions. . . . Human laws are no
more immutable than the things which they regulate. . . . And
if we examine the present state of Europe, we see that credit,
which formerly was useless, has now become necessary to everyone, indeed, absolutely indispensable." [114]

Of what use was it, then, for those who condemned "usury,"
to argue, for instance, that "the glory and the power of a State
do not consist in opulence; that wealthy Carthage was not the
equal of impecunious Rome; that Sparta flourished because it
loved poverty; and that Asian luxury corrupted virtuous
Greece? . . . To complete these antitheses," reply the authors
of *La Théorie de l'Intérêt de l'Argent,* "the political theorist
should add that, for the welfare of peoples, mendicity is preferable to prosperity, and that our future American trade cannot fail
to turn us into dishonest persons. . . . The question is not to
see what Sparta and Rome have been, or what we might be if
we were not what we are. The question is whether today, when
one-third, at least, of the inhabitants of the earth subsist only

on trade, they do or do not need moneylending at interest to be made lawful." [115]

A new world had been born. What purpose was served in regretting the old? Formerly, when "each man traded with his own capital, trade flourished," says an adversary of usury; "the fortunes of citizens were sound." Now, "the facilities" presented by interest-paying loans "encourage the less well-situated to undertake considerable trading ventures." [116] Formerly, when the "secret" of trade was as yet unknown, everything took place in an orderly fashion, whereas now, "thanks to that pernicious secret," says Père Gasquet, "a single trader will borrow up to 800,000 pounds without the public even being aware of it; that is, he finds a sure means of supplanting the multitude of traders and merchants, and channels a major part of trade to himself alone. What could be more detrimental to the public welfare! This enormous loan to a single individual, divided among 180,000 persons, could have enabled them to subsist to the benefit of society." [117]

Was it a good? Was it an evil? Even were it possible to put the question in this way at all, a common measure would still be lacking to decide it, since the two sides were no longer able to agree among themselves on what was good and what was bad. "The distinctive character of my religion," writes the author of the letter to the Archbishop of Lyons, "is . . . that it should not lead me to eternal felicity until it has made me happy in this world." [118] Was this still Christianity? "I wish there were more and better Christians," says a theologian, "and consequently that cupidity, which is so contrary to Christianity, should not be given so much opportunity to increase and be strengthened." [119] How were such contrary views to be reconciled?

The capitalists, who could not accept the position of the theologians, did not fail to find what they sought at the hands of the philosophers, whereupon the ministers of God accused the philosophers of complicity. "Our philosophers, like our moneylenders, glory little in being the extraordinary souls they are, superior to humanity. They prefer the slough of riches, that sordid self-interest which conceals from them the wisdom and the power of the precepts of religion." [120] And who were these philosophers who came to the rescue of the usurers? They were "true children of Belial, swollen with their vain knowledge, who no longer desire either yoke or dependence, and surrender blindly to all the aberrations of their minds." [121]

Nevertheless, where our theologian could see nothing but aberration, there was something else; a new order was developing, new forms of dependence, a new yoke. Loans at interest were not a "vice," and if the capitalist was a sinner, he was not normally a libertine, and trade was not one of those pleasures which the Church tolerated out of condescension to human weakness. The banker, whom it regarded as lost, was conscious of his duties, the duties of his profession, and he suffered regret and remorse if he failed to carry them out. He was, in his turn, a "man of order" who, later, after he had learned to beware of the "philosophers," might turn for support to the Church.

For the time being, however, there definitely seemed to be a profound rift between the Church and capitalism. The Church could not recognize the new order, and the capitalist resented the theologians who, "prejudiced against the profession of commerce, seek only to destroy it," [122] and treated respectable citizens as common criminals, accusing them of being usurers.

13 · THE BOURGEOIS ORDER

THE BOURGEOIS JUSTIFIED

The whole "course of the centuries, covering the life of all Christians and all men, is but a great caravan,"[1] says Nicole. There was therefore no point in attempting to outdistance others, which, in any case, ill befitted Christians who could not forget where they were going. Sometimes those who made up the caravan were arranged in one order of precedence, sometimes in another. It was of no great moment, since all, whether first or last, would reach the same goal. What mattered was that there should be order, that some should walk at the head, and others follow, so that everything might be done according to rule.

Thus all things here below had been ordained beforehand. Divine Providence had marked the framework within which the life of each individual must develop. The social order indicated to each his place, so that there might be no confusion. Divine Providence, in marking each one's destiny beforehand, had assigned him a particular station and a particular vocation. If the social structure with its various divisions were to collapse, it would have to be rebuilt. And everything would then revert once more to the same order, and the inhabitants would take up their various occupations once more, each according to his vocation; thus life here below, which for a Christian could be only a constant expectation of the next, would resume its regular course.

"It was by the most wise and most adorable of all counsels that God, in creating the world, and desiring to establish a society of men living together and destined to converse with one another, distinguished various conditions within it, and assigned them their functions and duties. Under this dispensation, there are superior and subordinate conditions, brilliant ones and obscure ones, all ordered by divine wisdom, and necessary for the maintenance of peace on earth and good order. For without that diversity which sets one in a position of command and keeps another in dependence, which causes one to appear in splendor, and reduces another to obscurity, what confusion there would be in the world, and what would become of human society!" [2]

God had thus willed that there should be different conditions in society; he had placed each man where he was, and, to please God, men must remain where they were and fulfill the duties of their station. There was no other way to salvation. "I say that man's whole prudence, even in the matter of salvation, may be summed up under two headings," explains Bourdaloue, "to advance in the perfection of his own station, and to avoid any other perfection, or any perfection contrary to this one, or one which prevents its practice." For that was God's will. "I have told you, Christians, that God's will is that each should be what he is in the world perfectly; that a king should be perfectly a king; that a father should perfectly fulfill the office of a father, a judge the function of a judge; that a bishop should perfectly exercise the ministry of a prelate; that all should walk perfectly in the paths marked out for them; that they should not be mingled, and that none should interfere in what is within the competence of another; for if things were so, and each was willing to be merely what he ought to be, we can say that the world would be perfect." [3]

Thus each individual, by perfectly fulfilling his own particular duties, would advance in Christian perfection and at the same time contribute his part to the maintenance of the social order. "There is no condition authorized by law," says Père Haineuve, "that is not in the order of Providence, which has ordained this diversity of conditions, without which the world and human society could not subsist. . . . Hence no one embraces any state, or is born in any condition of civil life, save by the order or permission of this same Providence, which has established inequality and subordination, as well as a diversity of conditions among men." [4]

Thus everything had been disposed to uphold the social order. "But this general disposition of Providence did not suffice, and a more specific one was required," insists Père Bourdaloue. "I mean that, among these different conditions, it was necessary that God, according to his designs . . . of predestination, should mark out for each man and should determine for him the particular station to which he was called. And that is what God did; so much so that there is no man who does not have his own specific vocation, which he must try to know well, and which he is necessarily compelled to follow." [5]

Every man who exercised a function, however humble, exercised it by order of the Lord. The Divinity had appointed him to his task, and saw to it that he carried out his duties. To carry out his duties well was to pray. "I maintain that to perform all one's duties faithfully; to work, to act in one's station in accordance with God's will and good pleasure, is to pray. . . ." "If God committed a task to you," says Père Bourdaloue, "and you carry out its functions assiduously, then, in so doing, you are praying. If Providence committed to you the conduct of a household, and you give it your care, then, in so doing, you are praying. The same applies to everything else." [6] Religion hallowed all the social duties; it sanctified all conditions. "Duties of state are thus in a sense true duties of religion; and if they differ from them in their object, they do not differ from them in the obligation which they impose on us. The sovereign on his throne, the father in his family, the master in his house, the judge in his court, the warrior at his post, the pilot on his ship, the farmhand in the field he cultivates, the artisan in his workshop—all in carrying out the duties of their state are discharging a true duty of religion." [7]

It would thus be a grave error to seek to oppose duties of

state to those of religion. "True piety," writes Massillon, "is the order of society; it leaves to each his own place; makes of the state in which God has placed us the sole way of our salvation; does not place a chimerical perfection in works which God does not ask of us; and considers as vices virtues which do not belong to our state. Everything that disturbs public harmony is an excess of man, and not zeal and a perfection of virtue. Religion disavows the most saintly works which one might substitute for duties; and a man is nothing before God when he is not what he is supposed to be." [8]

Order was always of divine institution, however imperfect and unjust it might appear. Some gained from it greater advantages than others. It could not be otherwise. There were rich men who enjoyed the good things of this world and lived in opulence; there were the poor, deprived of everything and living out their lives in penury. So it must be, if there was to be any order at all. "Thus there had to be a diversity of conditions, and especially there had to be poor, so that there might be subordination and order in human society," [9] says Père Bourdaloue.

Order was the all-important thing, and not the greater or lesser advantages that might accrue from it to this or that particular individual or class. Hence the Christian must carefully refrain from anything that might upset the established order. Was not religion itself, asks Massillon, "necessarily linked with law and order? It falls and is weakened when law and order breaks down. . . . As soon as the order of civil society gives way, all religion totters." [10]

Order was thus its own justification; that, for the Christian, must suffice. Men should abide by the established order and conform their lives and actions to it. This applied not only to injudicious reformers and seditious minds, who sought an imaginary perfection for the things of this world, but also to all those who on their own account wanted to get ahead and rise from their condition. The ambitious upset the social order, for ambition "carries us to a level to which we should not aspire, since it is above our condition," [11] says Bourdaloue. Ambition operated in contradiction to the designs of Divine Providence, which had ordained everything beforehand; it caused man to take God's place; it caused man to go his own way, instead of the way marked out for him by Divine Providence.

If the bourgeoisie pondered the teachings of Père Bourdaloue, it must have found its own condemnation in them. The bourgeois, according to Bourdaloue, could not claim that "natural and legitimate greatness which is established by God," and which belonged only to "princes, and all those who derive their superiority from birth or blood." He, personally, would never know any greatness but "an artificial one, whose only support is industry and human ambition." In trying to rise out of his condition, the bourgeois was seeking to correct the defect inherent in his birth; he was taking it upon himself to improve the designs of Divine Providence; he lacked humility and was entering into contestation with God. "There are two types of greatness, that which God has established in the world, and the other which is set up, of itself, the former being the handiwork of Providence, the latter the products of human ambition." [12] God had no part in bourgeois greatness. So long as the bourgeois remained in his own sphere, he was there by divine right, in the same way as all who had a rank or a place in society; but this ceased to be the case as soon as he lifted himself up. At that point, he was acting on his own responsibility. He was constituting himself his own providence; he was putting himself in the place of God. The movement which urged him on was a perpetual defiance of the Church, which maintained that it was his binding duty to confine his existence within the narrow limits which Divine Providence had set for him.

Was the bourgeois, then, no more than a climber, the spawn of sin, bearing within himself, under new forms, the ancient marks of mankind's corruption? No, he was not, or, if he was, he would always be ignorant of the fact. If he was ambitious, he was so in perfectly good conscience; he was ambitious as a matter of duty. His law was to get ahead, always to move forward. Therefore everything in this bourgeois life was carried out in the most orderly manner. Where, then, were the ambitious men of old times, courtiers without scruple, glorying in brilliant but short-lived successes? The Church's grandiloquence lost its edge when it addressed the bourgeois, who walked on with assured step, moved by an irresistible force that drove him onward.

Why was he portrayed as a depraved sinner, a man corrupted and succumbing to the temptations of self-love? In seeking to improve his position, he asked, was he not working for his children? That was his great argument; he justified himself in his children. If the clergy preached to him about the temptations of riches and accused him of being laggardly in the use of the means of salvation which Divine Providence had placed at the disposal of the rich, namely, almsgiving, he pointed to his children. "I have children, and for them I need all my wealth." [13] It was not for himself that he had got rich, he explained; he had worked for his family, for his posterity. Père Griffet puts his argument as follows: "But I am no longer master of the riches which you ask me to give to the poor; I owe them to the children whom God has given me; I have many of them, and I have in the first place to think of raising them, and then of settling them in life. . . . Must not everything give way before the call of blood? Must not paternal love have priority over the love of a neighbor whom we don't know?" [14]

Your children, the clergy replied, "will be rich enough, and you will leave them a large enough heritage, if you make them heirs of the prayers of the poor, and of the favor of Jesus Christ, which the infallible action of those prayers cannot fail to obtain for them." [15] But the bourgeois did not want to entrust the care of his family to anyone, not even God. "It will not be your ability, or your foresight, which will ensure these rich heritages for your children," says Père Croiset. "Alms have more virtue than all the glosses and contracts." [16] But the bourgeois could not believe this. His duty, he felt, was to be prudent and far-sighted, so that his children might later bless him and so that, in the meantime, he might enjoy the esteem of his neighbors. What argument could be advanced to convince him of his errors? What could be said to awaken in him the pangs of remorse of the sinner? He was working for his family, for his class; was he not in security of conscience?

"What does the world tell you? What does it require of you?

What sentiments does it inspire in you? Lift yourselves up, get richer, amass goods, buy offices, acquire honors, flee humiliations and poverty as the greatest evils on earth! That is what the world says. Read the Gospels, and see whether they do not teach us precisely the opposite." [17] But the bourgeois was not converted. Not from weakness of the flesh, but because he believed himself to be in the right as against the Church. He knew what he wanted and why he was entitled to want it. He, too, wanted order, a new order, which would be born of the efforts of his class and which the Church could not recognize.

"Today," says Père Croiset, "all conditions seem to be mixed together. The bourgeois who has just made his fortune is often indistinguishable from the man of quality, save by more brilliant luxury. . . . A propriety of order and Christian courtesy used to distinguish stations and conditions, even down to their clothing, in accordance with the spirit and moral teaching of Jesus Christ." Now, however, "confusion and disorder" [18] were rampant.

How, in all this, was a divine order to be recognized? God, we know, "ordered all conditions and placed a wise difference among them." Consequently, when "he has placed us in a position, our business is to remain fixed there, as a saint says, like statues in the niches in which the craftsman placed them; if he considers it fitting to move them, they suffer themselves to be moved; if he leaves them, they do not budge. There, Lord, that is how we should be in your hands! That is order, and nothing is more reasonable." [19]

But the statues had budged, and the Church lamented the confusion of conditions. Men were no longer following their vocations. They were seeking places here and there, according to their whim. Where was Divine Providence? How was one to continue to believe that God had some part in a social order where everything was topsy-turvy and where the bourgeois, born yesterday, and the product of his own industry, lifted himself above those whose rank was of divine right and whom Divine Providence had singled out above their peers?

Order, for the Church, was the *status quo,* which everyone could recognize because it was self-evident. Any constituted society had its order; men must respect the established order. For, once order had been instituted, God, "the first founder of all the states which make up the world and constitute human society," [20] forbade its violation on any pretext. The generations which succeeded one another must always be able to find the form and the rule of that order, so that the Christian might follow the path traced for him.

As a result, once transformations began to take place from within and values shifted, the Church, by identifying its God with an order that no longer had any justification for existence, was to compromise him, and the adherents of the new order, feeling that the Church merely protected abuses, ceased to ask its advice. Incapable of perceiving any order but that which existed and only very dimly perceiving the order which was emerging, what answer could the clergy give to those who were keeping abreast of the times?

There must be harmony between the Christian and the man who carries out the duties of his profession, Bourdaloue had said, "so much so that . . . the Christian cannot be separated from the trader, the Christian from the working man or craftsman, the Christian from the army officer, the Christian from the prince or monarch. For all these states, and every other state, if I may put it so, must be Christianized in our persons." [21]

The Church did not succeed in establishing harmony between the bourgeois and the Christian. The individual bourgeois might remain a Catholic; the bourgeoisie, the bourgeois State, did not. The bourgeois, seeing himself abandoned by the God of the Christians who appeared never to approve of him save to the extent that he stayed prudently within the narrow confines of his sphere, went on to the conquest of power without the cooperation of the Church and, without asking the advice of the God of the Christians, he asserted what he called his rights and established a new order.

THE TRIUMPH OF THE RESPECTABLE CITIZEN

On the ruins of the Gospel of Jesus Christ, "there arises a gospel of worldly probity, embracing all the duties of reason and religion. The Christian people are to be turned into a people of philosophers; all the virtues are summed up under the headings of the public weal, the proprieties of civil life, law and order, social tranquillity; no other laws, principles, norms of manners or conduct are known or recognized; people make it a point of honor to abandon the title of Christian and to merit the title and sustain the character of an upright man." [22] Thus Père Charles Frey de Neuville accuses his fellow citizens of seeking to limit "all the duties of religion to the duties of probity" and of imagining that "the true Christian can add nothing, or almost nothing, to the qualities of the upright man." [23] "When a man wants to speak highly of another," says the Pastor of Gap, "he says of him that he is an upright man; he does not say, and dare not say, that he is a genuine Christian, as though there were something discreditable in being a Christian." [24]

The bourgeois aimed at being an upright man, and nothing more. "You will tell me, no doubt, that you are upright men, but that you are not religious fanatics," says Abbé de Boulogne; "for that, my brothers, is the eternal refrain, the favorite maxim which, according to the self-styled sages of the times, will solve everything. You are not religious fanatics! No, indeed, since you are not Christians, since God is no longer anything for you!" [25] This was why, as the Pastor of Gap says, "most upright men in whom the so-called philosophical spirit has not absolutely extinguished the light of faith . . . have nothing now but a sterile faith which normally plays no part whatsoever either in their virtues or in their good deeds. Instead of Christian virtues, they have only moral virtues, like those of wise pagans; virtues, consequently, which are unavailing for the next life." [26] The education which they gave their children was proof enough. "I would wish," says the Pastor of Gap, speaking to his parishioners, "that you would season your conversations with a few words bearing some relation to religion and piety, words which *felt* Christian, if I may so express myself, and made it clear that you were Christians. . . . I will allow, Monsieur, that you give your children fine instruction on the way they should behave in the world. 'My son, have a sense of honor; be upright; . . . take care to earn a good reputation for yourself.

. . . Be gentle, honest, courteous, considerate, serviceable. . . . My daughter, be modest and reserved. . . .' Those are certainly very wise counsels, and thoroughly worthy of an upright man; yes, indeed, but a pagan father said the same things to his children. Why has religion no part in these instructions which in other respects are so excellent?" [27]

The bourgeois was an upright man without being a Christian. "Every day," says the Pastor of Gap again, "we see persons otherwise estimable, and leading well-ordered lives, who are basically nothing more than honest pagans, and have no Christian virtues at all." [28] The upright man knew his duty without asking the God of the Christians. He knew how to be "moral" without having to ask the Church.

To finalize his independence and prove conclusively to himself and to others that he knew how to order his life, the bourgeois would have liked to have his moral code set down in the form of a catechism. "For some time, now, we have been constantly hearing about the need for composing a catechism of morality, in which no use would be made of religious principles —antiquated incentives which it is time to set aside," says Necker,[29] who did not share this view, whereas Rivarol, who did, asserted that "a catechism of morality is today the first requirement of the nation. . . . The wise await it, the religious fanatics fear it, the government has made it necessary." [30]

But what did the bourgeoisie want to include in its catechism? A secular morality, of course, which would be that of the whole human race, the assumption being that "the civilized nations of the world are agreed on the essential points of morality, just as they differ on those of faith." [31] "It is said, and that is the fashionable sentiment nowadays," says Caraccioli, "that, independently of all religion, there is a certain love of justice which nature inspires in us, and which suffices at least to form an upright character." [32] Thus the bourgeois morality was of general human application. That was the interpretation which the bourgeois found on rereading the works of the philosophers, when he felt himself to be man, and not simply a bourgeois. From that sentiment he was to draw new strength to assert himself. Good sense, reason, nature, and humanity, he felt, were on his side.

Nevertheless, the eighteenth-century bourgeois was not the reasonable being whom he often represented to himself. He was not man in the abstract, he was a man of a particular period, the product of a particular set of economic and moral circumstances. Consequently, when he talked about man as he was and as he should be, it is man seen through bourgeois eyes that we recognize in the image he presented of the human condition . . . not man as such, but the respectable citizen, the representative of a certain class. Hence, too, his morality could not be of universal application, without distinction of social class. This, in any case, the eighteenth-century bourgeoisie came increasingly to realize; not everyone could be a pillar of society.

There must be "a religion for the people, and Christianity is without question the best that can be given them." [33] That was the view of the respectable citizen, as the Pastor of Gap has already told us. The bourgeois recognized without difficulty that the moral autonomy which he had gained for himself was not for everyone. For the populace, everything must remain as before; they must remain believers. We should have no illusions on this subject, explains Necker in his book, *De l'Importance des Opinions religieuses*. Social order required the existence of poor people.

"It is unavoidable, in the best regulated societies," writes Necker, "that some should enjoy, without labor and without trouble, all the conveniences of life, while others, in far greater number, should be forced to seek the most meager subsistence, the most limited reward, in the sweat of their brow." [34] Or again, "Will it be said, imprudently, that if distinctions of property are an obstacle to the establishment of a political morality, we should strive to destroy them? . . . One may dream of a state where things would be otherwise, and where equality reigned among men, but would one imagine that these primitive relations can be restored at a time when the disparity of means has considerably increased, and when all the superiority of state and power is consolidated by the immutable force of disciplined armies?" [35]

That, too, was why religion could not be dispensed with. "The successive abuses of force and authority, by undermining all the relations originally existing among men, have raised so artificial an edifice in their midst, in which there is such disproportion, that the idea of a God has become more necessary than ever, as the leveler of this confused assemblage of disparities of all kinds." In the emerging nations it might be different, "but in our old states of Europe, where the growth of wealth is constantly widening the differences in fortunes and the gap between conditions, . . . where poverty constantly jostles magnificence, a morality backed by religion is essential to hold back the multitudes who behold so many good things, so many objects of envy, and who, standing so near to everything they call happiness, may never aspire to it." [36]

We should therefore recognize the utility of religion. The rich had property which religion protected far better than could any emancipated morality. "God, giving his laws on Mount Sinai, has only to say, 'Thou shalt not steal' and, with the exalted idea of this God, . . . this commandment preserves sufficient authority for all time; but if political philosophy says, 'Thou shalt not steal,' it must add to that precept a series of arguments on the laws of property, on the inequality of conditions, and on the various relations of the social order." [37] It was therefore much safer to stick to religion and to entrust the defense of property to God rather than to philosophy.

Thus, in order to be able to profess a secular morality, the citizen must already possess some property; otherwise he must be content with the religion reserved for those who possessed none. And the more impoverished the latter became, the greater the efforts that must be made to preserve their faith. Necker says as much, "The more the weight of taxation keeps the people in a state of prostration and destitution, the more indispensable it is to give them a religious education." [38] But was this not an admission that religion was never more than an expedient, a lesser evil which men cannot do without if those who are unable to become pillars of society are to be kept to the straight and narrow path? That is what Rivarol says, in his letters to Necker. "I feel," he writes, "that if religion is necessary to the people, it is less to make them happy than to make them capable of enduring their misfortune. For it is the extreme disparities in wealth that must be blamed for the expedient of religions; when this world has been rendered unbearable to men, they must be promised another." [39] Or again, "If my lackey doesn't kill me in the depths of a forest because he fears the devil, I am not going to withdraw such a brake from that brutish soul any more than I would want to take from him his fear of the gallows; since I cannot make an upright man of him, I'll make him a religious one." [40]

Thus the bourgeois, having learned prudence, proposed to reserve his morality for himself; the rest might remain religious until further notice. This suffices to show the closeness of the link between the new morality, whatever the general forms in which it was clothed, and the spirit of a class. Not that the respectable citizen, as he developed his principles, always realized the boundaries that would confront him once he attempted to apply them. The bourgeoisie had created a new conception of life for itself. It was quite natural that, to ensure the triumph of that conception, its authors should present it in generalities and relate it to a universal order. They sought to broaden it rather than to delimit its boundaries. The bourgeois spoke of "man" and "humanity"; he tended to invoke "nature." However, if a man were to be "upright," he found it very useful, if not essential, to be propertied. In any case, was it not altogether natural to own property, and did not the bourgeois condition correspond to the intentions of nature, which desired its children to be happy and provided them with the necessary means to that end?

In reducing bourgeois morality to its social and economic dimensions, it has not been our intention to detract from its value. It was precisely because the respectable citizen was but a sublimation of the honest bourgeois, and not an abstract figure produced by a moral catechism, that he constituted a reality: the new man of the modern bourgeoisie as contrasted with the man of former times, as conceived by the Church. This new man had proved himself; his own existence was to be his supreme argument. He had proved what only life itself could bear out: that by living as he had, one could succeed. He could point to flourishing towns and villages; he could show that well-being had spread wherever he had been allowed to use his abilities unimpeded. And it seemed that a jealous God no longer reserved happiness for the next life alone, now that his children were capable of conducting themselves as reasonable and enterprising men. The world which the bourgeois had created testified in his favor. It was his world. It was not the product of the churchgoers. He had created it in defiance of the godly, who spoke to him only of the vanity of human efforts in the face of death. He, personally, had believed in life and had succeeded.

"Everywhere one could hear the sound of chisel and hammer, and not even darkness could quell the eagerness of those who were having splendid mansions built for themselves. All along the streets you could see wood being polished, marble being cut. Floors were being raised upon floors, as though to create a rampart against death."[41] So a writer of the period, who took the part of the Church, describes the activity he witnessed in Paris around 1772. The bourgeois had been confident of his own strength and had become master of the world. The great and the poor, the former to justify their rank and wealth, the latter to console themselves for having none, turned to the church and rendered it homage; but what reason had the bourgeois for doing likewise? A child of this world, he had grown up without the assistance of the Church. The God of the Christians had never wanted to recognize him; what he was, he owed to himself; he had appointed himself his own providence, and was not prepared to recognize any other.

Notes

NOTES

Part I. The Church and the Development of the Bourgeois Conscience

1. THE HUMBLE BELIEVER

1. Abbé Réguis, *La Voix du Pasteur: Discours familiers d'un curé à ses paroissiens pour tous les dimanches de l'année* (1773), IV, 230. The sermons of Abbé Réguis, Pastor of Gap, are one of the most valuable sources of information on the attitudes of the various social classes in a small town under the *ancien régime*.

2. *Ibid.*, p. 213.

3. Abbé Pluche, *Le Spectacle de la Nature* (1750), VIII, Part II, 348 ff.

4. *Ibid.*, p. 362.

5. Réguis, *op. cit.*, IV, 213.

6. Pluche, *op. cit.*, VIII, Part II, 371 ff.

7. Jacques-Bénigne Bossuet, *Réflexions sur un Écrit de M. Claude,* ed. Guérin (1862), V, 371.

8. Pluche, *op. cit.*, VIII, Part II, 170, 214, 360.

9. Pastoral Instruction of Msgr. l'Evêque-Duc de Langres on *Excellence de la Religion* (1786), p. 144.

2. THE "ENLIGHTENED"

1. Bossuet, *Réflexions sur un Écrit de M. Claude,* ed. Guérin (1862).

2. Abbé Pluche, *Le Spectacle de la Nature* (1750), VIII, II, 298 ff.

3. *Ibid.*, pp. 169 ff.

4. *Ibid.*, p. 145, 166.

5. *Ibid.*, p. 265.

6. Abbé Réguis, *La Voix du Pasteur* (1773), I, 218 ff.

7. Jean-Baptiste Massillon, "Sermon on the Word of God," *Oeuvres,* ed. Lefèvre (1838), I, 165.

8. Réguis, *op. cit.,* I, 213 ff.

9. *Ibid.,* pp. 297 ff.

10. De Boulogne, "Sermon on Faith," *Oeuvres posthumes,* I, 191.

3. BOURGEOISIE AND POPULACE

1. Bossuet, *Conférence avec M. Claude sur la Matière de l'Eglise.*

2. Nicolas-Sylvestre Bergier, "Foi," from "Dictionnaire de Théologie," in *Encyclopédie méthodique,* III.

3. *Ibid.,* "Implicite," IV.

4. *Ibid.,* "Foi," III.

5. Censure of the Theological Faculty of Paris against Rousseau's novel, *Emile, ou de l'Education* (1762).

6. Pelvert, *Lettre d'un Théologien à M**** (1776), pp. 142 ff., in which the doctrine of some modern writers against unbelievers is examined.

7. Abbé Fleury, "Grand Catéchisme historique," *Oeuvres* (1837), p. 434.

8. Abbé Réguis, *La Voix du Pasteur,* I, 1803, 73 ff.

9. Henry-Marie Boudon, *La Science sacrée du Catéchisme* (1749), pp. 16 ff.

10. Caraccioli, *La Religion de l'honnête Homme* (1776), p. 212.

11. Boudon, *De la Sainteté de l'Etat ecclésiastique* (1765), p. 181.

12. *Ibid.,* p. 358.

13. Champion de Pontallier, *Le Théologien philosophe* (1786), I, 130.

14. Boudon, *La Science sacrée du Catéchisme* (1749), p. 82.

15. Boudon, *De la Sainteté de l'Etat ecclésiastique, op. cit.,* pp. 174 ff.

16. Boudon, *La Science sacrée du Catéchisme, op. cit.,* pp. 78 ff.

17. Boudon, *De le Sainteté de l'Etat ecclésiastique, op. cit.,* p. 176.

18. Grivel, *Théorie de l'Education* (1783), III, 136.

19. Bossuet, *Discours sur l'Histoire universelle.*

20. Molinier, "Sermon on the truth of the Christian religion," *Sermons choisis sur les Mystères . . .* (1730), I, 248.

21. Abbé Réguis, *La Voix du Pasteur* (1773), IV, 218.

22. *Ibid.,* III, 243 ff.

23. Philipon de la Madelaine, *Vues patriotiques sur l'Education du Peuple, tant des Villes que des Campagnes* (1783), pp. 235 ff.

24. *Ibid.*, p. 239.

25. Réguis, *op. cit.*, IV, 232 ff.

26. Robert de Lamennais, "Reflections on the state of the Church in France," *Oeuvres* (1844), V, 46.

27. Massillon, "Sermon for Christmas Day," *Oeuvres*, ed. Lefèvre (1838), I, 88.

28. De la Chalotais, *Essai sur l'Education nationale* . . . (1763).

29. Massillon, "Sermon for the feast of the Incarnation," *Oeuvres*, ed. Lefèvre (1838), II, 32.

30. Molinier, "Sermon on the truth of the Christian religion," *Sermons choisis sur les Mystères* . . . (1730), I.

31. Trublet, *Essais sur divers sujets de Littérature et de Morale* (2nd ed., 1737), p. 429.

32. Massillon, "Sermon on the truth of religion," *Oeuvres, op. cit.*, I, 142.

33. *Ibid.*, "Sermon for Christmas Day," p. 88.

34. Molinier, *op. cit.*, I, 246.

35. Fumel, *Instruction pastorale de Msgr l'Evêque de Lodève sur les Sources de L'Incrédulité du Siècle* (1765), p. 5.

36. Msgr l'Evêque-Duc de Langres, *Instruction pastorale sur l'Excellence de la Religion* (1786), p. 6.

37. Abbé Réguis, *La Voix du Pasteur* (1773), IV, 356.

38. Massillon, "Sermon for Christmas Day," *op. cit.*, I, 88 ff.

39. Jean-Baptiste Beauvais, "Funeral oration for Count du Muy," *Oeuvres* (1807), IV, 346.

40. Caraccioli, *La Religion de l'honnête Homme* (1766), p. 169.

41. *Ibid.*, p. 224.

42. Molinier, "Sermon on the truth of the Christian religion," *op. cit.*, I, 161.

43. Augustin Barruel, "Collection ecclésiastique," *Considérations sur les Limites de la Puissance spirituelle et de la Puissance civile*, ed. the Archbishop of Toulouse (1791), II, 476.

44. Jauffret, *De la Religion à l'Assemblée Nationale*, pp. 4 ff.

45. Parishioners of Landemont in Bas-Anjou to the National Assembly, Archives Nationales, DXIX (1789), 23.

46. Report made by one of the judges of the District Court of Challans in connection with disturbances and risings occurring in several parishes of the said district, Archives Nationales, DXXIX (1791), 15.

47. B. Lambert, *Réflexions sur l'État actuel de l'Eglise* (1787), p. 2.

48. Gros de Besplas, *Les Causes du Bonheur public* . . . (1774), II, 90.

49. Bayle, *Oeuvres diverses,* I, 173.

50. Réguis, *op. cit.,* I, 217.

51. *Ibid.,* I, 430.

52. *Ibid.,* I, 44.

53. Caraccioli, *op. cit.,* p. 198.

54. Réguis, *op. cit.,* I, 308 ff.

55. *Ibid.,* III, 375.

56. Bergier, "Fête," from "Dictionnaire de Théologie," in *Encyclopédie méthodique,* III.

57. *Ibid.,* "Culte."

58. Réguis, *op. cit.,* II, 76, 223.

59. *Ibid.,* II, 76.

4. PRIESTS AND LAITY

1. Fénelon, *Traité du Ministère des Pasteurs,* Ch. 2.

2. *Nouvelles Ecclésiastiques,* February 27, 1780.

3. Le Franc de Pompignan, Bishop of Le Puy, *Défense des Actes du Clergé de France concernant la Religion* (Published in the Assembly records, 1765), p. 247.

4. Isaac-Joseph Berruyer, *Histoire du Peuple de Dieu, depuis la Naissance du Messie* (1755), I, iv ff.

5. Réguis, *La Voix du Pasteur* (1773), III, 267 ff.

6. Champion de Pontallier, *Le Théologien philosophe* (1786), I, 128, 129.

7. Vincent-Toussaint Beurier, *Conférences ou Discours contre les Ennemis de notre Sainte Religion* (1779), p. 508.

8. *Ibid.,* p. 522.

9. *La Religion Chrétienne méditée dans le véritable Esprit de ses Maximes* . . . (1763), V, 275.

10. Beurier, *op. cit.,* pp. 522 ff.

11. Réguis, *op. cit.,* III, 250.

12. *Ibid.,* I, 404 ff.

13. *Les Héxaples ou les Six Colonnes sur la Constitution Unigenitus* (1721), IV, 257, 259.

14. Réguis, *op. cit.,* III, 247.

Part II. *God, Sin, and Death*

6. DEATH

1. Bossuet, "Address to the Daughters of the Visitation on Death."

2. Bossuet, "Preparation for Death."

3. Bossuet, "Address to the Daughters of the Visitation on Death."

4. Bossuet, "Funeral Oration for Henri de Gornay."

5. Bossuet, "Sermon on Death," *Oeuvres*.

6. Pierre Nicole, *Essais de Morale* (1753), IV, 57.

7. *Ibid.*

8. Bossuet, "Preparation for Death," first prayer.

9. Pascal, *Pensées*, ed. M. Turnell (New York, Harper & Brothers, 1962), No. 11, p. 105.

10. Bossuet, "Funeral Oration for Madame Yolande de Monterby."

11. Bossuet, "Sermon on Death," *op. cit.*

12. Nicole, *op. cit.*, IV, 63.

13. *Ibid.*, p. 37.

14. Père Gégou, "Traité de la Préparation à la Mort," in Houdry, *La Bibliothèque des Prédicateurs*, VI, 474.

15. Père de la Colombière, "De la Mort," *Ibid.*, pp. 499 ff.

16. *Ibid.*, p. 475.

17. Nicole, *op. cit.*, IV, 37 ff.

18. Houdry, *op. cit.*, VI, 476.

19. Duguet, *Lettres sur divers Sujets de Morale et de Piété* (6th ed., 1726), II, 375 ff.

20. Houdry, *op. cit.*, VI, 489. Author anonymous.

21. Père Estienne Chamillard, *Ibid.*, p. 540.

22. *L'Art de toucher le Coeur dans le Ministère de la Chaire* (1783), II, 269.

23. Père de la Colombière in Houdry, *op. cit.*, VI, 612.

24. A book entitled *Le Chrétien inconnu, Ibid.*, III, 594.

25. Réguis, *La Voix du Pasteur: Discours familiers d'un curé à ses paroissiens pour tous les dimanches de l'année* (1773), IV, 191, 207.

26. "Essais de Sermons pour les Dimanches," in Houdry, *op. cit.*, III, 573.

27. M. Joly, "Les Prônes," *Ibid.*, p. 574.

28. Massillon, "Funeral Oration for the Dauphin," *Oeuvres,* ed. Lefèvre (1838), I.

29. Réguis, *La Voix du Pasteur* (1773), IV, 203.

30. Feugère, *Bourdaloue, sa Prédication et son Temps* (1889), p. 268.

31. Griffet, *Sermons,* III, 42 ff.

32. Beurier, *Conférences ou Discours contre les Ennemis de notre Sainte Religion* (1779), pp. 560 ff.

33. Massillon, "Sermon on Religious Doubts," *Oeuvres,* I, 389.

34. Molinier, *Sermons choisis sur les Mysteres . . .* (1730), IV, 261 ff.

35. Massillon, "Sermon for Christmas Day," *Oeuvres,* I.

36. *Ibid.*, "Sermon on Religious Doubts," p. 392.

37. Griffet, *op. cit.*, III, 39 ff.

38. Bayle, "Des-Barreaux," *Dictionnaire historique et critique,* II, 616.

39. Cambacérès, "Sermon on Hell," *Sermons* (1787), II, 331.

40. Massillon, "Sermon on Religious Doubts," *op. cit.*, I, 397.

41. Cambacérès, "Sermon on the Word of God," *op. cit.*, I, 397.

42. Hyacinthe de Montargon, *Dictionnaire apostolique* (1768), V, 509 ff.

43. Molinier, "Sermon for the First Monday in Lent," *op. cit.*, IV, 269.

44. Abbé L. François, *Preuves de la Religion de Jésus-Christ contre les Spinozistes et les Déistes* (1751), I, 24.

45. Père Louis le Comte, *Nouveaux Mémoires sur l'état présent de la Chine* (1696), II, 303 ff.

46. Griffet, *op. cit.*, III, 38 ff.

47. Pascal, *Pensées,* ed. M. Turnell (New York, Harper & Brothers, 1962), No. 11, p. 108.

48. Caraccioli, *Le Tableau de la Mort* (1760), p. 148.

49. De Boulogne, *Oeuvres posthumes,* I, 297.

50. Fénelon, "Letter of September 17, 1691," *Lettres spirituelles.*

51. Fénelon, *Oeuvres* (1837), III, 540.

52. "Ordonnance de M. l'Evêque de Chartres, portant la Condamnation du livre intitulé: 'Analysis Orationis mentalis . . . ' " in Du Pin, *Histoire ecclésiastique du XVIIᵉ siècle* (1727), III.

53. Bossuet, *Instruction sur les États d'Oraison.*

54. *Nouvelles Ecclésiastiques,* July 25, 1773.

55. *Ibid.*, July 17, 1762.

Y a-t-il quelque Remède aux Maux d l'Eglise de France? (1778), p. 102.

48. *Les trois Etats de l'Homme* (1784), p. 280.

49. Cordier, *Eclaircissement sur la Prédestination.* Quoted in *Nouvelles Ecclésiastiques,* October 8, 1748.

50. *Le vrai Sens des Cent Une Propositions* (1742).

51. Hyacinthe de Montargon, *Dictionnaire apostolique* (1768), V, 100.

52. *Ibid.,* III, 255 ff.

53. Fumel, *Le Culte de l'Amour divin.* Quoted in *Nouvelles Ecclésiastiques,* November 6, 1777.

54. Mathisse, canon of the collegial church of Nantes, *Panégyrique de la Bienheureuse Angèle Merici.* Quoted in *Nouvelles Ecclésiastiques,* April 11, 1744.

55. Bergier, *Dictionnaire de Théologie,* from the *Encyclopédie méthodique,* IV, 496. Article: Justice.

56. *Ibid.,* II, 133. Article: Choice.

57. Colbert, *Oeuvres,* II, 603.

58. *Ibid.,* p. 788.

59. *Le vrai Sens des Cent Une Propositions,* pp. 44 ff.

60. *Les Héxaples,* II, 181 ff.

61. *Ibid.,* IV, 338.

62. Bergier, *op. cit.,* II, 134. Article: The elect.

63. *Les Héxaples, ou les Six Colonnes sur la Constitution Unigenitus* (1721), IV, 285.

64. Colbert, *Oeuvres,* I, 576.

65. *Les Héxaples,* II, 621.

66. *Ibid.,* III, Part I, 445 ff.

67. Soanen, *Lettres,* VI. Letter dated May 8, 1738.

68. *Les Héxaples,* II, 505.

69. *Ibid.,* I, foreword, xxxvii.

70. *Ibid.,* p. xlvi.

71. *Ibid.,* p. xx.

72. Mésenguy, *Mémoire justificatif,* p. 169.

73. *Les Héxaples,* III, Part I, 249.

74. *Ibid.,* p. 283.

75. *Ibid.,* pp. 61 ff.

76. *Traité de l'Equilibre de la Volonté* (1719). Quoted in Pelvert, *Lettres d'un Théologien* (1776), p. 427.

77. *Quatrième Gémissement d'une Ame vivement touchée de la Constitution de Notre Saint Père le Pape Clément* (1714), pp. 192 ff.

78. Nouvelles Ecclésiastiques, XVII, 99, June 19, 1786.

79. Quatrième Gémissement . . . , p. 197.

80. Réponse de M*** à M. l'Evêque de *** sur cette question: Y a-t-il quelque Remède aux Maux de l'Eglise de France? (1778), p. 114.

81. Hyacinthe de Montargon, Dictionnaire apostolique (1768), III, pp. 269, 274.

82. De Boulogne, Oeuvres posthumes, I, p. 251.

83. Hyacinthe de Montargon, op. cit., III, 213.

84. L'Esprit de Nicole (1765), pp. 461 ff.

85. Le Ciel ouvert à tout l'Univers (1782), p. 156.

86. Cambacérès, "Sermon on Hell," Sermons (ed. 1787), II, 297 ff.

87. Elisée, Sermons, IV, 292.

88. Charles Frey de Neuville, Sermons, III, 255.

89. De Boulogne, "Sermon on the Last Judgment," Oeuvres Posthumes, I.

90. Bergier, Dictionnaire de Théologie, from the Encyclopédie méthodique, IV. Article: Justice.

91. Les trois Etats de l'Homme (1784), p. 61.

92. Ibid., pp. 71 ff.

93. Ibid., p. 92.

94. Ibid., p. 96.

95. Deuxième lettre du R. P. de Gennes, prêtre de l'Oratoire, à M. l'Evêque d'Angers (1719).

96. Quesnel, Ninety-fifth Proposition.

97. J. B. Gaultier, Le poème de Pope intitulé "Essai sur l'Homme," convaincu d'Impiété (1746), p. 111.

98. Quesnel, Le Nouveau Testament, en français, avec des Réflexions morales (1736), VII, 360.

99. Bayle, Dictionnaire historique et critique, V. Second explanatory note.

100. Toussaint, Les Moeurs (1749-, pp. 8 ff.

101. Pascal's Pensées, ed. M. Turnell. (New York, Harper & Brothers, 1962), No. 317, p. 196.

102. Arnauld, "Réfutation de la fausse Relation du Père Ferrier, jésuite," Oeuvres, XXII, 314.

103. Les Héxaples, ou les Six Colonnes sur la Constitution Unigenitus (1721), I, p. xxii.

104. Nicole, Essais de Morale (1753), XII, 513 ff.

105. Quesnel, op. cit., VII, 354.

106. Yvon, *L'Accord de la Philosophie avec la Religion* (1776). Quoted in *Nouvelles Ecclésiastiques,* February 27, 1777.

8. THE IDEA OF SIN

1. Charles Frey de Neuville, *Sermons,* I, 100.

2. Bossuet, *Défense de la Tradition et des Saints Pères,* ix, Part II, Ch. xxii.

3. Quesnel, *Le Nouveau Testament, en français, avec des Réflexions morales* (1736), VI, 114 ff.

4. Duguet, *Lettres sur divers Sujets de Morale et de Piété,* V, Letter xlix.

5. Arnauld, "Apologie pour les Saints Pères," *Oeuvres,* XVIII, 934.

6. Colbert, *Oeuvres,* II, 585.

7. *Les Héxaples, ou les Six Colonnes sur la Constitution Unigenitus* (1721), p. 197.

8. *Ibid.,* p. 175.

9. *Mémoires de Trévoux* (1782), July, p. 1601.

10. Du Pain, *Traité philosophique et théologique sur l'Amour de Dieu* (1717), pp. 95 ff.

11. *Les Héxaples,* IV, 191.

12. Patouillet, *Apologie de Cartouche ou le Scélérat, justifié par la grâce du sieur Quesnel,* p. 81.

13. Nicole, *Essais de Morale* (1753), V, 262.

14. Fumel, *Instruction pastorale de Monseigneur l'Evêque de Lodève sur les Sources de l'Incrédulité du Siècle* (1765), p. 331.

15. Quoted in *Nouvelles Ecclésiastiques,* October 23, 1745, p. 171.

16. Père de Bouhours, *Sentiments des Jésuites touchant le Péché philosophique* (1694), pp. 73 ff. Third Letter.

17. *Ibid.,* pp. 77 ff.

18. *Les Héxaples,* II, 437 ff.

19. *Réponse de M*** à M. l'Evêque de *** sur cette Question: Y a-t-il quelque Remède aux Maux de l'Eglise de France?* (1778).

20. Arnauld, "Seconde Apologie de Jansénius," *Oeuvres,* XVII, 140.

21. *Réponse de M*** à M. l'Evêque de *** sur cette Question: Y a-t-il quelque Remède aux Maux de l'Eglise de France?* (1778).

22. *Instruction pastorale de Monseigneur l'Archevêque de Lyon*

sur les Sources de l'Incrédulité et les Fondements de la Religion (1776), p. 136.

23. Duguet, *Explication du livre de la Genèse* (1732), I, 382.

24. Pascal's *Pensées*, ed. M. Turnell. (New York, Harper & Brothers, 1962), No. 246, p. 170.

25. Pelvert, *Lettres d'un Théologien* (1776), p. 38.

26. Bossuet, *Elevations sur les Mystères*, Seventh Week, Third Elevation.

27. Arnauld, "Apologie pour les Saints Pères," *Oeuvres*, XVII, 63.

28. *Nouvelles Ecclésiastiques*, April 17, 1757.

29. *Discours sur les Nouvelles Ecclésiastiques* (1759). Thirtieth Discourse.

30. *Les Héxaples*, III, Part II, 825.

31. *Discours sur les Nouvelles Ecclésiastiques* (1759). Thirtieth Discourse.

32. *Nouvelles Ecclésiastiques*, July 10, 1779.

33. *Ibid.*, May 2, 1763. *Mandement . . . de . . . l'Archevêque de Lyon, portant condamnation des trois parties de l' "Histoire du Peuple de Dieu."*

34. *Les trois Etats de l'Homme* (1784), p. 36.

35. Arnauld, "Seconde Apologie de Jansénius," *Oeuvres*, XVII, 331.

36. *Ibid.*, pp. 329 ff.

37. *Ibid.*, p. 846.

38. *Réponse de M*** à M. l'Evêque de *** sur cette Question: Y a-t-il quelque Remède aux Maux de l'Eglise de France?* (1778), p. 122.

39. *Nouvelles Ecclésiastiques*, April 25, 1774.

40. *Ibid.*, April 11, 1774.

41. Bossuet, "Sermon on the Respect Due to Truth."

42. Bossuet, "Funeral Oration for Nicolas Cornet."

43. Bossuet, "Sermon on the Respect Due to Truth."

44. Massillon, "Sermon on the Evidence of the Law," *Oeuvres*, I, 450.

45. *Ibid.*, "Sermon on the Samaritan woman," *Oeuvres*, p. 363.

46. Lamy, *Entretiens sur les Sciences* (1683). Seventh Discussion.

47. Fleury, *Discours sur l'Histoire Ecclésiastique*. Sixth Discourse.

48. Lefranc de Pompignan, "Lettres à un Evêque sur divers Points de Morale," *Oeuvres posthumes* (1802), I, 230 ff.

49. Bayle, *Dictionnaire historique et critique*, III, 735. Article: Loyola.

50. Lefrance de Pompignan, *Oeuvres posthumes* (1802), I, 277.

51. Bossuet, *Elevations sur les Mystères*. Seventh Week, Third Elevation.

52. *Les Héxaples, ou les Six Colonnes sur la Constitution Unigenitus* (1721), II, 435.

53. *La Religion Chrétienne méditée dans le véritable Esprit de ses Maximes,* I, 406 ff.

54. Tronson, *Examens particuliers sur divers Sujets propres aux Ecclésiastiques* (ed. 1811), I, 321 ff.

55. *Ibid.,* II, 317.

56. *Ibid.,* I, 100.

57. *Ibid.,* II, 259 ff.

58. *Ibid.,* pp. 208, 212.

59. Bossuet, *Treatise on Concupiscence.*

60. Nicole, *Essais de Morale* (1753), XIII, 390.

61. Pacaud, "Address on the feast of the Purification," *Discours de Piété sur les importants Objets de la Religion* (1745), III, 91.

62. Nicole, *op. cit.,* XII, 301 ff.

63. Arnauld, "Seconde Apologie de Jansénius," *Oeuvres,* XVII, 310.

64. Quesnel, Fourty-forth Proposition.

65. Le Pelletier, *Nouvelle Défense de la Constitution,* pp. 237 ff.

66. Colbert, *Oeuvres,* II, 587.

67. *Les Héxaples,* I, 287.

68. *Ibid.,* pp. 283 ff.

69. Colbert, *Oeuvres,* II, 587.

70. *Le vrai Sens des Cent Une Propositions,* p. 30.

71. Le Pelletier, *op. cit.,* p. 242.

72. *Ibid.,* p. 254.

73. Arnauld, "Seconde Apologie de Jansénius," *Oeuvres,* XVII, 352.

74. *Nouvelles Ecclésiastiques,* January, 1747.

75. *Ibid.,* December 11, 1745.

76. *Ibid.,* April 24, 1786.

77. *Ibid.,* December 11, 1745.

78. *Mémoires de Trévoux,* V, August, 1754.

79. *Nouvelles Ecclesiastiques,* January, 1752. Twenty-third Address.

80. Pascal's *Pensées,* ed. M. Turnell. (New York, Harper & Brothers, 1962), No. 433, p. 231.

81. *Ibid.,* No. 143, p. 146.

82. Nicole, *op. cit.*, VI. Miscellaneous thoughts, para. 26.
83. *Nouvelle Défense de la Constitution,* pp. 112 ff.
84. *Ibid.,* p. 215.
85. *Parallèle de la Doctrine des Paiens avec celle des Jésuites* (1726), pp. 138 ff.
86. Toussaint, *Eclaircissement sur Les Moeurs* (1762), p. 132.
87. Toussaint, *Les Moeurs* (1749), p. 14.
88. *L'Alambic Moral* (1773). Article: Man.
89. Desserres de la Tour, *Du Bonheur* (1767), p. 46.
90. Rivarol, *Oeuvres* (1808), II, 145.
91. Toussaint, *Les Moeurs,* 1749, p. 139.
92. Pacaud, *op. cit.,* III, 29.
93. Meyniel, *Maximes de Droit naturel sur le Bonheur* (1791).
94. Desserres de la Tour, *op. cit.,* p. 168.
95. Coyer, *Plan d'Education publique* (1770), p. 249.
96. Meyniel, *op. cit.,* p. 19.
97. *L'Alambic Moral* (1773). Article: Man.
98. Montazet, *Instruction pastorale de Monseigneur l'Archevêque de Lyon sur les Sources de l'Incrédulité et les Fondements de la Religion* (1776), quoted by Albert Monod, *De Pascal à Chateaubriand* (1916), p. 477.
99. Montesquieu, *Pensées et Fragments inédits,* II, 488.

Part III. The Bourgeoisie and the Social Teachings of the Church

9. THE CHURCH AND THE SOCIAL CLASSES

1. Bossuet, "Sermon on Final Impenitence."
2. Bossuet, "Panegyric in Honor of St. Francis of Assisi."
3. Massillon, "Sermon on the Respect which the Great Owe to Religion."
4. Bossuet, "Funeral Oration for Maria Theresa of Austria."
5. Collet, *Traité des Devoirs des gens du Monde et surtout des Chefs de Famille* (1763), pp. 282 ff.
6. Abbé Poulle, "Sermon on Almsgiving," *Sermons* (1781), I.
7. Collet, *op. cit.,* p. 281.
8. Nicole, *Essais de Morale* (ed. 1753), VI, Fourth treaties, para. 13.

9. Lamourette, *Considérations sur l'Esprit et les Devoirs de la Vie religieuse* (1785), pp. 102 ff.

10. Houdry, *La Bibliothèque des Prédicateurs,* VII, 203.

11. Bossuet, "Sermon on the Love of Pleasures."

12. Massillon, "Sermon on the Obstacles to Truth in the Hearts of the Great."

13. Bossuet, "Sermon on Ambition."

14. Bossuet, "Sermon on the Love of Pleasures."

15. Bossuet, "Sermon on the Profession of Madame de la Vallière."

16. Bossuet, "Funeral Oration for Henrietta of England."

17. Massillon, "On the Affliction of the Great who Abandon God."

18. *Ibid.*

19. Massillon, "Sermon on the Temptations of the Great."

20. Bossuet, "Sermon on Final Impenitence."

21. Bossuet, "Address to the Daughters of the Visitation on Death."

22. *Ibid.*

23. Cf. Feugère, *Bourdaloue,* p. 373.

24. Bourdaloue, *Oeuvres,* ed. Didot, II, 100.

25. *La Religion Chrétienne meditee dans le veritable Esprit de ses Maximes* (1763), pp. 64 ff.

26. Bossuet, "Sermon on Final Impenitence."

27. Massillon, "Sermon on the Respect which the Great Owe to Religion."

10. ALMSGIVING

1. Bossuet, "Panegyric in Honor of St. Francis of Assisi."

2. Griffet, *Sermons,* II, 398.

3. Bourdaloue, *Oeuvres,* I, 177.

4. Nicole, *Essais de Morale* (1753), XII, 371 ff.

5. Griffet, *op. cit.,* pp. 398 ff.

6. Massillon, "Sermon on the Humanity of the Great toward the People."

7. Bossuet, "Sermon on Final Impenitence."

8. Bossuet, "Panegyric in Honor of St. Francis of Assisi."

9. Bourdaloue, *Oeuvres,* II, 79.

10. *Ibid.,* I, 177.

11. Massillon, *Oeuvres,* I, 373.

12. Bossuet, "Panegyric in Honor of St. Francis of Assisi."

13. Bourdaloue, *Oeuvres,* II, 79.

14. Feugère, Bourdaloue, "Sermons sur l'Aumône," p. 217.
15. Le Chapelain, "Addresses on the obligation and extent of alms-giving," *Les Avocats des Pauvres* (1814), II, 487.
16. Bossuet, "Panegyric in Honor of St. Francis of Assisi."
17. Hyacinthe de Montargon, *Dictionnaire apostolique* (1768), I, 268.
18. *Ibid.*, p. 269.
19. Abbé Poulle, *Sermons*, I, 154 ff.
20. *Encyclopédie de Pensées, de Maximes et Réflexions . . .* (1761).
21. Hyacinthe de Gasquet, *L'Usure démasquée* (1766), p. 420.
22. Réguis, *La Voix du Pasteur* (1773), IV, 511.
23. Réguis, *La Voix du Pasteur* (1773), IV, 339.
24. Griffet, *Sermons*, II, 415 ff.
25. Charles Frey de Neuville, *Sermons*, III, 365.
26. Mésenguy, *Abrégé de l'Histoire de l'Ancien Testament* (1747), X, 45.
27. De la Rue, "First sermon on Almsgiving," *Les Avocats des Pauvres* (1814), II, 289.
28. *Ibid.*, Fléchier, "On the Precept of Almsgiving," p. 159.
29. *Ibid.*, Le Chapelain, "Address on the Obligation and Scope of Almsgiving," p. 445.
30. *Ibid.*, De la Colombière, "Sermon on Almsgiving," p. 254.
31. Griffet, *op. cit.*, II, 318.
32. *L'Art de toucher le Coeur*, I, 304.
33. Champion de Pontallier, *Le Trésor du Chrétien*, II, 564.
34. Hyacinthe de Montargon, *Dictionnaire apostolique* (1768), I, 251 ff.
35. Desserres de la Tour, *Du Bonheur* (1767), pp. 139, 144, 149.
36. Gaspard Terrasson, quoted by J. Candel, *Les prédicateurs français dans la première moitié du XVIIIe siècle* (1904), p. 133.
37. Charles Frey de Neuville, *op. cit.*, I, 421.
38. Réguis, *op. cit.*, IV, 334.
39. Poulle, *Sermons*, I, 150 ff.
40. *Ibid.*, p. 148 ff.
41. Bourdaloue, *Oeuvres*, III, 95.

II. CHRISTIAN LIFE AND MIDDLE-CLASS LIFE

1. Arnauld, *De la fréquente Communion* (1739), pp. 748 ff.
2. Nicole, *Essais de Morale* (1753), XIII, 457 ff.

3. Pascal's *Pensées,* ed. M. Turnell, (New York, Harper & Brothers, 1962), No. 740, p. 338.

4. *L'Esprit de Nicole,* p. 297 ff.

5. Nicole, "On the Gospel for the Feast of the Circumcision," *op. cit.,* IX.

6. *L'Esprit de Nicole,* p. 581 ff.

7. Nicole, *op. cit.,* X, 202 ff.

8. Quesnel, *Le Nouveau Testament, en français, avec des Réflexions morales* (1736), VI, 108.

9. Nicole, *op. cit.,* IV, 307.

10. *Nouvelles Ecclésiastiques,* June 18, 1788.

11. Nicole, "On the Epistle for Midnight Mass," *op. cit.,* IX.

12. *Ibid.,* "On Greatness," II, ch. VI.

13. Jean Crasset, *Considérations sur les principales Actions Chrétiennes* (1732), pp. 64 ff.

14. *Ibid.,* p. 66.

15. *Ibid.,* p. 67.

16. Croiset, *Réflexions Chrétiennes,* I, V.

17. *Ibid.,* p. 13.

18. *Ibid.,* p. 4.

19. *Ibid.,* p. 8.

20. Bourdaloue, *Oeuvres,* I, 561.

21. *Ibid.,* "Sermon on the Feast of St. Francis de Sales," II, 562.

22. *Ibid.*

23. Houdry, *La Bibliothèque des Prédicateurs,* III, 91.

24. *Ibid.,* VI, 791. Père Croiset.

25. Bourdaloue, *Oeuvres,* II, 36.

26. *Ibid.,* III, 611 ff.

27. Mésenguy, *Abrégé de l'Histoire de l'Ancien Testament* (1747), III, 428.

28. Quesnel, *Pensées* (1842), p. 90.

29. Bourdaloue, *Sermons,* I, 323.

30. Houdry, *op. cit.,* III, 94. Manuscript Sermon.

31. *Ibid.,* VIII, 71.

32. *Nouvelles Ecclésiastiques,* October 1, 1748.

33. Griffet, *Sermons,* II, 211 ff.

34. Cambacérès, "Sermon on Virtue," *Sermons* (1787), III, 46.

35. *Ibid.,* p. 18.

36. Houdry, *La Bibliothèque des Prédicateurs,* VIII, 293. Père Caussu.

37. Froger, pastor of Mayet, diocese of Le Mans, *Instruction de*

Morale, d'Agriculture et d'Economie pour les Habitants de la Campagne (1769), p. 219.

38. *Ibid.*, p. 15.

39. *Ibid.*, p. 19.

40. *Ibid.*, p. 248.

41. *Ibid.*, p. 257.

42. Froger, *op. cit.*, p. 260 ff.

43. Abbé de Bonnaire, *Le Règle des Devoirs que la Nature inspire à tous les Hommes* (1768), II, 319.

44. De Beauvais, *Sermons,* II, 260.

45. Toussaint, *Les Moeurs* (1749), p. 96.

46. Quesnel, *Le Nouveau Testament, en français, avec des Réflexions morales* (1736), VI, 259.

47. Quesnel, *Pensées* (1842), p. 92.

48. Réguis, *La Voix du Pasteur* (1773), I, 4 ff.

49. De Boulogne, *Oeuvres posthumes,* I, 297.

50. Fleury, *Moeurs des Israélites et des Chrétiens* (1766), p. 57.

51. Pacaud, "Address on Almsgiving," *Discours de Piété sur les importants Objets de la Religion* (1745), II, 256.

52. Nicole, "On the Gospel for Midnight Mass," *Essais de Morale* (1753), IX.

53. *L'Esprit de Nicole,* p. 78.

54. Réguis, *op. cit.*, I, 190.

55. Mésenguy, *Abrégé de l'histoire de l'Ancien Testament,* I, 71.

56. Bourdaloue, "Sermon on Idleness."

57. Quoted by Abbé Etienne Brémont in *Représentation adressée à M. N. . . à l'occasion de son ouvrage De l'Importance des Opinions religieuses* (1788), p. 216.

58. Hyacinthe de Gasquet, *L'Usure démasquée* (1766), p. 146.

59. Mésenguy, *op. cit.*, I, 72.

60. Réguis, *op. cit.*, I, 193 ff.

61. *Ibid.*, IV, 511 ff.

62. Houdry, *La Bibliothèque des Prédicateurs,* VIII, 71.

63. Nicole, "Treatise on Christian vigilance," *op. cit.*, IV, Ch. VII.

64. Abbé Boileau, *Pensées choisies* (1718), pp. 380 ff.

65. *Ibid.*, p. 372.

66. Nicole, *Essais de Morale* (1753), IV, 324.

67. Houdry, *La Bibliothèque des Prédicateurs,* VII, 665, and VIII, 285.

68. *L'Art de toucher le Coeur dans le Ministère de la Chaire* (1783), II, 242 ff.

69. *L'Alambic Moral*. Article: Remedy.

70. Houdry, *op. cit.*, VII, 667.

71. *Ibid.*, VIII, 616.

72. Griffet, *Sermons*, II, 39 ff.

73. *Gazette du Commerce*, II, 612, Sept. 22, 1764.

74. De Boulogne, *Oeuvres posthumes*, I, 332.

75. A. Touron, *De la Providence* (1754), p. 193.

76. Duguet, *Explication du livre de la Genèse*, IV, 21 ff., 1732.

77. Hyacinthe de Montargon, *Dictionnaire apostolique* (1768), V, 291 ff.

78. Réguis, *La Voix du Pasteur* (1773), IV, 345 ff.

79. *Ibid.*, III, 444.

80. Champion de Pontallier, *Le Trésor du Chrétien*, I, 74.

81. *La Religion Chrétienne méditée dans le véritable Esprit de ses Maximes*, I, 294.

82. Réguis, *op. cit.*, IV, 129.

83. *La Religion Chrétienne méditée dans le véritable Esprit de ses Maximes*, I, 294.

84. Beauvais, *Sermons*, II, 165.

85. Hyacinthe de Montargon, *op. cit.*, V, 574 ff.

86. Bourdaloue, "Sermon on Riches."

87. Mésenguy, *Abrégé de l'histoire de l'Ancien Testament*, X, 43.

88. Houdry, Père Cheminais, "Sermon on Restitution," *La Bibliothèque des Prédicateurs*, V, 529.

89. Bourdaloue, "Sermon on Riches."

90. De la Rue, "First Sermon on Almsgiving," *Les Avocats des Pauvres*, II, 342.

91. Griffet, *Sermons*, II, 125 ff.

92. *Mémoires de Trévoux*, April, 1756.

93. Réguis, *La Voix du Pasteur* (1773), IV, 126 ff.

94. *Ibid.*, p. 136.

95. *Ibid.*, pp. 130.

96. Houdry, "Manuscript Sermon on the Right Use of Riches," *op. cit.*, VIII, 301.

97. Gros de Besplas, *Les Causes du Bonheur public* (1774), II, 74 ff.

98. *Ibid.*, p. 411.

99. Fontenay, *Lettres sur l'Education des Princes* (1746), p. liv.

100. *Ibid.*, pp. 52 ff.

101. J. Croiset, S.J., *Parallèle des Moeurs de ce Siècle et de la Morale de Jésus-Christ* (1743), I, 232 ff.

102. Bossuet, *Politique tirée de l'Ecriture Sainte*.

12. THE CHURCH AND CAPITALISM

1. Thomassin, *Traité du Négoce et de l'Usure* (1697), pp. 96 ff.

2. *Ibid.,* pp. 111 ff.

3. Jean-Arthur de la Gibonais, *De l'Usure, Intérêt et Profit qu'on tire du prêt* (1710).

4. Bayle, *Dictionnaire historique et critique,* V, 755, fourth explanatory note.

5. Mésenguy, *Abrégé de l'Histoire de l'Ancien Testament* (1747), VI, 145.

6. Croiset, *Réflexions Chrétiennes sur divers Sujets de Morale* (1752), II, 299 ff.

7. Houdry, Extract from Père Croiset's, "Réflexions Chrétiennes . . . ," *La Bibliothèque des Prédicateurs,* I, 534.

8. Croiset, *op. cit.,* II, 261.

9. *Ibid.,* p. 264.

10. *Ibid.,* p. 299.

11. *Ibid.,* pp. 261 ff.

12. *Ibid.,* p. 126.

13. Croiset, *Parallèle des Moeurs de ce Siècle et de la Morale de Jésus-Christ* (1743), I, 303.

14. Croiset, *Réflexions Chrétiennes sur divers Sujets de Morale* (1752), II, 126 ff.

15. *Ibid.,* pp. 121 ff.

16. *Ibid.,* p. 129.

17. *Ibid.,* I, 133.

18. Croiset, *Parallèle des Moeurs de ce Siècle et de la Morale de Jésus-Christ* (1743), I, 303.

19. Croiset, *Réflexions Chrétiennes sur divers Sujets de Morale* (1752), II, 264.

20. *Ibid.,* p. 299.

21. Prigent, *Observations sur le Prêt à Intérêt dans le Commerce* (1783), pp. 239 ff.

22. *La Théorie de l'Intérêt de l'Argent* (1780), pp. 239 ff.

23. Prigent, *Observations sur le Prêt à Intérêt dans le Commerce* (1783), p. 211.

24. Mespolié, *Trois sortes d'Examens très utiles pour faire une Confession générale et particulière* (1706), p. 60.

25. Croiset, *Réflexions Chrétiennes,* II, 265.

26. Liger, *Lettres critiques et dissertation sur le Prêt de Commerce* (1774), p. 24.

27. *Recueil des pièces de poésie et d'éloquence présentées à l'Académie des Belles-Lettres de Marseille, pour prix de l'année* (1755), *Discours de M. Guys, directeur de l'Académie.*

28. Nicole, *Essais de Morale* (1753), XIII, 56.

29. Soanen, "Sermon on the Infamies of the Age," *Sermons sur différents Sujets prêchés devant le Roi,* I.

30. Boulanger, "Le Christianisme dévoilé," *Oeuvres* (1791), VII, 296.

31. *Ibid.,* p. 47.

32. J.-B. de Bonzèle, *La Guerre aux Vices,* p. 167.

33. Nicolas Petitpied, *Lettres touchant la matière de l'Usure* (1731). First Letter.

34. Hyacinthe de Gasquet, *L'Usure démasquée* (1766), p. 62.

35. *Ibid.,* p. 18.

36. *Ibid.,* p. 48.

37. *Ibid.,* p. 4.

38. Petitpied, *op. cit.,* p. 151. Fourth Letter.

39. Hyacinthe de Gasquet, *op. cit.,* p. 407.

40. *Ibid.,* pp. 5 ff.

41. *Ibid.,* pp. 385 ff.

42. Abbé Rougain, *Les nouveaux Patrons de l'Usure,* p. 567.

43. *La Théorie de l'Intérêt de l'Argent,* 1780, p. 178.

44. *Lettre à Monseigneur l'Archevêque de Lyon, dans laquelle on traite du Prêt à Intérêt à Lyon* (1763), p.16.

45. *Ibid.,* p. 23.

46. Hyacinthe de Gasquet, *op. cit.,* pp. 172 ff.

47. *Défense des Contrats et Rentes rachetables des deux côtés communément usités en Hollande* (1730).

48. Louis Bulteau, *Traité de l'Usure* (1720), pp. 178 ff.

49. *Ibid.,* pp. 8 ff.

50. *Ibid.,* pp. 201 ff.

51. *Ibid.,* p. 180.

52. *Ibid.,* p. 179.

53. *Suite de la Défense des Contrats de Rentes rachetables des deux côtés* (1730), p. 47.

54. *Traité des Prêts de Commerce* (1738), p. 55.

55. Abbé Rougain, *op. cit.,* pp. 568 ff.

56. Abbé de Laporte, *Le Défenseur de l'Usure confondu* (1781), pp. 206 ff.

57. *Ibid.,* pp. 292 ff.

58. Hyacinthe de Gasquet, *op. cit.,* p. 386.

59. *Ibid.*, pp. 446 ff.

60. Croiset, *Réflexions Chrétiennes,* I, 135 ff.

61. Feu Joly de Choin, *Instructions sur le Rituel* (1780), II, 408 ff.

62. Hyacinthe de Gasquet, *op. cit.*, p. 390.

63. Souchet, *Traité de l'Usure* (1776), p. 120.

64. Prigent, *Observations sur le Prêt à Intérêt* (1783), p. 235.

65. *Ibid.*, pp. 237 ff.

66. Prigent, *op. cit.*, p. 1.

67. Turgot, "Mémoire sur les Prêts d'Argent," *Oeuvres* (1844), I, 118.

68. *Lettre à Monseigneur l'Archevêque de Lyon dans laquelle on traite du Prêt à Intérêt à Lyon* (1763), p. 44.

69. *Ibid.*, pp. 36 ff.

70. Hyacinthe de Gasquet, *L'Usure démasquée* (1766), p. 400.

71. Abbé Rougain, *Les nouveaux Patrons de l'Usure*, pp. 544 ff.

72. *Lettre à Monseigneur l'Archevêque de Lyon* . . . , pp. 39 ff.

73. Turgot, *op. cit.*, p. 118.

74. Hyacinthe de Gasquet, *op. cit.*, pp. 344 ff.

75. Jean Arthur de la Gibonnais, *De l'Usure, Intérêt et Profit qu'on tire du Prêt* (1710), pp. 464 ff.

76. *Ibid.*, pp. 174 ff.

77. Jean Arthur de la Gibonnais, *op. cit.*, p. 315.

78. Liger, *Lettres critiques et dissertation sur le Prêt de Commerce* (1774), p. 24.

79. Prigent, *op. cit.*, pp. 231 ff.

80. *Ibid.*, p. 219.

81. Rougain, *op. cit.*, p. 570.

82. Prigent, *op. cit.*, pp. 215 ff.

83. Turgot, *op. cit.*, p. 137.

84. Prigent, *op. cit.*, p. 222.

85. *Ibid.*, p. 219.

86. *Ibid.*, pp. 214 ff.

87. *La Théorie de l'Intérêt de l'Argent* (1780), p. 64.

88. Hyacinthe de Gasquet, *op. cit.*, pp. 335 ff.

89. *Ibid.*, pp. 343 ff.

90. Prigent, *op. cit.*, pp. 221 ff.

91. Hyacinthe de Gasquet, *op. cit.*, p. 35.

92. *La Théorie de l'Intérêt de l'Argent*, pp. 200 ff.

93. *Ibid.*, pp. 19 ff.

94. *Ibid.*, p. 146.

95. Prigent, *op. cit.*, pp. 242 ff.

96. *L'Usure condamnée par le Droit naturel. Réponse à M. Formey* (1752). Quoted in *Lettre à l'Archevêque de Lyon* . . . , p. 60.

97. *La Théorie de l'Intérêt de l'Argent*, p. 184.

98. *Ibid.*, p. 180.

99. Jean Arthur de la Gibonnais, *op. cit.*, p. 458.

100. Turgot, *op. cit.*, p. 128.

101. Liger, *op. cit.*, p. 20.

102. *Ibid.*, p. 34.

103. Abbé de Laporte, *Le Défenseur de l'Usure confondu* (1781), p. 276.

104. *La Théorie de l'Intérêt de l'Argent*, pp. 164 ff.

105. Souchet, *Traité de l'Usure* (1776), p. 198.

106. Hyacinthe de Gasquet, *op. cit.*, p. 298.

107. *La Théorie de l'Intérêt de l'Argent*, p. 243.

108. *Ibid.*, pp. 255 ff.

109. *Ibid.*, pp. 175 ff.

110. *Lettre à l'Archevêque de Lyon*, p. 91.

111. *Ibid.*, p. 41.

112. Hyacinthe de Gasquet, *op. cit.*, pp. 452 ff.

113. Rougain, *op. cit.*, p. 547.

114. *Lettre à l'Archevêque de Lyon* . . . , p. 28.

115. *La Théorie de l'Intérêt de l'Argent*, pp. 201 ff.

116. Souchet, *op. cit.*, p. 123.

117. Hyacinthe de Gasquet, *op. cit.*, pp. 353 ff.

118. *Lettre à l'Archevêque de Lyon* . . . , p. 45.

119. Rougain, *op. cit.*, p. 486.

120. Souchet, *op. cit.*, p. 49.

121. Rougain, *op. cit.*, p. 548.

122. *La Théorie de l'Intérêt de l'Argent*, p. 184.

13. THE BOURGEOIS ORDER

1. Nicole, *Essais de Morale* (1753), XIII, 54 ff.

2. Bourdaloue, *Oeuvres,* II, 96.

3. *Ibid.*, p. 101.

4. Houdry, *La Bibliothèque des Prédicateurs*, VI, 20 ff. Père Haineuve.

5. Bourdaloue, *Oeuvres,* II, 96.

6. Feugère, *Bourdaloue, sa Prédication et son Temps* (1889), p. 283.

7. Griffet, *Sermons,* II, 208.

8. Massillon, "Sermon on the Dangers to the Piety of the Great."

9. Bourdaloue, *Oeuvres*, II, 79.

10. Massillon, "Sermon on the Dangers to the Piety of the Great."

11. Bourdaloue, *Oeuvres*, II, 96.

12. *Ibid.*, pp. 162 ff.

13. Hyacinthe de Montargon, *Dictionnaire apostolique* (1768), I, 287.

14. Griffet, *Sermons*, II, 435.

15. *Ibid.*, p. 441.

16. Croiset, *Réflexions chrétiennes*, II, 167.

17. Réguis, *La Voix du Pasteur* (1773), III, 9.

18. Croiset, *Parallèle des Moeurs de ce Siècle et de la Morale de Jésus-Christ* (1743), I, 191.

19. *Sermons du Père Hubert, prêtre de l'Oratoire, pour le Carème* (1725), II, 22 ff.

20. Hyacinthe de Montargon, *op. cit.*, V, 570.

21. Bourdaloue, *Oeuvres*, III, 289.

22. Charles Frey de Neuville, *Sermons*, III, 226.

23. *Ibid.*, p. 272.

24. Réguis, *La Voix du Pasteur* (1773), IV, 505 ff.

25. De Boulogne, *Oeuvres posthumes*, II, 195.

26. Réguis, *op. cit.*, IV, 505.

27. *Ibid.*, I, 11 ff.

28. *Ibid.*, p. 16.

29. Necker, *De l'Importance des Opinions religieuses* (1788), pp. 25 ff.

30. Rivarol, *Oeuvres*, II, 161.

31. *Encyclopédie*. Article: Morality.

32. Caraccioli, *La Religion de l'honnête Homme* (1766), p. 107.

33. Réguis, *op. cit.*, III, 375.

34. Necker, *op. cit.*, p. 34.

35. *Ibid.*, p. 46.

36. *Ibid.*, pp. 58 ff.

37. *Ibid.*, p. 63.

38. *Ibid.*, p. 58.

39. Rivarol, *Oeuvres*, II, 136.

40. *Ibid.*, p. 138.

41. Caraccioli, *Voyage de la Raison en Europe* (1772), p. 192.